I0418905

Street
Photography

Gordon Lewis

Street
Photography

The Art of Capturing the Candid Moment

rockynook

Gordon Lewis
gordon.lewis.mail@gmail.com
shutterfinger.typepad.com
shutterfinger.zenfolio.com
etsy.com/shop/ShutterfingerPhoto

Project Editor: Maggie Yates
Copyeditor: Maggie Yates
Layout: Petra Strauch
Cover Design: Helmut Kraus, www.exclam.de
Printer: Friesens Corporation
Printed in Canada

ISBN 978-1-937538-37-8

1st Edition 2015
© 2015 Gordon Lewis

Rocky Nook, Inc.
802 E. Cota Street, 3rd Floor
Santa Barbara, CA 93103

www.rockynook.com

Library of Congress Cataloging-in-Publication Data

Lewis, Gordon, 1953--
 Street photography : the art of capturing the candid moment / Gordon Lewis. -- 1st edition.
    pages cm
 ISBN 978-1-937538-37-8 (softcover : alk. paper)
1. Street photography. I. Title.
 TR659.8.L49 2015
 778.9'4--dc23
                        2014048710

All rights reserved. No part of the material protected by this copyright notice may be reproduced or utilized in any form, electronic or mechanical, including photocopying, recording, or by any information storage and retrieval system, without written permission of the publisher.

Many of the designations in this book used by manufacturers and sellers to distinguish their products are claimed as trademarks of their respective companies. Where those designations appear in this book, and Rocky Nook was aware of a trademark claim, the designations have been printed in caps or initial caps. All product names and services identified throughout this book are used in editorial fashion only and for the benefit of such companies with no intention of infringement of the trademark. They are not intended to convey endorsement or other affiliation with this book.

While reasonable care has been exercised in the preparation of this book, the publisher and author(s) assume no responsibility for errors or omissions, or for damages resulting from the use of the information contained herein or from the use of the discs or programs that may accompany it.

This book is printed on acid-free paper.

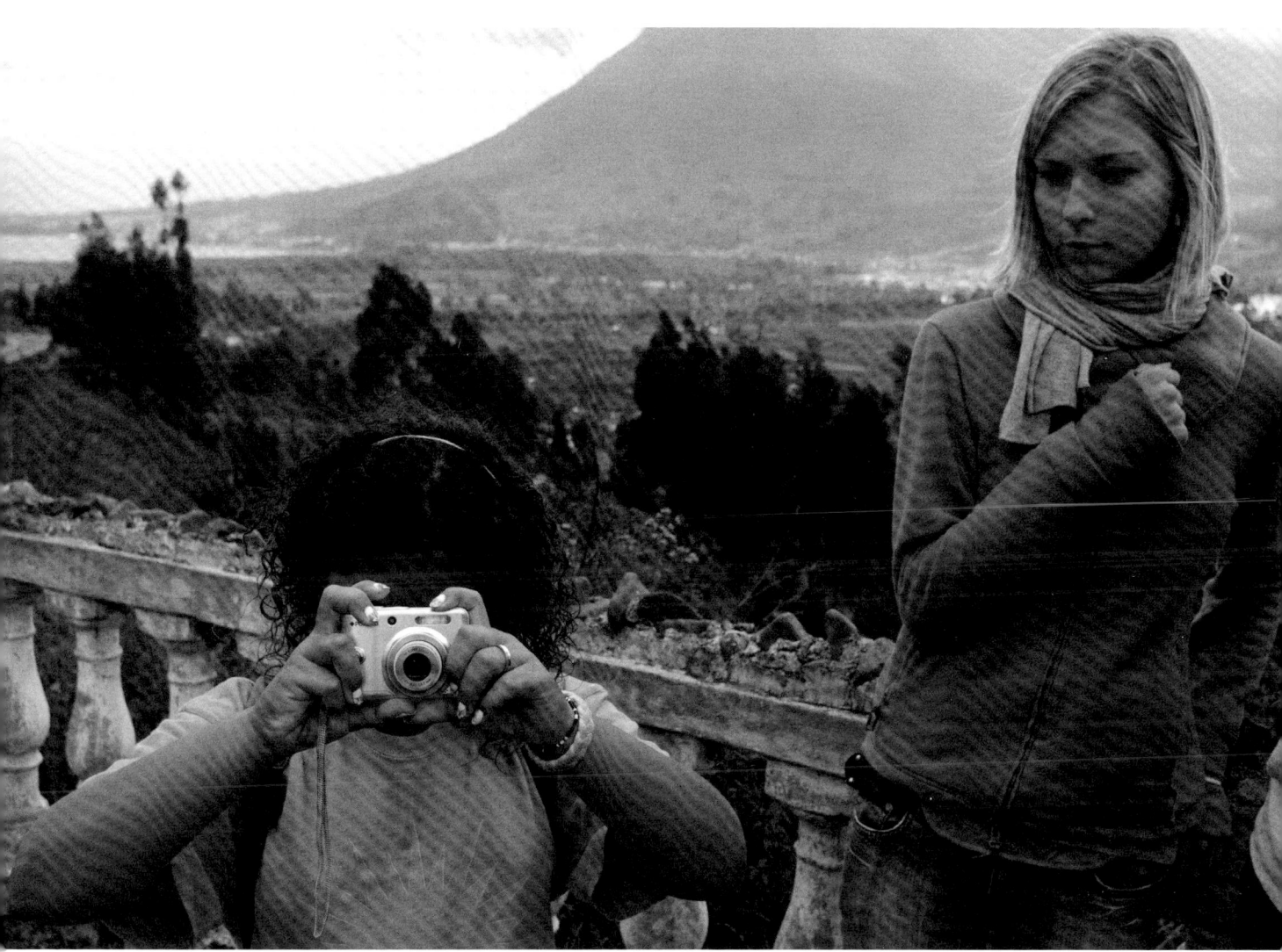

Photo enthusiast, Quito, Ecuador 2010

Table of Contents

Foreword

This book is the result of over 40 years of practice as a dedicated street photographer. My interest in this photographic genre began in the late 1960s, when I was a student in high school, before I was even aware that such a thing as "street photography" existed. I simply felt moved to take candid pictures of people and things that interested me, wherever I might happen to find them. This interest continued during my undergraduate years at Harvard, when I became aware that there were master photographers who shared the same inspiration and passion—photographers such as Henri Cartier-Bresson, Elliott Erwitt, Roy deCarava, and Gordon Parks. From them and their work I drew deeper inspiration, insight, and encouragement. This passion for capturing candid expressions of life continued through the '80s and '90s, when I lived in Los Angeles, a city where pedestrians and their habitats are few and far between. The introduction of digital photography and a move to Philadelphia, as fine a city for street photographers as one can hope to find, gave me new subjects and a new digital medium with which to capture them. My desire to share my work and thoughts with a larger audience inspired me to launch *Shutterfinger*, a blog about photography. *Precipitation* (page 113), a photo I published on a different blog (*The Online Photographer*), attracted the attention of George Barr, who included it in his book, *Why Photographs Work* (Rocky Nook, 2010). This photo caught the eye of Rocky Nook's publisher, Gerhard Rossbach, who asked if I would be interested in writing a book on street photography.

To be honest, I wasn't sure I'd be able to muster the sustained effort it would take to pull off an entire book. I write full-time for a living, so the idea of adding to my writing load (as well as time spent sitting in front of a computer) was not instantly appealing. The common doubts, fears, and insecurities involved with writing a book also contributed to my reluctance. The realization that this would probably be my only opportunity to publish my work for a broad audience motivated my decision to go for it, despite my doubts. I hope you'll enjoy the following work as much as I enjoyed producing it. I hope these photographs inspire you to try, enjoy, practice, and improve your own street photography. May the only limit to the amazing photographs you will capture be the time and interest you have in capturing them.

Acknowledgements

Thanks to Mike Johnston for *The Online Photographer*; George Barr for *Why Photographs Work*; Gerhard Rossbach, Matthias Rossmanith, and Maggie Yates for their patience, persistence, and good humor; Dean Collins (RIP) for opening my eyes to lighting and color; Colin Sprang for teaching me darkroom basics; Ned Bunnell and Chuck Westfall for access to pro equipment; Steve Barnes and Darnell Gadberry for their continued friendship; and most especially my wife, Claudia, for her continuing love and support.

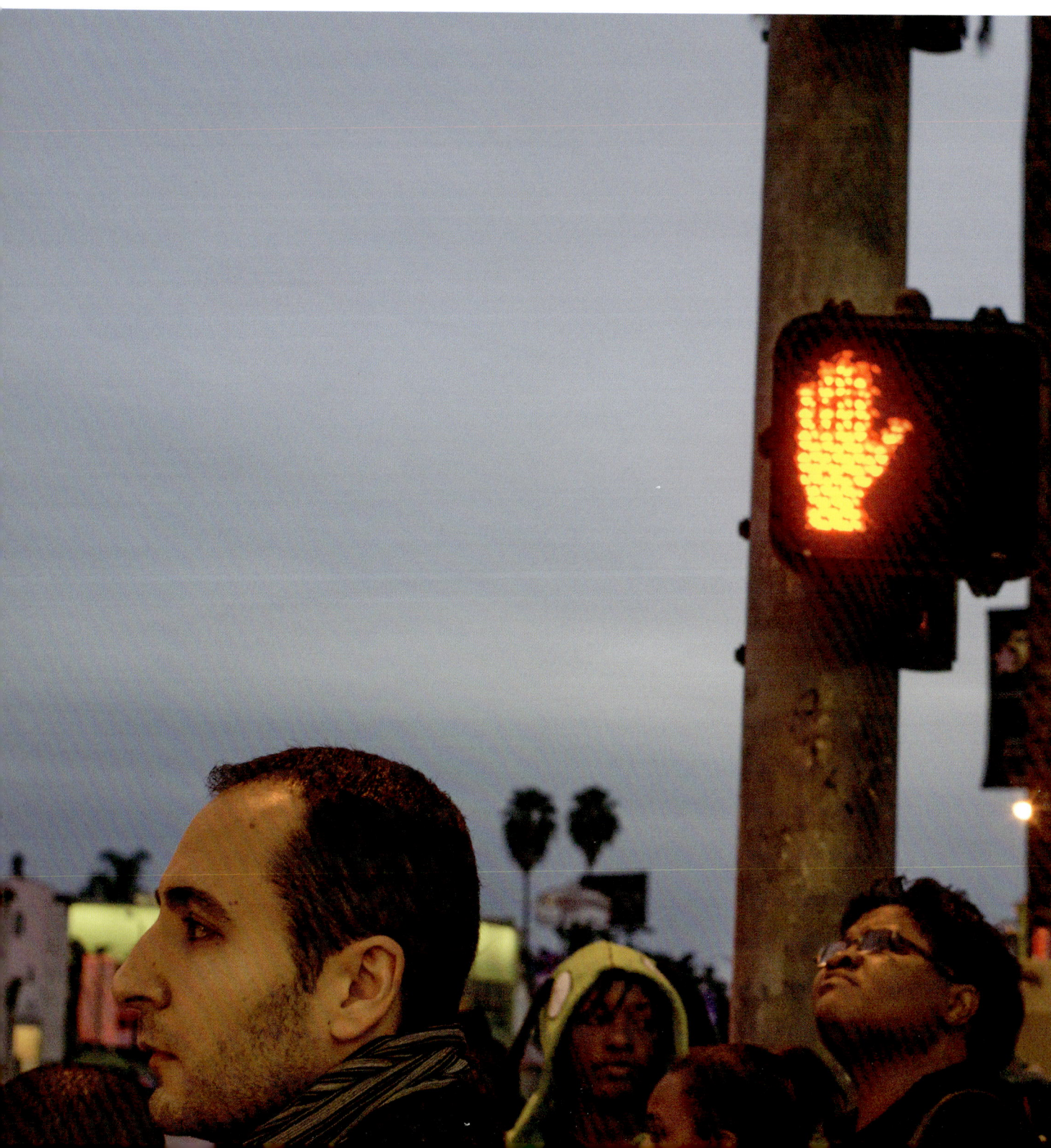

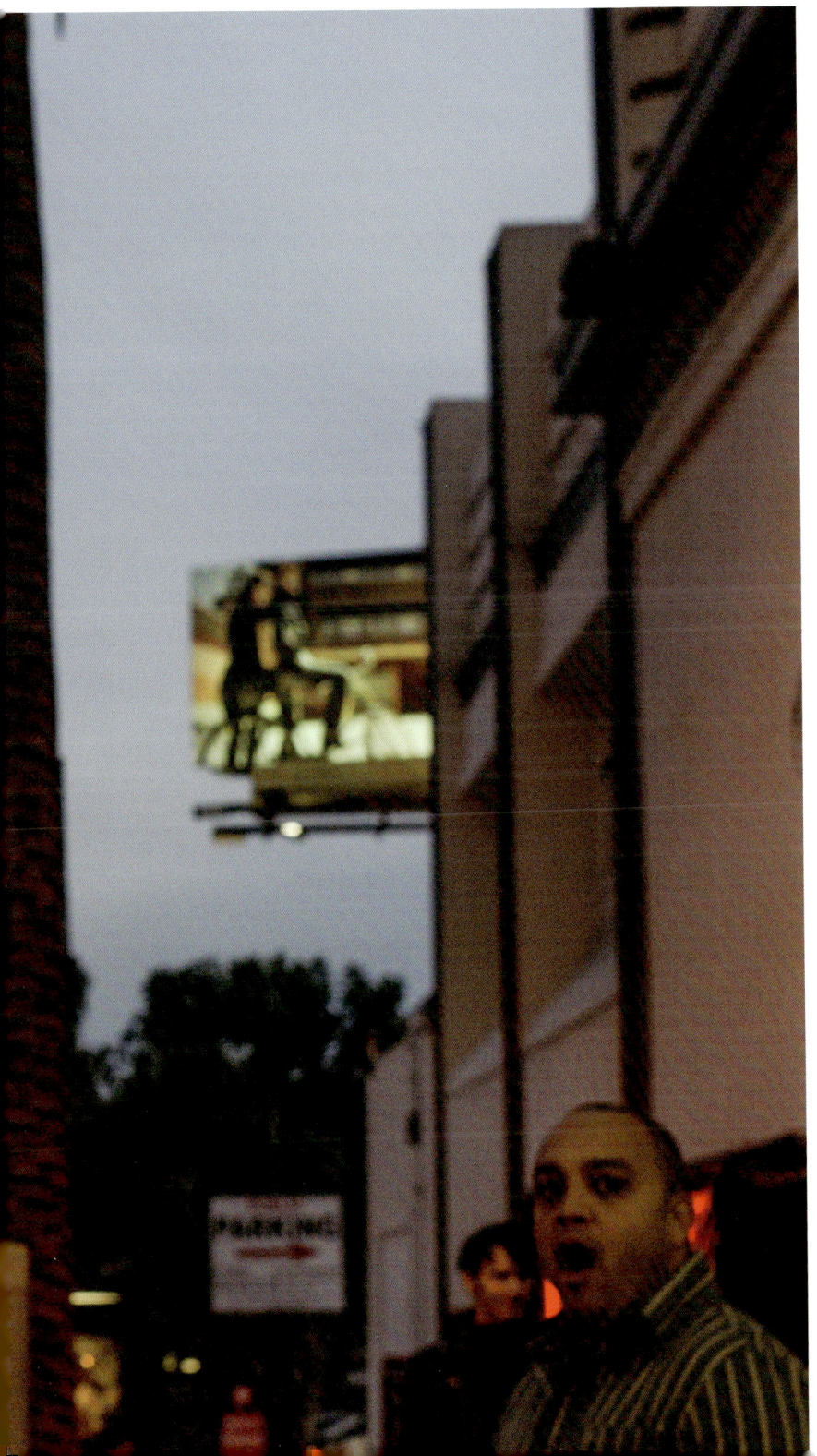

Chapter 1

The Allure of Street Photography

People have been practicing street photography for practically as long as there have been cameras and streets. Although its popularity has risen, fallen, and risen again over the decades, street photography has never disappeared completely. In fact, digital imaging has made street photography as popular (at least among photographers) as it has ever been. For some photographers however, the reasons behind this popularity are a mystery: some may wonder why anyone would want to wander the streets photographing random strangers without their knowledge or permission, and whether the results are worth the effort. This chapter will not try to convince anyone who has no interest in street photography why they should embrace it. After all, it's a big world and there are plenty of other subjects and styles to explore. You should do whatever you love most. This chapter is instead for the curious. It explores why so many photographers love street photography—and why, if you've never done it before, you might want to try it for yourself.

It's Easy

What better and easier time to practice street photography than now? Cameras are built into cell phones that anyone can carry everywhere, all the time. Dedicated cameras are available in practically every size, weight, and configuration you like at a wide range of prices. Better yet, all you really need is a camera and a lens. Anything else is not only optional, but often a hindrance.

Most cameras have the ability to handle focus or exposure automatically. Is the image a little too light, too dark, or blurry? You'll be able to tell immediately, and depending on what type of camera and settings you're using, correct the exposure after the fact. You can shoot literally thousands of images and store them on something that's not much larger than a postage stamp. Once you have all the basic equipment you need—camera, lens, memory card, computer, software, etc.—the incremental cost is practically nil. That's important when you're practicing an art where even the best photographers take a large number of images in the pursuit of capturing that one fascinating moment.

As for access to subject matter, I'll grant you that it's easier to practice street photography if you live in a bustling metropolis than if you live in the wilderness. That said, roughly 80% of the American population now lives in or near urban and suburban areas. Subject matter is close at hand, available for free, and, for all practical purposes, inexhaustible.

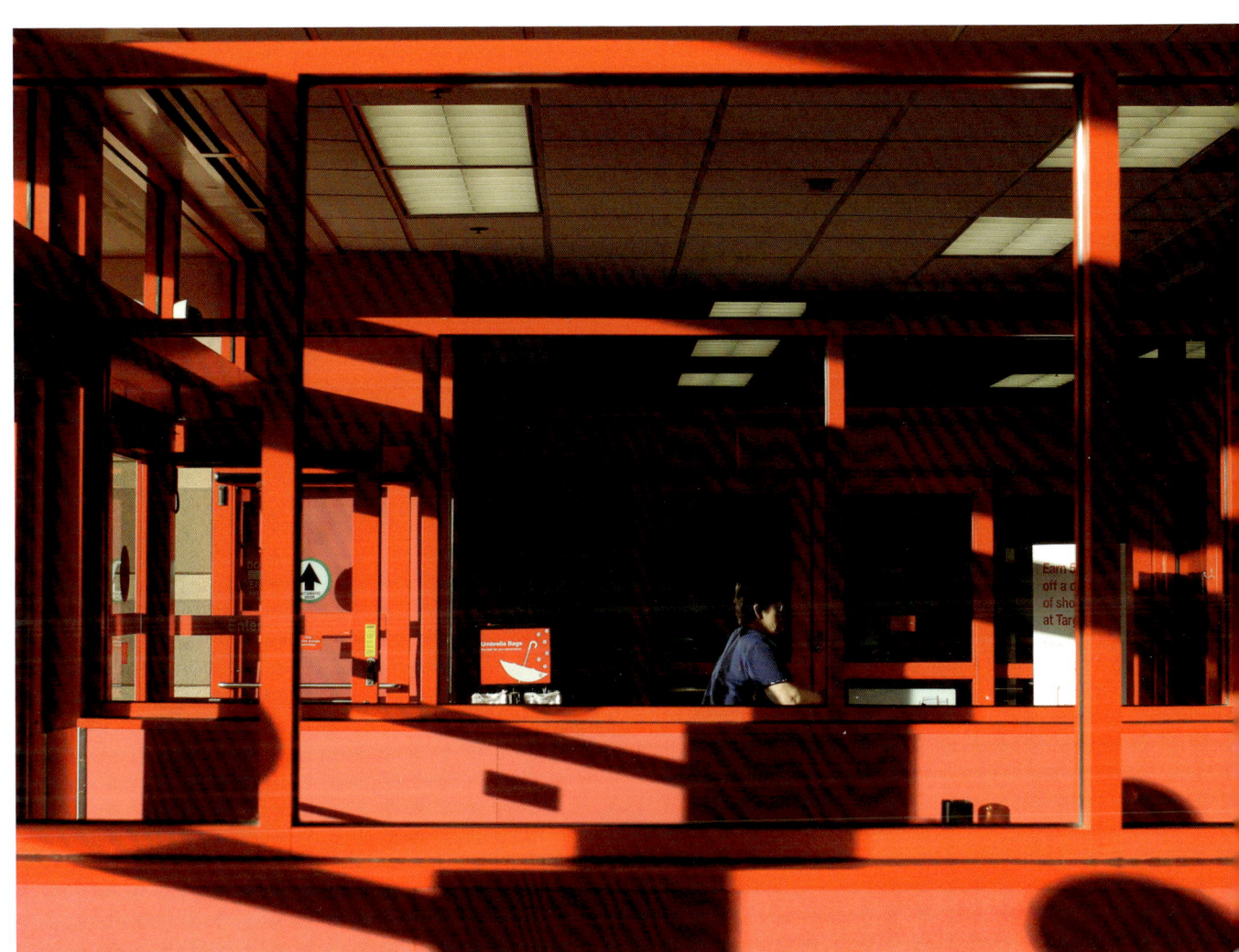

Entering Target, Abington, PA 2014
As I entered a local department store, I noticed the late afternoon light casting dramatic shadows on the red walls. As is often the case, I had my camera slung over my shoulder. A kid in a blue T-shirt added the perfect accent. No lights, no tripod, just point-and-shoot.

It's Challenging

Although it has never been easier to *practice* street photography, producing excellent photographs is a challenge. Your subjects and everything around them will either be in constant motion or likely to move without warning. The light is constantly changing. Just when you need your camera to obey your will, it may decide it has a mind of its own. The only thing you have any real control over is how to frame the shot and when to release the shutter.

For some personality types these conditions will be enough to drive you mad. You would probably be much happier in a nice, clean studio that lets you control every aspect of an image to your heart's content. For others, this unpredictability and serendipity is precisely the attraction. You never know what you'll see or what to expect. Every day, even every moment, is an adventure. Some days you can spend hours on the streets and come home empty-handed. Other days you'll find one amazing photo opportunity after another. What makes it all worthwhile is reviewing an image you just shot and discovering that you have captured a moment in time and space that would have been impossible to imagine, much less anticipate.

It Improves Your Reflexes

Another attraction and benefit of street photography is that it helps develop your ability to be alert, aware, and in the moment. You never know when or where the perfect moment will present itself—but with practice you can anticipate it to the degree that you develop a "sixth sense." You become able to adjust your camera and raise it to your eye without conscious effort; to grab a shot before other photographers are even aware there's a shot to take; to create the impression of order and intent out of random events.

Regardless of whether you're starting out with quick reflexes or slow, the constant practice of street photography will only make your reflexes faster. You'll find that it's a skill that comes in handy for any sort of action photography you do, from sports to wedding candids. It can even come in handy for portraiture, where the slightest change in expression can make the difference between a keeper and a photo that's destined for the trash.

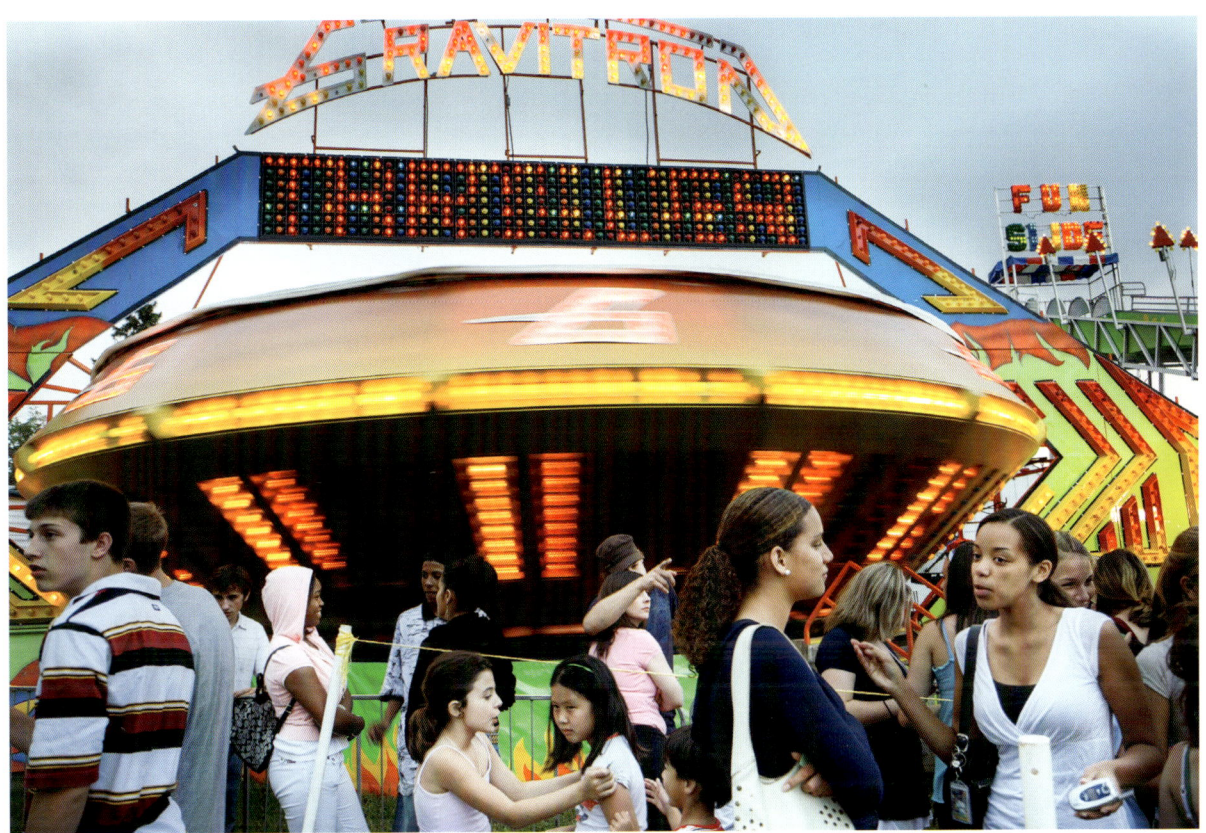

Carnival Scene, Abington, PA 2012
One of the most difficult challenges in street photography is creating a cohesive composition with multiple people in the frame. The various groups of people interacting with each other makes this image one of my more success-ful attempts to show connectivity through composition.

It Improves Your Technique

It's one thing to be able to nail your focus, exposure, and color balance in controlled lighting situations, when your camera is mounted on a tripod. It's quite another when the quality, contrast, source, and direction of the light can change from one moment to the next. Second chances are rare in street photography. This helps develop a strong incentive to refine your technique to the point that you can instantly adjust to whatever lighting and subject you're faced with, get the shot by whatever means necessary, and pull success from the jaws of failure.

It Develops Self-Confidence

Let's face it—for some people the very idea of taking photographs of perfect strangers, with or without their knowledge, is just as unnerving as it is appealing. What if you get caught looking? What if someone gets upset or yells at you? What if you get arrested and jailed for domestic espionage? What if an angry mob chases you down the street, screaming for blood?

As exaggerated as these fears might sound, the fear itself feels very real. It's also very common. Even the masters have experienced it. I'm no master, but I've been practicing street photography for over 40 years now, and I still feel that anxiety myself from time to time. However, the more often you confront these fears by taking pictures

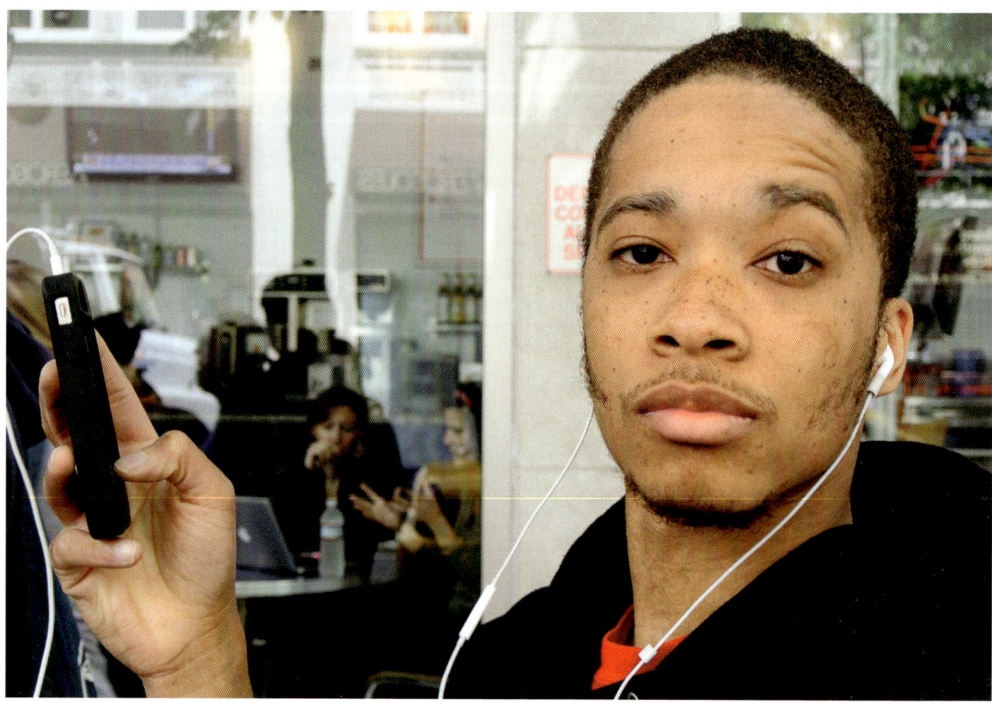

Cell Phone Aficionado, Philadelphia, PA 2012
This young man was in the middle of selecting music on his cell phone when I raised my camera to photograph him. He glanced at me with a cocked eyebrow, smiled, and then returned to what he was doing.

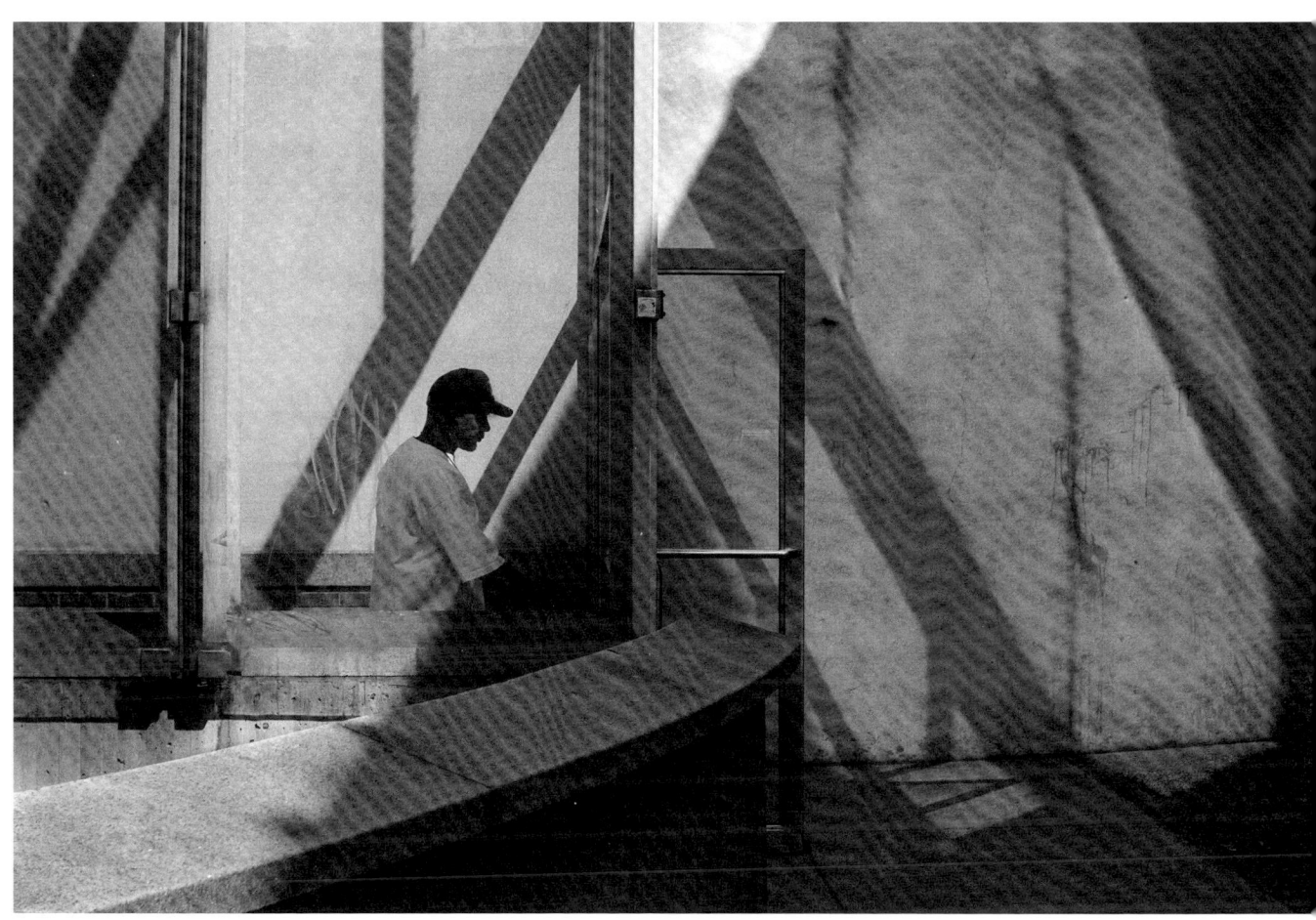

SEPTA Exit, Philadelphia, PA 2008
I knew the shadows cast by this structure could make a great composition if I
had a person placed in exactly the right spot. If I had released the shutter a
fraction of a second too soon or too late, this image would not exist. Ten seconds
later a cloud passed over the sun and the shadows vanished.

even when you're nervous and anxious, the less power your fears will have over you. In other words, you may never overcome your nervousness, but you will become better at taking pictures even though you're nervous about it.

You will also discover, as I have, that actual confrontations, or even dirty looks, are quite rare. Most people are flattered to be considered worthy of a photograph, especially if they think you're a serious photographer with no ulterior motives.

Aside from the confidence you develop from photographing people without checking first to see if it's okay, you'll also develop confidence as you improve your technical abilities as a street photographer—which in turn bolsters the confidence it takes to release the shutter.

It Documents Life

No one knows better than the dedicated street photographer how impermanent life can be. People grow older. Fashions change. Old buildings disappear, and new ones take their place. Things happen on the street that will never happen the same way or look the same way again, if only because you can't live the same moment twice. Documenting the world around you is one of the most effective ways you have of looking back into the past, remembering, reliving, and maybe even gaining a fresh perspective on life in the present.

Street photography is not purely documentary or photojournalistic, however. When done well, there's a strong element of individual style and artistic statement. It's because of **Eugène Atget** that we can see the streets of Paris in the unsentimental, deromanticized

way he saw them. It's because of **Henri Cartier-Bresson** that we learned to appreciate those spontaneous yet ambiguous "moments-between-moments." **Elliott Erwitt** showed us life at its most humorous and absurd. **Diane Arbus** invited us to look at people we would normally turn away from. **Saul Leiter** proved that not only was it possible to produce street photos in color, it could be done with artistry. Whatever you photograph will show the people who view your work how you see the world and what you considered important enough to document.

It's Insightful

Just as success in street photography requires the ability to notice and pay attention to what's going on *around* you, it's just as important to notice what's happening inside yourself. It's hard to improve as a street photographer without developing insights into human behavior, including your own. How do people behave when they think no one is watching them? How do they react when they notice someone with a camera nearby? How do they react when they notice you've just photographed them? Conversely, what street shooting situations excite you most? Which make you the most nervous? What themes do you have a passion for? When and how do you do your best work? As you improve and deepen in your practice, it will become obvious that your work says as much about you as it does about your subjects. You could discover something you didn't know, or confirm something you suspected but lacked the evidence to prove.

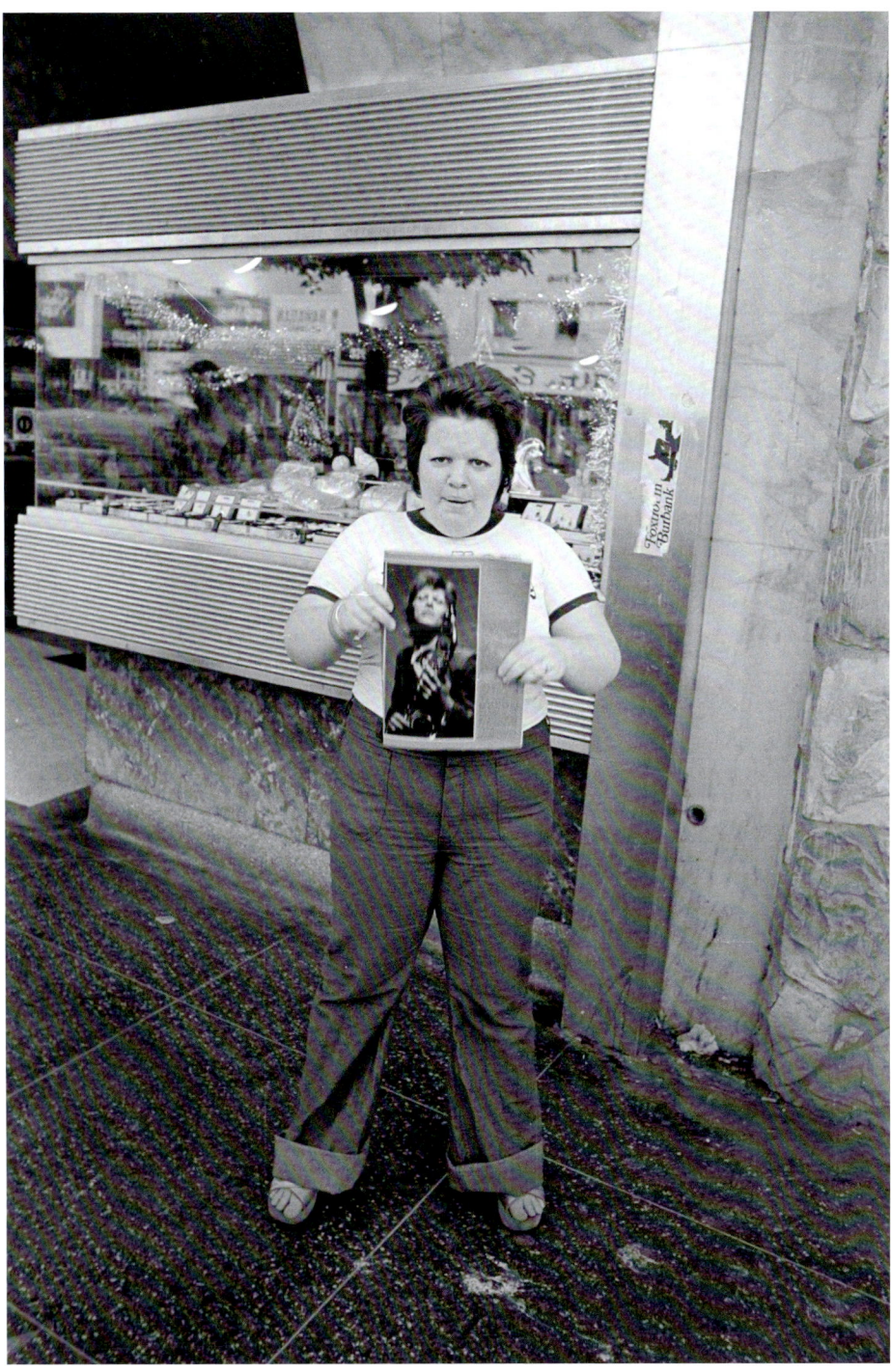

Bowie Fan, Hollywood, CA 1973
This Ziggy Stardust era David Bowie fan was walking down Hollywood Boulevard, carrying a photo of Bowie, and wearing the same hairstyle. She was happy to pose for a quick snapshot. This image becomes more historical with every passing year.

It's Satisfying

There's a certain satisfaction that comes from taking on a goal and, despite the challenges, reaching that goal or even surpassing it. There's also the satisfaction you get from pulling off one of those once-in-a-lifetime shots; the type that can make a whole week of coming up with nothing seem worthwhile. You might even occasionally feel the satisfaction that comes from having other people praise your work. Actual fame, or even just wide recognition, will be hard to come by. Only a small percentage of photographers are skilled enough and have a large enough body of work to merit serious attention. Of those, the few who are "famous" are well known only among other photographers and collectors. Few street photographers are well known among the general public—which is fitting. Imagine how difficult it would be to practice an art that requires you to walk among people without attracting attention if you were truly famous.

It's a Way to Make an Artistic Statement

The masters of street photography became acknowledged as such not because they were lucky enough to collect a random assortment of individually strong photographs, but because their body of work expressed a strong, unified, and often passionate point of view. **Henri Cartier-Bresson** was originally influenced by the Surrealist school of art, but he took on more of a photojournalistic style after World War II. **Brassaï** was enamored of night scenes; **Bill Brandt** with working class British life. **Elliott Erwitt** is known for his love of dogs and the humorous side of life. The masters have consistent themes, subjects, and visual styles that distinguish their work. I will explore this topic more deeply in the chapter on Style. For now, let's leave it at this: the best and most lasting street photos express ideas and emotions that transcend or even elevate their subjects. What ideas and visual styles do *you* feel passionate about, and what emotions do you want to express?

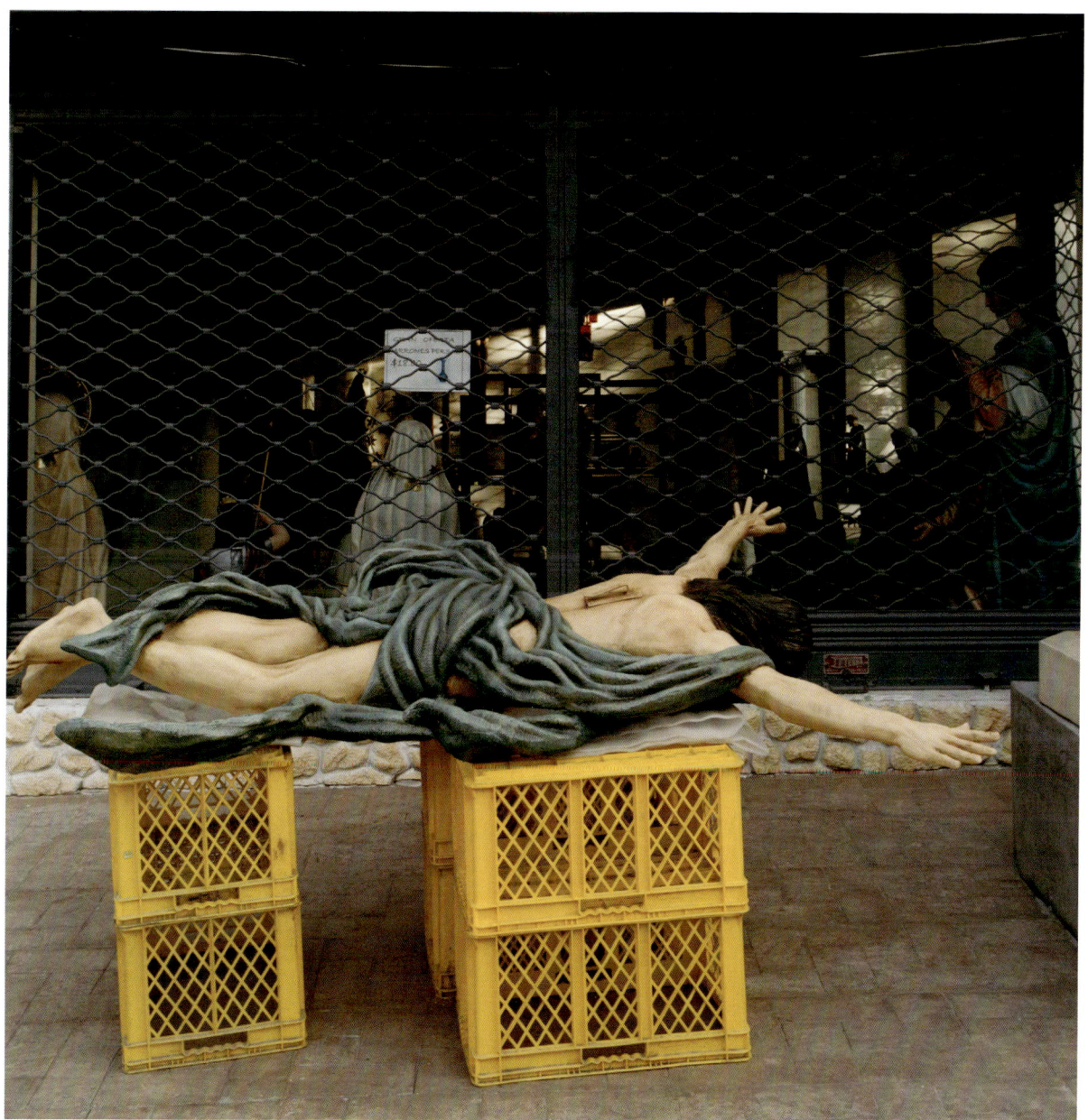

Flying Jesus, Quito, Ecuador 2010
This statue of Jesus was not yet mounted to a cross. Placed horizontally on crates, it looked as if He was flying. How could a puckish street photographer resist?

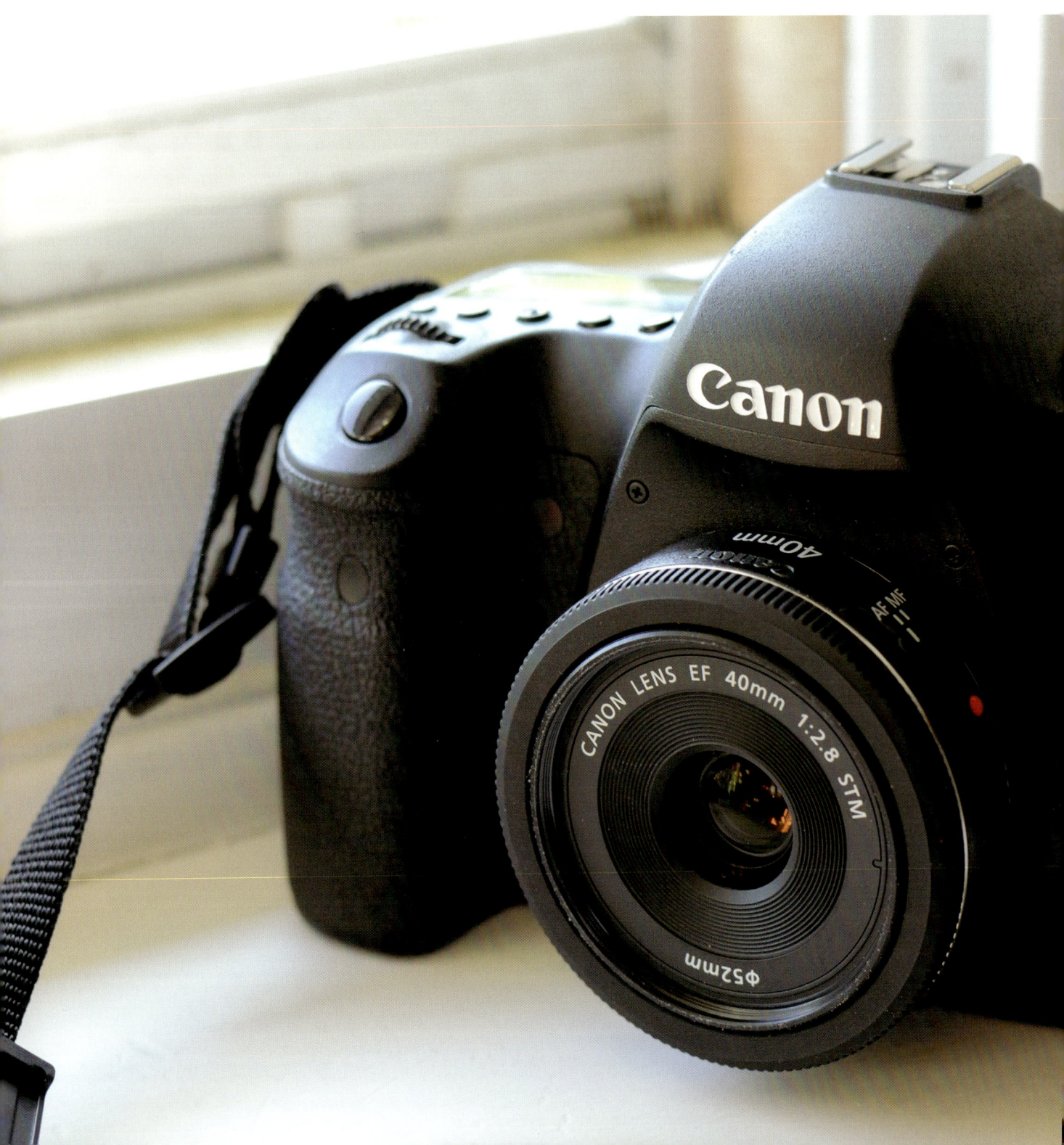

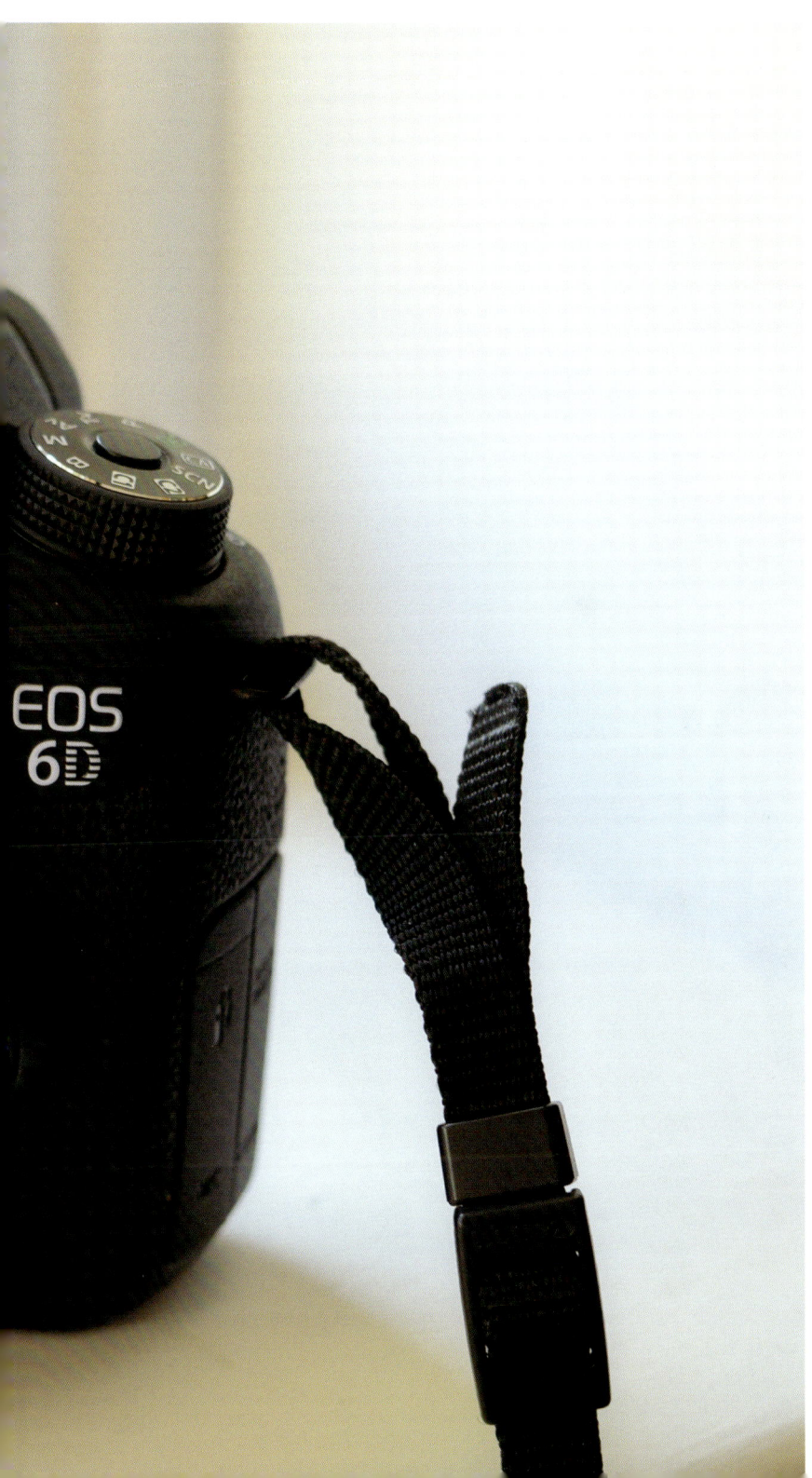

Chapter 2
Tools

Primary Considerations

One of the attractions of street photography is that it requires so little equipment. Successful street photographers have been known to use only one camera and one or two lenses during their entire careers. Better yet, unlike more specialized types of photography such as architecture or macro, you have a lot of flexibility in camera choice. I have used everything from a Pentax 67 film SLR (whose body weighs only 1,660 grams and has a mirror that sounds like a door slamming) to a Leica M4 rangefinder (550 grams and whisper quiet) with equal success. The chances are that whatever reasonably portable camera and lens you already own is suitable for street photography, as long as you're

comfortable with it and happy with the results. That being said, most street photographers, myself included, prefer to use cameras and lenses that meet most (if not all) of the following criteria:

Small Size and Low Weight

Street photography requires that you carry your gear, often for long periods of time. It's obviously more comfortable to carry a small, lightweight load than a large, heavy one, even if you're strong and fit. Heavy cameras tend to get left at home when you're headed out the door with no specific photographic purpose in mind. A small camera incurs no such burden, which increases the likelihood you'll

Notice how the more gear this photographer carries and the larger it is, the more "serious" he looks?

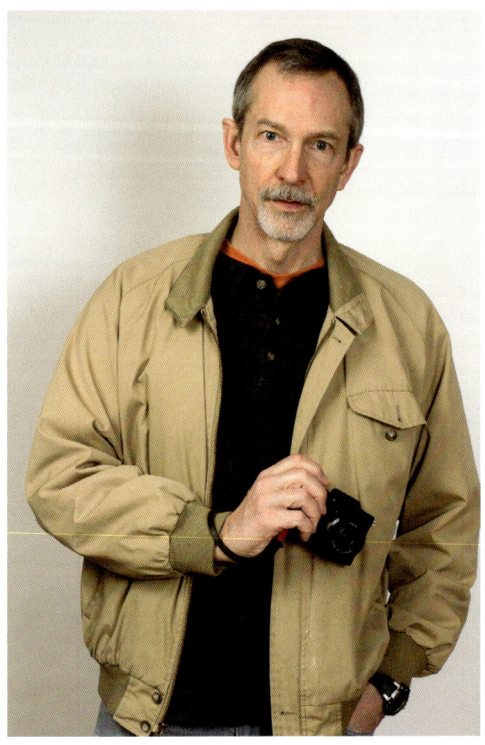
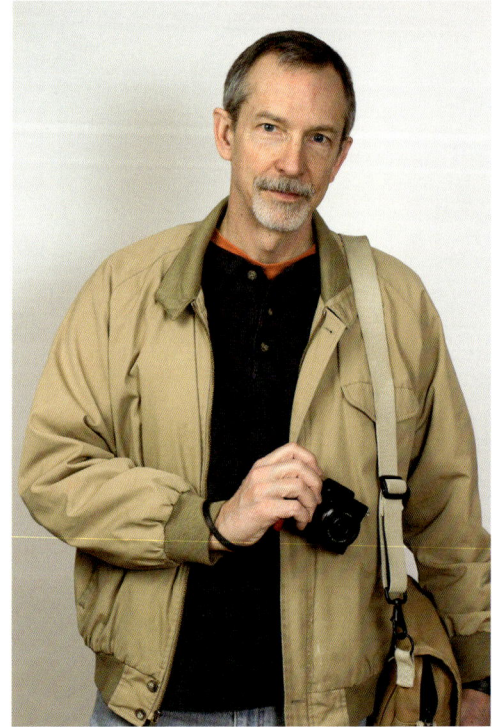

have it with you when a serendipitous photo opportunity presents itself.

Another benefit of small cameras is that they generally attract less attention on the street than large ones. People assume—often correctly, I might add—that the larger your camera and lens, the more expensive they are, and therefore the more serious your intent. This makes people self-conscious, possibly even nervous, suspicious, or angry. A small, nondescript camera is much less intimidating. People will generally assume you're just another tourist or harmless amateur, if they notice you at all.

By *small*, I mean a camera and lens you could block from view with the palm of your hand, not one so small that usability and image quality suffer. Remember: You want

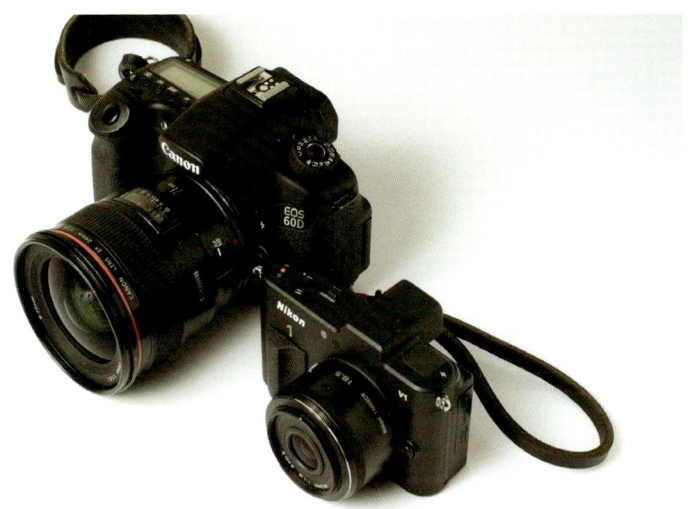

Small is relative. That said, it should be obvious which camera would be easier to conceal and carry for long periods of time.

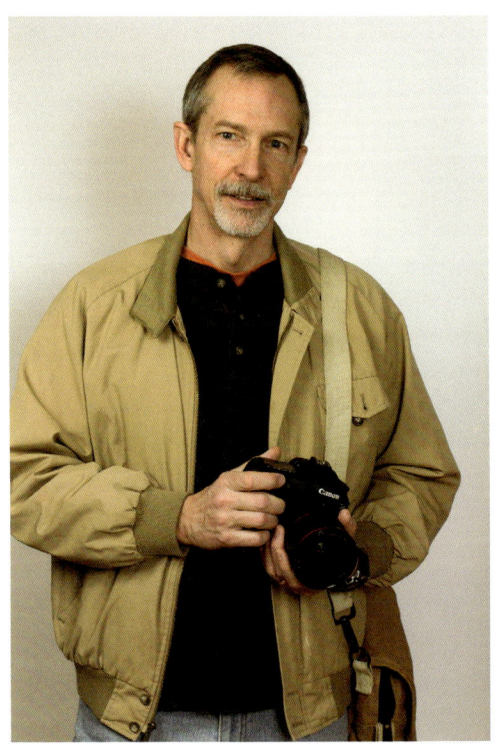

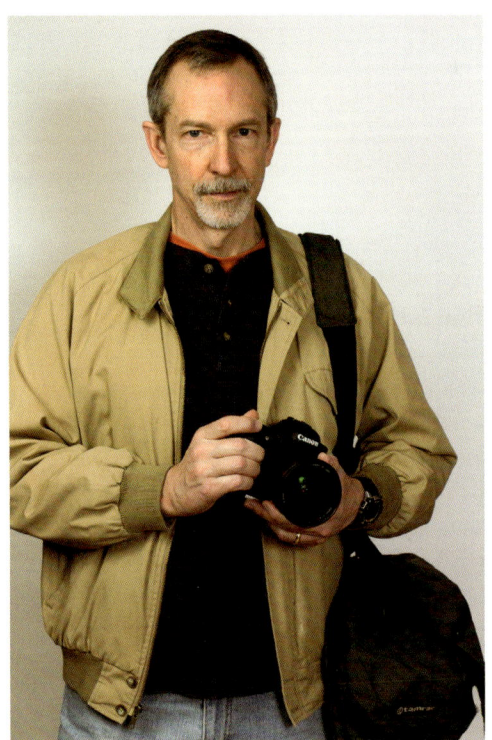

a *balance* of features, not one or two at the expense of others.

Speed

One of the constant challenges of street photography is that you often have no more than a few seconds to capture an image. This calls for a camera that does what you need it to, as close to instantly as possible. The last thing you want in this sort of situation is a camera that is slow to turn on, has noticeable shutter lag, or is slow to zoom or focus.

Fast focus, even if it's not perfectly accurate, improves your ratio of successful photographs. Slow focus results in frequent missed shots. It's as simple as that. If you take a close look at some of the classic street photography shots, they often are not in perfect focus; there might be some subject or camera motion. However, if the photographer managed to catch the right moment at the right time, none of these "defects" matter. I'll have more to say about how to reduce focusing time in the chapter on Technique. In any case, the faster your camera is to begin with, the better.

Simple Operation

As with size, simplicity is a relative term. Some cameras have complex menus that allow you to program the camera to your preference. Cameras like these can be quite simple to use once you've set them up; it's just the setting-up that can be difficult. Not only do you have to know the best way to set up your camera, you also have to determine if your camera can, in fact, be set up this way and, if not, how close you can get to those ideal settings.

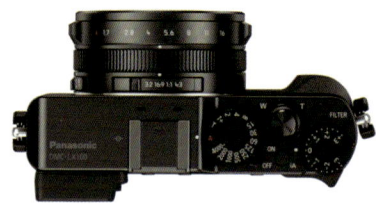

The benefit of direct controls such as these is that you can see at a glance, even if the camera is off, what aperture, shutter speed, and exposure compensation this camera is set to

Another thing that contributes to simple operation is direct access to key parameters such as focus, shutter speed, aperture, and ISO. This generally means a camera with dedicated, single-function buttons or dials, as opposed to one where you have to scroll through menus. A touchscreen interface with direct access to these parameters should work just as well (in theory). In practice, touchscreens can be difficult to see and use in bright light.

Beware of controls that change function depending on what mode the camera is in; for example, a button that controls ISO when you're in one mode but exposure compensation when you're in another. A similar problem is awkwardly placed controls such as a power switch that's hard to reach or a pop-up flash button that's too easy to press by accident. Either one can result in confusion and stress when you're trying to make quick adjustments in the heat of the moment.

Quiet

It stands to reason that a quiet camera will attract less attention than a loud one. In practice however, you'll often find yourself in environments where there is so much noise and activity that the sound of your camera will be barely noticeable. There are exceptions of course: high-pitched shutters are generally more noticeable than low-pitched ones. Continuous, multiframe exposures are more noticeable than a single exposure. Cameras are easier to hear when they're close to your ears as opposed to far away. All that being said, I still prefer a quiet shutter, if only because it makes *me* feel more confident and less self-conscious. You may feel the same way.

So, if quiet is good, is silent even better? Not necessarily: The problem with silent shutters (there are a few mirrorless cameras that have them) is that they provide no auditory feedback. This makes it difficult to know if and when the shutter did, in fact, release. Completely silent cameras have their uses, but they are by no means essential for street photography.

Reliability

A reliable camera is one that either does what you expect it to or gives you fair warning that something is amiss. For example, the battery power display should not indicate 75 % full power one minute and 25 % full power two minutes later. The shutter should release when you press the shutter button, not lock up or misfire. Given the same lighting and composition, the color balance and exposure should be the same from one shot to the next—not changing unpredictably.

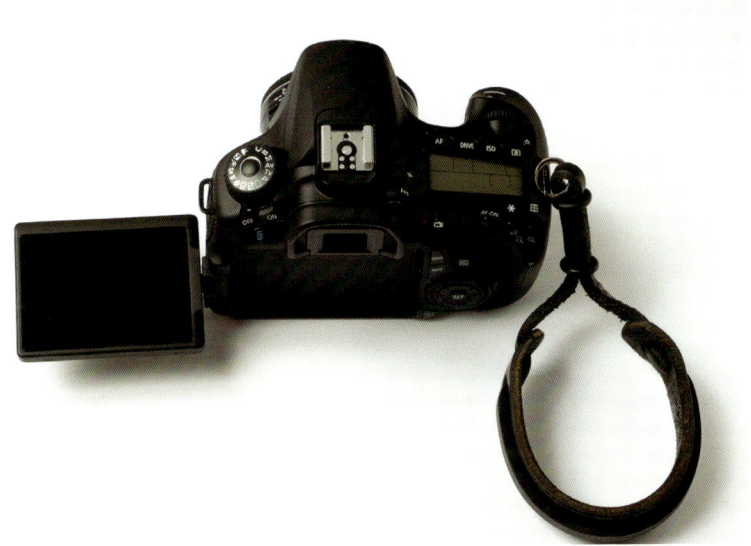

Clear Viewfinder

There are many different ways of viewing and framing an image. The most common and easiest to use is the eye-level viewfinder because we view life at eye-level. However, holding a camera at eye-level can present a problem for street photographers because it's an obvious sign that you intend to photograph whoever or whatever your camera is aimed at. Some street shooters therefore prefer the option of a waist-level viewfinder. Instead of being parallel to the lens axis, a waist-level viewfinder is *perpendicular* to the lens axis. Assuming your subject is standing in front of you, you will have to look downward to focus and frame, which makes it look to observers as if you're fiddling with your camera rather than framing and getting ready to shoot. This can be quite a boon to those who prefer a stealthy approach to street photography.

This waist-level viewfinder swivels to the side. Others are hinged to flip upward from the back of the camera.

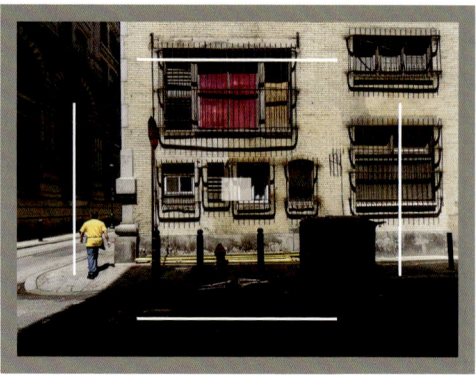

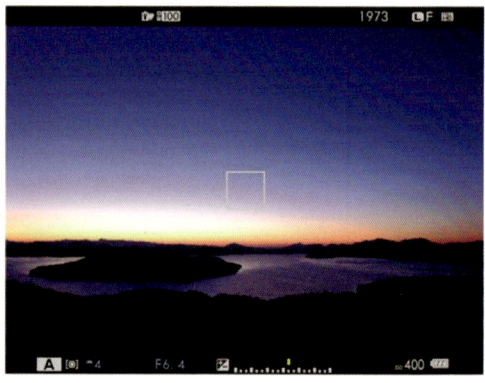

Bright-line viewfinders such as this one indicate the approximate image borders with framelines. Viewfinders with parallax compensation move the framelines downward and to the right as you focus closer.

One of the main benefits of electronic viewfinders is that they "gain up" (become brighter) as the ambient light becomes dimmer. With an optical viewfinder, the lower the ambient light level, the darker the viewfinder.

Most eye-level viewfinders show you the exact framing (or close enough) that you will capture with the image sensor or film. What you see is truly what you get, as least as far as framing is concerned. A dwindling number of cameras, such as the Leica M-series and Voightlander rangefinders, provide a "looser" frame that consists of marked lines or corners within a larger window. Framelines are less precise, but they have the benefit of allowing you to see *outside* the frame and thereby anticipate when someone or something is about to intrude on your composition.

A third option to consider is the difference between optical and electronic viewfinders. With an optical viewfinder, you're looking at the actual photons reflected from the subject and transmitted through your camera's lens or viewfinder. With an electronic viewfinder, you're looking at how the image sensor and an LCD display inside your camera *interpret* the photons reflected by your subject. In practice, optical viewfinders are easier to use

outdoors in bright light because they aren't susceptible to being overpowered by direct sunlight. Electronic viewfinders are often better indoors and under available light because they "gain up" (get brighter in low light) to provide a close approximation of how the final image will look.

None of these viewfinder options are inherently better or worse; it's more a matter of what types of subjects you prefer, and under what conditions you like to shoot. What's most important is that your camera's viewfinder facilitates the types of shots you take rather than inhibiting them.

Secondary Considerations

Once you've satisfied these basic utility factors, you can focus on factors that are more a matter of preference than necessity. In other words, use whatever functions you like and stop using the ones you don't like. What follows are my opinions on the pros and cons of various available equipment options.

Digital Cameras

Most street photographers use digital cameras these days—and for good reasons. These include:

- *Instant feedback*
  You can see immediately after you release the shutter whether you got what you expected or, if not, whether you need to adjust the composition, exposure, focus, ISO, or white balance. Instant feedback greatly reduces the odds that a whole day's outing will be ruined by one or two easily correctable problems.

- *Low incremental cost*
  Once you have everything you need for digital photography—camera, lens, memory card, computer, etc.—you can take literally thousands of photographs without incurring any additional cost. This in turn reduces the cost of failed attempts and learning experiences, which are common even among experienced street photographers.

- *Exposure flexibility*
  If you shoot raw files (as opposed to JPEGs) you have a lot of latitude to adjust and enhance your images post-exposure. That means you can shoot quickly if necessary, without having to worry too much about perfect exposure or white balance. You can even use software that gives your images a "film look" as opposed to your camera's normal rendering. This is especially convenient for photographers who shoot with digital and film cameras and want a consistent look from both.

- *Ease of sharing*
  You don't have to print a digital photograph to show it to someone. You can display it with your camera's LCD display, on your home computer, or on a tablet. You can upload it to your own website or a photo-sharing site such as Flickr, SmugMug, or Picassa.

- *Custom configurations*
  Many digital cameras allow you to program the features you want to assign to various controls, and specify how these controls will operate. Assuming you know the best way to configure your camera for street photography, this can greatly increase your shooting speed and accuracy.

- *Portability*
  Some digital cameras are literally small enough to fit inside a mobile phone. You're more likely to carry a pocket-size camera for long outings than a large, heavy one, and small cameras generally draw less attention. The downside is that what you gain in portability you lose in image quality and adaptability. There are plenty of options, from large to tiny. Like Goldilocks in the tale of the three bears, it's up to you to decide what size is "just right."

Film Cameras

Given all the advantages of digital, you might wonder why anyone would prefer shooting with film. As it turns out, there are still a lot of good reasons, some of which you may find persuasive:

The Film Look

Film has characteristics that, although they may be easy to replicate, are hard to duplicate with digital media. One of them is grain: film images are comprised of tiny random particles of silver halide. The higher the film speed (ISO), the larger these particles will be. Whether the film grain is visible or not will depend on how much you enlarge the image. Smaller formats, such as 35mm, require greater enlargement to reach a given size than larger formats, such as 120. Therefore, assuming all things are equal, smaller formats produce a more obvious film grain than larger formats. For photographers who like the gritty, slightly impressionistic look of large film grain, this is a good thing. Those who don't like this look have the option of finer-grained (lower ISO) films. Digital cameras can approximate and simulate either look, but the results will never be identical because the look of real film grain varies depending on the film, developer, film processing, enlarger, or scanner being used. This can

Store Window, Philadelphia, PA 2010
Shot on Kodak Ultra-max 400 35mm color negative film (now discontinued)

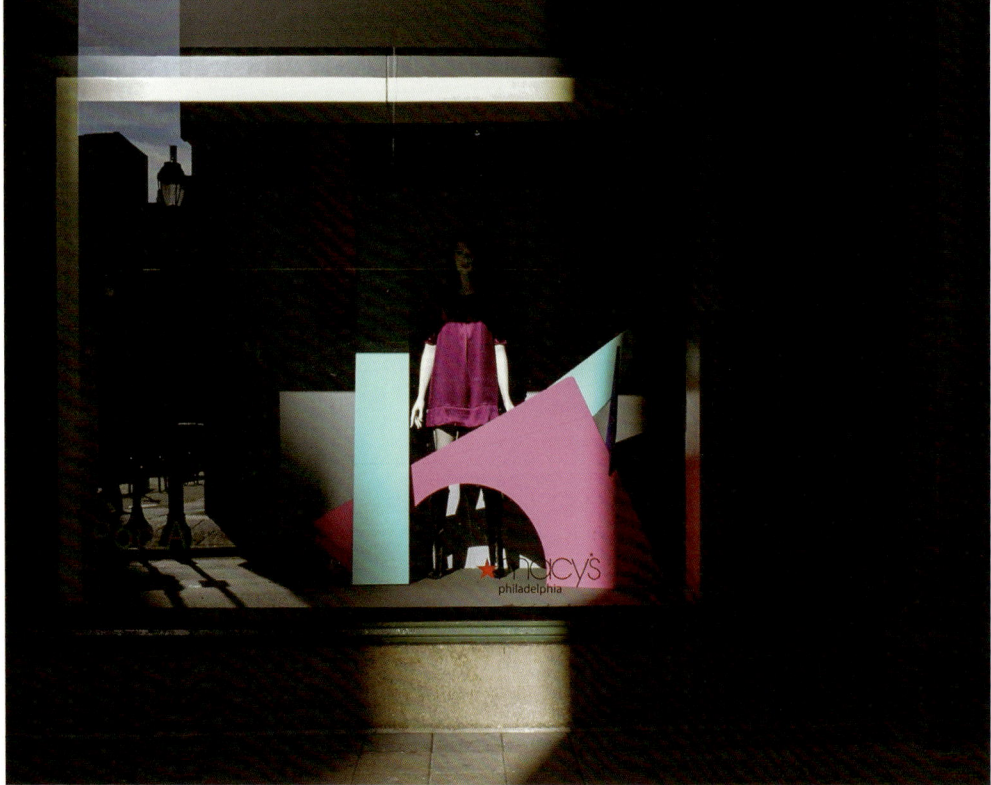

be an attractive feature for photographers who are looking for a way to give their photographs a unique look.

Another valued characteristic of film is the way it reproduces colors and tones. Some films are high in contrast; others are the exact opposite. Some feature bold, saturated colors while others feature soft, muted colors. Black-and-white films don't render color at all. You can pick the look you like and know that you'll get it roll after roll, without having to use computers or software.

Color transparency films are similar to digital sensors in the way they react to overexposure: once the highlights are overexposed, you can't recover them. Negative films are more forgiving than digital media or color transparencies: you can expose two stops over the recommended ISO and not only will you retain the highlights, you'll generally get finer grain and more shadow detail. This can happen accidentally, or you can do this intentionally to give yourself a safe margin of error. Either way, this flexibility comes in handy for street shooting.

If you're using black-and-white film and doing your own developing, you have full control over how you process your film and print the results (*print* in this case refers to JPEGs for viewing on the Internet as well as literal prints). It's common for two different photographers to both use the same film, such as Kodak Tri-X, and produce results that look completely different.

Economy
Film is not necessarily more expensive than digital. Although you do have to pay for film and processing, you save yourself the potentially considerable expense of buying a digital camera, the associated hardware,

software and peripherals, and their periodic upgrades. If you don't own a film camera, it's not hard to find someone who is either willing to give you a student model camera for free or sell it at next to nothing. This doesn't generally apply to professional film cameras such as Leicas, Nikons, Hasselblads, etc., but even these sell for a lot less than their digital equivalents. In any case, there's a certain comfort in using a camera that's already technically obsolete. No one is introducing new film cameras any more, so prices have already depreciated. Assuming you take good care of it, there's little worry that your camera will lose half its value within a year after you've bought it, and in the case of used top-of-the-line film cameras, you can often sell them for only slightly less than you originally paid.

A final, often overlooked factor is that the incremental cost of shooting film encourages better shooting discipline. A camera that allows you only 12, 24, or 36 exposures at a time, all of which you have to pay to process, encourages you to be more thoughtful about when to release the shutter button.

Thoughtfulness and restraint alone don't guarantee better images, but they do reduce your number of throwaways.

Simplicity and Direct Control
Manually operated film cameras have only three or four controls: shutter speed, aperture, focus, and perhaps an ISO setting for the exposure meter. You can't get much simpler than that. Even if you opt for a film camera with autofocus, there's still no searching through complicated menus—just a few more buttons, dials, or levers. What you give up in automation you gain in direct control and simplicity. There's no computer to do your thinking for you, and no setting changes

unless you change them yourself. Better yet, many of the older film cameras require batteries only to power the light meter, not the camera itself. This means that even if the battery fails, you'll still be able to operate the camera and grab that once-in-a-lifetime shot. It's a different story with the more fully automated film cameras that have LED displays, and options such as metering pattern (spot, center-weighted, matrix, etc.) focus method and film advance mode (single-shot or continuous). You get more features and options at the cost of more battery dependence and complexity.

Lenses

Lens choice is largely a matter of comfort and practicality. As with cameras, you want something reasonably small and light, not only because large, heavy lenses are tiring to carry for long periods, but also because they attract undue attention. Unless you're doing a lot of shooting indoors or in low light, you generally won't need a maximum aperture faster than f/4, which also helps minimize size, weight, and cost. If you *do* plan to shoot in low light, however, then the faster your lens is, the better. A fast maximum aperture allows lower ISOs and/or faster shutter speeds.

Although lenses with optical image stabilization (also known as vibration reduction) will reduce the amount of blur caused by camera shake, they will do nothing to prevent blur caused by *subject* motion.

Focal length is flexible: moderate wide-angle lenses (28–35mm in 35mm film format equivalent) are best for crowded and narrow streets because they provide a useful field of view even at close distances, without causing obvious geometric distortion. Normal focal lengths (45–60mm in 35mm equivalent) are good, general-purpose lenses with a field of view similar to that of the human eye. With practice you should be able to anticipate how an image will be framed even before you raise your camera to your eye.

Telephoto lenses (85mm or more in 35mm format equivalent) are problematic for street photography mainly because of their size, weight, and conspicuousness, but also because their narrow field of view requires you to be further away from your subject for the shot to be successful. Although this might seem to be an advantage, especially for those of you who are nervous about photographing strangers, a greater distance from your subject increases the odds that someone will step in front of your camera at a critical moment.

Zoom lenses have the benefit of speed, convenience, and flexibility. Instead of having to switch lenses to change focal lengths, you can simply zoom in or out to adjust your framing without running the risk of dropping a lens or exposing your image sensor to dust. Unfortunately, this speed, convenience, and flexibility comes at a price: zooms are generally larger, heavier, and more expensive than a prime lens with a similar focal length and aperture. They also encourage a tendency to frame subjects without regard for optimum

From left to right, these lenses are an 18.5mm f/1.8 Nikkor for the Nikon V1 mirrorless camera, 85mm f/2 AIS manual focus Nikkor, and 85mm f/1.8 auto focus Canon EF

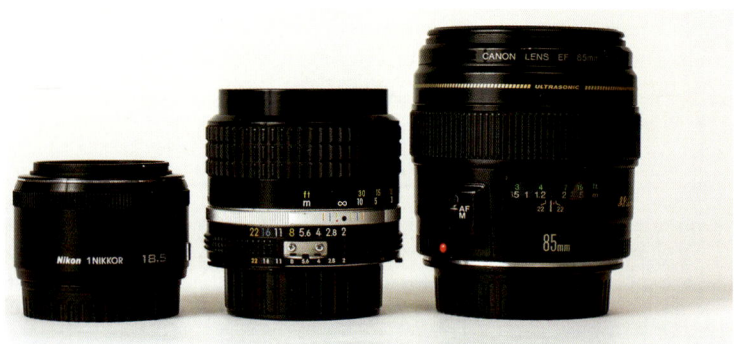

focal length, distance, and image perspective. Sometimes it's better to keep the same focal length and step forward or back to change your field of view than to zoom in or out.

Last but not least among lens features is autofocus. Autofocus has obvious benefits for the street photographer. Some cameras, particularly those optimized for sports photography, can focus faster and more accurately than you could ever hope to on your own. This assumes the camera knows exactly what you want in focus, which is not always the case. When you add in the fact that some cameras and lenses focus slowly, inaccurately, or both, it becomes obvious that autofocus is not infallible. That's why many experienced street photographers prefer lenses that at least provide the option of quick and easy manual focus. This means direct (rather than electronic) manual focus via a focusing ring, printed distance scale, and focusing index mark. You can manually set the distance you expect your subject to be at—4 meters, for example—then set a small enough aperture that depth of field will mask minor focusing errors. This works best with wide-to-normal focal length lenses, which have more depth of field at equal distances than telephoto lenses. You will find more information about this and useful variations in the Techniques chapter.

Electronic Flash

Believe or not, there are many successful street photographers (**Bruce Gilden**, to name just one) who use electronic flash. They use it at night, as the primary source of illumination, and in broad daylight, for shadow fill. Either way, it provides a distinctive look to your photos that you can't get any other way.

Whether or not you like this look and are willing to do what it takes to get it is purely up to you. But the option is available.

Tripod

I almost never use a tripod for street photography, mainly because they are bulky, limit speed and mobility, and can be hazardous to other pedestrians. When I do use a tripod, it's mainly at night, when the sidewalks are less crowded and I want to be able to use as slow a shutter speed and as small an aperture as I like without fear of camera movement.

Camera Bag

In my experience, the best camera bag for street photography is one that holds your camera, one or two lenses, and little else. Anything larger will tempt you to carry more, which will weigh you down and make you more conspicuous to your subjects. Avoid bags with big flashy logos that announce "Camera inside!" Not only will they attract attention from subjects, they may attract the attention of thieves and the authorities, as well. Light padding in your bag will protect against most bumps and abrasions; heavy padding simply adds weight and bulk.

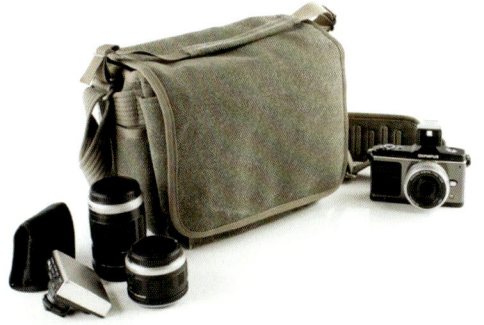

Retrospective 5 shoulder bag from ThinkTank Photo website. If it weren't for the camera and lenses sitting next to it, this would look like any generic messenger or shoulder bag—which is a good thing.

Water-resistance, though not essential, definitely comes in handy if you ever find yourself having to carry your equipment in rain or snow.

Camera Carrying Method

How you choose to carry your camera and lenses is mainly a matter of personal preference and convenience. Some prefer a neck or shoulder strap, others prefer a wrist strap, and others prefer no strap at all.

Neck or Shoulder Strap

⊕ When you're not shooting, a neck strap frees both hands to do something other than hold the camera. The camera is not visible when carried over the shoulder and behind the back.

⊖ Heavy equipment can cause discomfort and pain in the neck and shoulders. A loose strap can catch on objects such as doorknobs. Leaning forward with a camera around your neck can cause it to swing forward like a pendulum.

Wrist Strap

⊕ The camera is always at hand and ready to shoot. The camera is not visible when carried behind the back.

⊖ As long as you are carrying the camera, one hand is occupied. Heavy equipment is tiresome to carry.

Comfortable Shoes

Laugh if you will, but after spending a few hours walking the pavement in stiff, tight, uncomfortable shoes, you will be wincing in pain. The more physically comfortable you are, the longer you can wander around and the more enjoyable the experience will be.

Glasses or Contact Lenses

It should be obvious that good vision is a prerequisite to good photography. However, as our eyes age, they lose the ability to focus on nearby objects. You may reach a point in your life where your optometrist can either correct your vision for nearby objects *or* distant objects, but trying for both becomes a compromise, even with bifocals. This becomes a problem when you need distance vision to see your subjects but close-up vision to see the display and controls on your camera. There is no one solution that is ideal for everyone, so you will simply have to experiment to find out what works best for you and requires the least amount of fumbling.

WHAT ABOUT USING A CAMERA PHONE?

There is something to be said for the convenience of using a mobile phone with a built-in camera for street photography. As long as you've got your phone you've got a camera—and the images today's camera phones can produce are surprisingly good, especially when used in daylight. And you certainly won't attract attention using one. Mobile phones are as common as hands and feet these days. No one will pay the slightest attention to you aiming one in their direction, if they notice you at all.

The main limitation of mobile phones is lack of flexibility: you're locked into one lens, one aperture, and no direct controls other than the shutter button. Everything else has to be accessed via menus, assuming there are any controls at all.

In short, although a camera phone is certainly better than no camera at all, my personal opinion is that using it as your one-and-only camera limits your options to an unacceptable degree.

In Summary and to Reiterate…

You should not get too caught up in worrying about what type of equipment is best for street photography. Practically anything you have will work, as long as it's reasonably portable and quick. You'll have much more success with a simple camera and a tireless interest in documenting life on the streets than you will with $10,000 worth of equipment that sits at home under lock and key. It's all about getting the shot. How you get it and the equipment you use are of secondary importance.

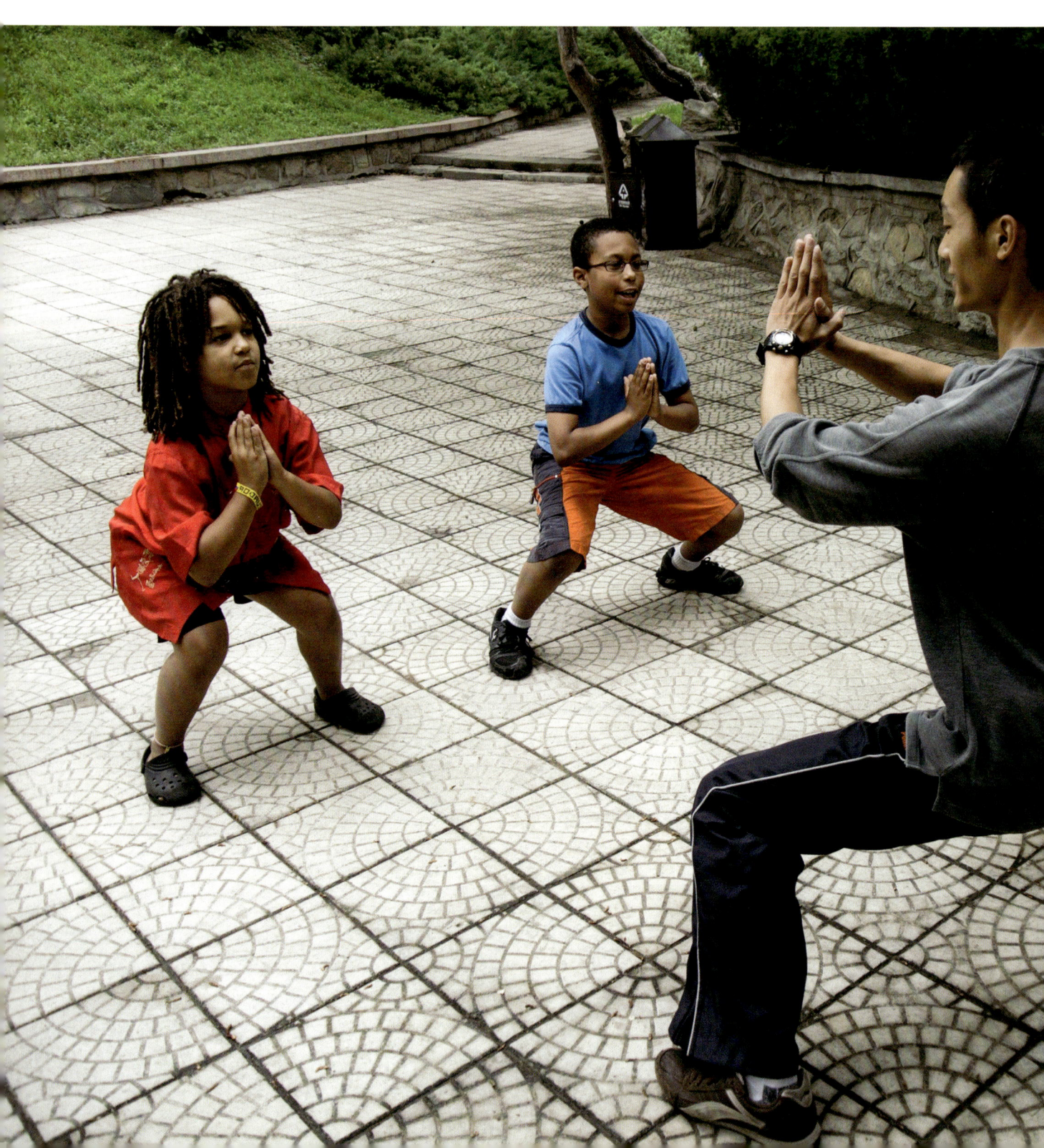

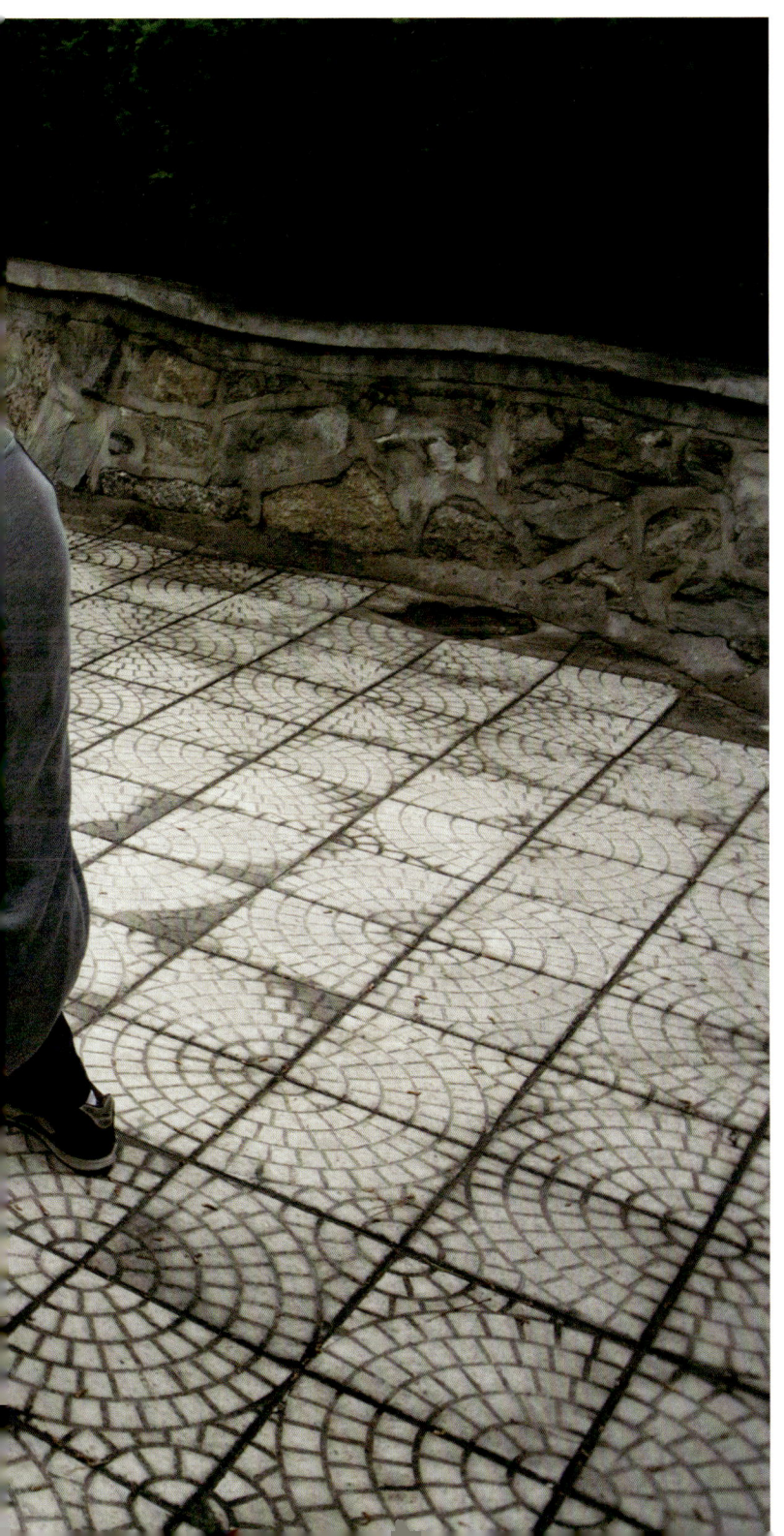

Chapter 3
Techniques

One of the reasons so many photographers decide to try their hand at street photography is because it is—or at least it *appears* to be—so easy. If you're using one of today's fully automatic cameras, you simply point, frame, and shoot. More often than not the result will be a decently exposed, properly focused, but if truth be told, mediocre image.

The real challenge lies in producing photographs that, aside from meeting basic technical requirements, are actually interesting, fascinating, wondrous, humorous, poignant, or amazing. This requires a degree of artistry and creativity, an interest in human behavior, and a feel for timing, light and shadow, and color and composition. I can point you in the right direction, but only you can decide how deeply you want to explore this craft. Keep in mind that the primary objective of any technique you use should be to capture what street photography master **Henri Cartier-Bresson** called "the decisive moment"—the split second when a significant, spontaneous event combines with a pleasing composition of elements to produce a satisfying photograph.

This, of course, implies that you are taking candid photos and that your subject is not waiting patiently for you to focus, zoom, and release the shutter. When you're shooting on impulse, you will need to reduce or eliminate anything that might delay you from being able to produce a reasonably sharp, well-exposed photograph in as little time as possible. In this chapter, I'll describe proven techniques for how to do just that.

I will also provide tips on how to capture such events without attracting negative attention. Keep in mind that unless you are literally invisible or hiding, you will be standing in plain sight with a camera in your hands.

With the right technique, few people, if any, will notice or care if you're taking pictures of them. Of those who do, practically none will be annoyed enough to confront you. In the 40 years I've been practicing street photography, I can count on the fingers of one hand the number of times that someone asked me to stop taking pictures. I compare this to the dozens of times someone on the street has asked or even playfully demanded that I photograph them. I have been only too happy to comply. There is no rule that says *all* street photographs have to be candid, which is why this chapter will conclude with tips for how to improve your street photos when your subjects are aware that you are photographing them and cooperative with the process.

Reduce the Lag

As should be obvious from looking at some of the best examples of street photography, the difference between a great image and a mildly interesting one may be only a matter of seconds. Expressions are fleeting. The lighting can change in an instant. Your subject can change position. Someone can step in front of your camera. The less time it takes you to raise your camera to your eye and shoot, the greater the odds are that you will capture that once-in-a-lifetime shot.

This isn't quite as simple as it might sound. For example, if your camera is battery dependent, you will need to make sure it's switched on. If it has a power-saving feature, it will automatically go to sleep after a few minutes of no activity. Some cameras awake from sleep the instant you tap the shutter button; others may take a second or two. Others refuse to let you release the shutter unless and until the image is in focus, which can introduce unexpected delays. The good news is that you can overcome almost all of these delays, as long as you're aware of them and know how to set your camera to avoid them.

Power Management

If your camera needs a battery to power anything other than the exposure meter, you won't be able to take a photograph unless the camera is switched on. Some cameras have the power switch located next to the shutter button, which makes it easy to switch on with your index finger without having to change your grip, but others have a less conveniently placed switch.

One answer to this problem is to simply leave the power switch set to On. Unfortunately, leaving the power on while you're wandering about presents problems of its own, especially if your camera has a high current draw. (Cameras with totally electronic viewfinders fall into this category.) Not only will this increase the drain on battery power, it will cause the battery to heat up, which can noticeably increase image noise. A solution for this is to carry several backup batteries. If the one you're using gets hot or depleted, you can swap it for another.

To reduce current draw, most cameras will conserve battery power by automatically and temporarily shutting themselves down after a few minutes of inactivity. If you have a camera that takes a second or two to rouse itself from slumber, you'll need to develop the habit of waking it up the instant you even suspect you might want to take a photograph. Keep in mind, however, that this will never be as fast as a camera that is always on.

Shutter Lag

Shutter lag is the time difference between the point when you trigger the shutter and the point when the photo is actually taken. The lag may be due to the time it takes your camera to focus, meter, set white balance, charge the built-in flash, etc. Some cameras, such as the Leica M7 film rangefinder, have a lag of only 12 milliseconds. Others, such as low-end cell phone cameras or digital point-and-shoots, have delays of a half-second or more. When reviewing your pictures, if you find that you're always capturing the gesture or expression *after* the one you wanted, your camera has too much shutter lag. Unfortunately, there is not much you can do to reduce it, so it's always a good idea to use a camera with as little shutter lag as possible.

Viewfinder Lag

Many digital cameras these days have no optical viewfinder. Instead, they offer the electronic equivalent of an eye-level viewfinder as well as the normal Live View LCD option. A built-in sensor detects when you are raising the camera to your eye and automatically switches from the Live View LCD to the eye-level electronic viewfinder. The longer the lag between however long it takes you to raise the camera to your eye and when the camera switches from one viewfinder to the other, the greater the chance that neither one will be on and you'll be shooting blind. One solution, if your camera has this option, is to switch off one of these two viewfinders; that way, the one you choose to use will always be on and ready to shoot.

Another, more subtle form of electronic viewfinder lag is when the image you see in the viewfinder is a few milliseconds delayed from the actual scene. If you don't notice any delay in your photographs, however, then it's not a problem.

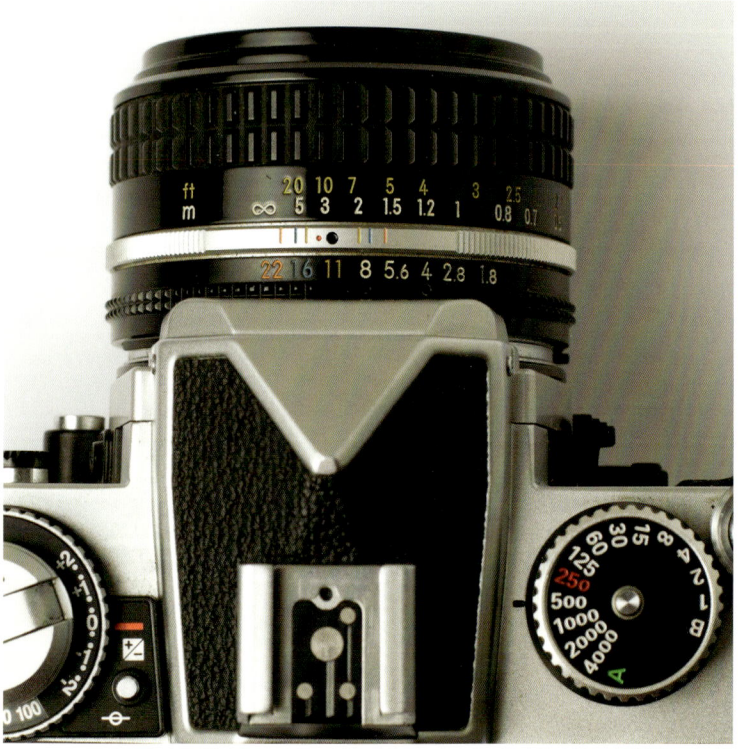

Depth-of-field scales are rare and vestigial these days. This example is from a 50mm f/1.8 AIS Nikkor, produced in the early 1980s. The color-coded lines on the lens-mounting ring correspond to the colors of the f/stops below f/8 on the aperture ring. For example, f/11 is yellow and f/16 is blue. The line to the left of the focus index indicates the furthest point of acceptable focus. The line on the right indicates the nearest. With the focusing ring set to 3 meters (10 feet) and the aperture set to f/11, the range of acceptable focus would therefore be 2–5 meters (6–18 feet).

Keep in mind that acceptable focus is relative to the degree of enlargement, viewing distance, focal length, sensor size, and other variables. On the other hand, you will find it's far better to have a fascinating image in acceptable focus than a boring image in perfect focus.

Zooming

Zoom lenses can be a great convenience. They can also result in lost shots if, instead of releasing the shutter, you are zooming in or out. It's much faster to simply preset a suitable focal length for the environment you're in and leave it at that. Some of the most acclaimed street photographers avoid zooms altogether, in favor of fixed focal length lenses. With practice, you can become so familiar with the fixed angle of view that you know what you'll see before you even raise the camera to your eyes. You lose framing flexibility, but you gain speed and the ability to previsualize.

Focusing

The autofocus systems in today's cameras are so good that most can snap into focus in a split-second. DSLRs with sports-tuned continuous focus systems can even maintain focus as your subject walks toward or away from you. Unfortunately, this does not mean that autofocus is infallible. In real-world street photography, your compositions will often include groups of people standing at different distances from your camera. Your camera's autofocus system has no way of knowing exactly where to focus unless you position the focus point over your intended subject. That's fine if you have the time to do so, but it results in missed shots if you don't.

There are two easy ways around this, assuming you have the right equipment. The first requires an autofocus camera that has a preset snap focus option. This allows you to set the camera to focus at a preselected distance—3 meters (10 feet), for example. With a medium-to-wide focal length and a small enough aperture, such as f/11, you will have enough depth of field that objects as close as 2 meters (6 feet) and as far away as 5 meters (16 feet) will still be in reasonably sharp focus.

Your second option is to use basically the same technique by prefocusing manually. If the lens you're using has a manual focusing ring and a focusing scale, just set the ring to your distance of choice (refer to the image on the opposite page). If it also has a depth-of-field scale, you will be able to estimate the nearest and furthest distances at which the image will be in acceptable focus. If it doesn't have these features, you can prefocus visually; for example, by focusing on an object that's approximately 3 meters away. If you're using an autofocus lens, make sure it's set to manual focus; otherwise the focus may shift when you press the shutter button. If you're using a zoom, make sure to not move the zoom ring either, because that will also shift the point of focus.

Exposure

The automatic exposure metering systems in today's cameras are accurate enough to handle most, if not all, lighting situations you're likely to encounter on the street. With experience, you will discover which situations your camera's meter has trouble with and how to compensate. You might, for example, dial in +1 stop of exposure compensation if your subject is brighter than average or -1 stop if your subject is darker than average. This requires actively monitoring your exposure settings. Otherwise you run the risk of accidentally over- or underexposing an image beyond retrieval.

One of the most effective (but least used) ways to avoid this is to set your exposure manually, based on the ambient light

conditions for wherever you happen to be shooting. Ambient light is the amount of light falling onto a subject or scene, independent of the subject's reflectance. Setting your camera to a fixed shutter speed and aperture based on the ambient light level will therefore prevent exposure variations caused by reflections from your subjects. For example, based on the "Sunny f/16" rule of thumb, the normal exposure setting at ISO 100 for a bright sunny day is roughly 1/100 at f/16 or the equivalent (meaning 1/125 at f/16, 1/250 at f/11, 1/500 at f/8, 1/1000 at f/5.6, etc.). On a heavily overcast day or in the concrete canyons of a major city, you would reduce the shutter speed (that is, use a longer shutter speed) or increase (widen) the aperture by two stops.

Your Camera is Ready, Now What About *You?*

It goes without saying that your camera won't take pictures on its own. At minimum, it needs you to aim, focus, and release the shutter. This is not likely to happen on a crowded street if you have fundamental issues with the act of taking candid photographs of strangers in public places. You must have the desire and the motivation to practice street photography. If you do, you'll soon find which of the following approaches you're most comfortable with, and which yields the most positive results for you.

Mindset

Unlike studio photography, where you can control lighting, framing, color, subject matter, and composition, street photography is completely impromptu. You venture out in public with some idea of where you're going and what you might see, but you have no control over what might happen. The best opportunities for interesting photographs often appear and disappear in a matter of seconds. If you don't capture those moments, you will never have the same chance again. Because of this reality, successful street photography requires the mindset of a hunter or fisherman: you need to be calm yet alert; open to whatever good fortune happens to send your way; and ready to focus your attention the instant you see the potential for a memorable image. It's important to be aware of your surroundings. You don't want to become so focused on the photograph you're trying to capture that you step off a curb into the path of an oncoming car, walk into a pole, or trip over a crack in the sidewalk.

You will also need to be at peace with the idea of taking photographs of people without their knowledge or permission. Some photographers find this immoral or unethical; others don't. As I mentioned, I have no interest in trying to persuade people who believe street photography is wrong to change their minds. This book is meant to provide information to help those who want to improve their street photography skills. The first step, if you have jittery nerves, is simply to practice overcoming your nervousness. The more candid shooting you do and the more open and casual you are about it, the more comfortable you'll become.

Locations

The best locations for street photography will be covered in chapter 4: Locations and Events. For the purposes of general technique, however, you can either walk around looking for

appealing locations and subjects, or stick to one location you like and wait for appealing subjects to appear. As long as you and your camera are ready, either option has equal odds of success. I personally don't take pains to hide my camera or bag. Most people either don't notice or care, even when I'm holding the camera in my hands in plain sight. That being said, the larger your camera and lens are, the more attention you're likely to attract. One exception to this is if you're one among many other photographers. This is common when you're shooting at popular tourist locations, where everyone is so busy snapping pictures and taking videos that no one will pay you any particular attention.

Clothing and Attitude

Given that you will be standing in plain sight with a camera in your hands, there is no point in trying to hide the fact that you're a photographer. On the other hand, there's no need to draw extra attention to yourself, either. The tactic I find most successful is to hide in plain sight. This means you should:

- Wear nondescript clothing that is consistent with your surroundings. (Avoid bright colors or bold patterns, if they will stand out.)
- Maintain a calm, relaxed, yet alert demeanor.
- Avoid any actions that make you look nervous or furtive. If people perceive that you're acting as if you have something to hide, they will naturally assume you do, and will view you with suspicion.

I take a few pictures when the opportunity presents itself, then return to my relaxed, watchful attitude. Curious onlookers will occasionally ask me what I'm doing and why. My response is always short and honest, yet positive. For example: "I'm a photographer, it's a nice day, and I like to walk around and photograph the people that make this such a great city." Many people who see me wandering around will actually invite me to take their picture—which, of course, I am only too happy to do.

There are, of course, locations and situations where it's normal and well justified for people to be suspicious of photographers. For example, photographers should be cautious about taking pictures of children other than their own unless they have been invited to do so by the parents. Photographers should also be careful about photographing in front of high-security buildings, on private property, or in high-crime locations. Aside from the slight risk of having your equipment stolen, people who have good reason not to want to be photographed can get very upset when they see a photographer lurking around. Even if you have the legal right to photograph in such locations, life is too short to waste it in arguments with overzealous security personnel or paranoid subjects.

First-Shot Response

Your first-shot response is simply the time it takes you to raise your camera, frame, and shoot. If you've taken the trouble to minimize all the potential lag sources, you should be able to get a reasonably sharp and well-exposed shot in less than a second. Some of the best street photographers are so quick they can raise and lower their camera in less than a second. This is faster than many subjects can react, particularly if they didn't

notice you to begin with. It's also fast enough that some will doubt whether you actually took a photo at all, especially if you avoid eye contact.

Avoiding Eye Contact

Although there is nothing wrong with a subject being aware that you have photographed them, you don't necessarily have to announce the fact. To add some ambiguity to the situation, consider looking beyond the person you intend to photograph, as if your interest is in something behind them. If someone does make eye contact, you can simply smile, nod, and keep shooting whatever it was that was "behind" them. This is particularly effective if you're using a wide-angle lens in a location packed with people: because the field of view is wider than someone might expect, subjects will assume they aren't in the frame when in fact, they are.

Keep in mind that this approach is less effective if, for example, your subject is seated across from you in a subway train and she is the only person you could possibly be photographing. If that's the case, then you might want to try an equally effective option: shooting from the hip.

Shooting From the Hip

If you're fortunate enough to own a camera that has a rear LCD that you can flip upward to convert into a waist-level viewfinder, you'll find that shooting from the hip is an excellent way to shoot discreetly. While you are actually focusing and framing a shot, it will appear to your subject that you're just another shutterbug who's looking down and fumbling with your camera. Even this subterfuge may not be necessary if you're shooting with a small, nondescript digital camera that has no eye-level viewfinder. As long as you extend the camera at arm's length to view and shoot, you'll look like just another amateur snapping away with a cheap camera. Some street shooters take this approach one step further—they point the camera at their subjects, finger on the shutter button, without using any viewfinder at all. I have tried this myself and can confirm that, as you might imagine, it takes a lot of practice (and yes, luck) to get consistently good results. On the other hand, the results you do get will have a distinctive perspective and manner of framing that you don't often get with typical eye-level shots.

Swimming Upstream

A popular technique for photographers shooting on crowded sidewalks or boardwalks is to position yourself opposite the flow of foot traffic, so your subjects are moving toward you. This allows plenty of opportunities to observe people as they approach, and to photograph them as they pass by. If they notice you at all, they will often be in such a hurry or so indifferent that they would rather continue on their way than pause to ask why you photographed them.

Keep in mind that if you use this approach, the people you are photographing will often be in motion. If your camera has an effective continuous focus feature, you can use this to lock and maintain focus as your subject moves toward you. Lacking such a feature, I find I can get equally good results by prefocusing on a spot that is at the distance I expect the subject to be when I release the shutter.

Wait and See

Another technique that works well for many photographers is to find a promising setting—a billboard, a bus stop, a street performer gathering an audience—and wait for the right subject or composition to appear. Aesthetically speaking, the right subject can be someone wearing clothing that contrasts or complements the background, someone who stands in the perfect spot, or someone who has the perfect expression. You have to be careful, though, that the resulting images don't become clichéd or formulaic. Even if you have a particular composition or moment in mind, you should always be open and ready for serendipity; sometimes those unexpected moments turn out far better then anything you might have planned.

Keep Your Distance

There is no rule that says you have to be within a few feet of your subjects to produce good street photos. You could be across the street or even half a block away. Assuming there is nothing but open space between you and your subject, you could even use a short telephoto or zoom lens to make up for the distance. Aside from reducing your anxiety level

OPPOSITE PAGE:
Mom and Son, Marina del Rey, CA 1998
I was waiting for my car to exit a car wash when this mother and son sat directly opposite me. I liked the way their arms were intertwined but didn't want to disturb the mood. My camera was already resting in my lap, so without raising it to my eye I simply pointed the lens at them and released the shutter.

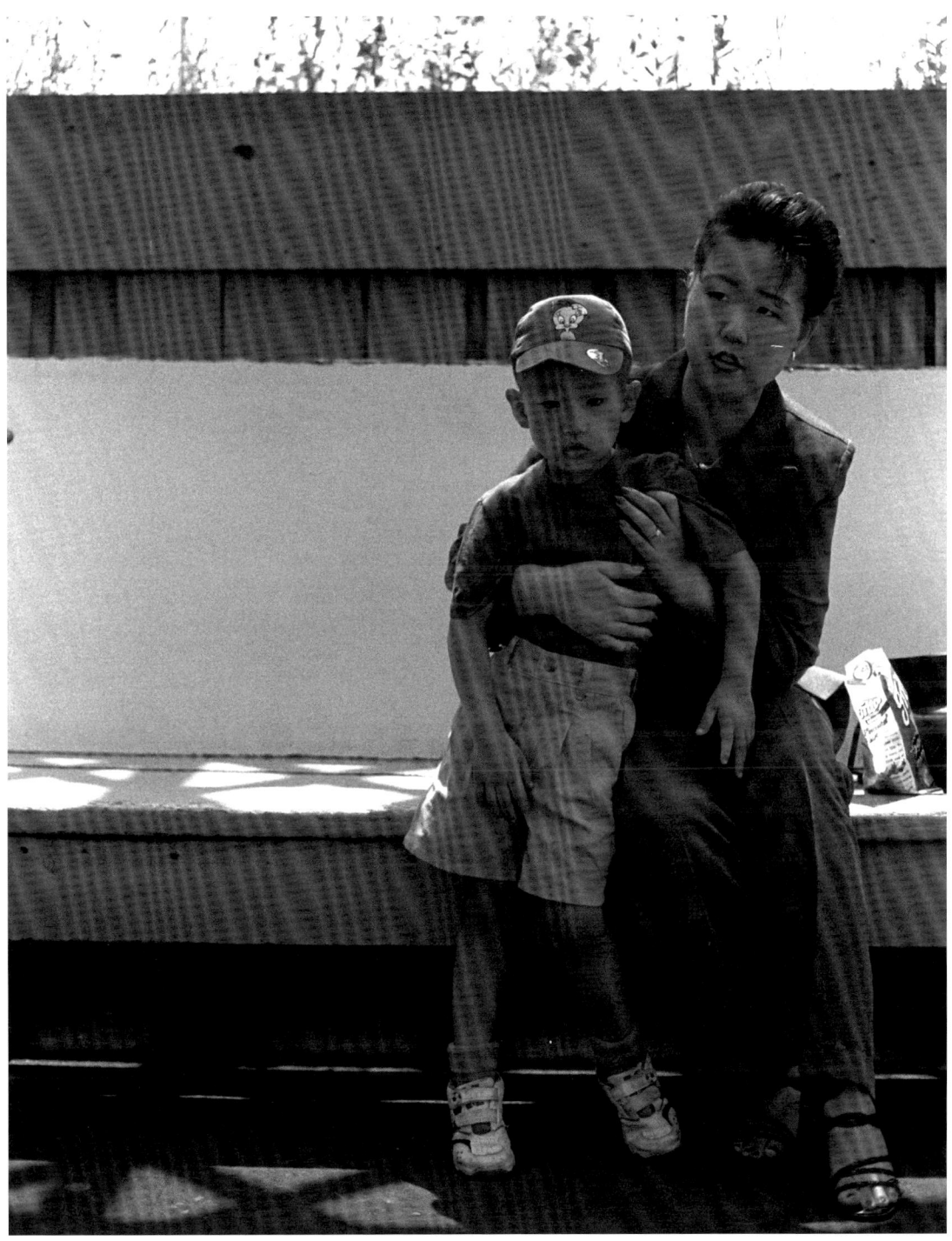

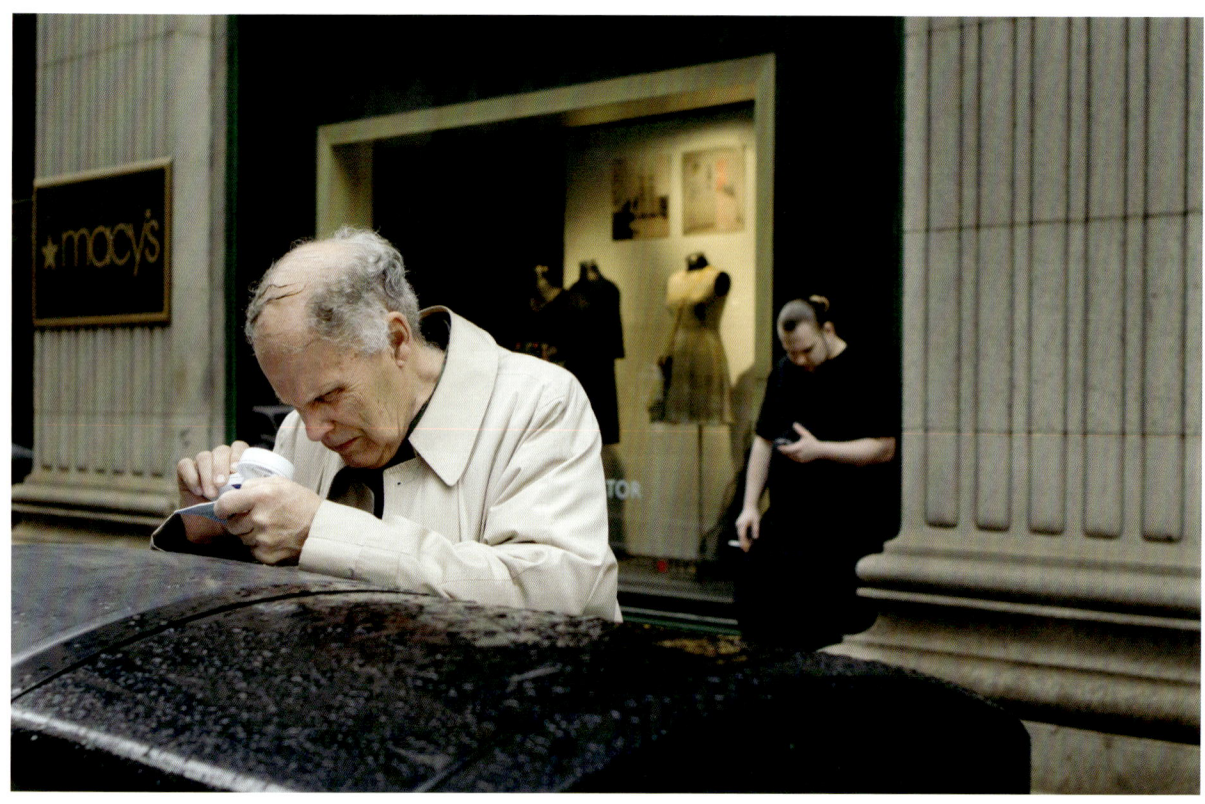

Take a Closer Look, Philadelphia, PA 2012
This is generally as close as I would be to someone who wasn't aware I was photographing him or her. He was focusing so intently on the piece of paper he was reading and my camera was so quiet that he never noticed me.

or that of your subjects, distance allows you to include more of the environment, which can be an important documentary element in your photographs. You may notice from my photos that, although I don't use this approach exclusively, I use it often enough that it's a key element of my style. Feel free to do the same.

TO ASK OR NOT TO ASK?

A common complaint voiced by critics of street photography is that it's rude and exploitive to take photographs of people without their permission. My personal point of view is that it depends on how physically close you are to your subject. I wouldn't dream of sticking a camera in someone's face and snapping away without their permission. On the other hand, if I'm a few feet away and can photograph them without disturbing or disrespecting them, I see no harm in doing so. As the distance increases to several yards and you're photographing groups of people, crowds, or figures that are simply elements in a larger composition, it's ridiculous to seek permission. Let common courtesy and common sense be your guide and you'll seldom go wrong.

And Now a Word for the Direct Approach...

There is also no rule that says your subjects have to be unaware that you're photographing them. In fact, the closer you are to someone, the more likely they are to notice you, especially if you point a camera in their direction. Some of the best street photos feature people looking directly at the camera, either because the photographer asked before taking their picture or because they gave their tacit approval by smiling, laughing, or simply continuing to do whatever it was they were doing.

The benefit of the direct—as opposed to a purely candid—approach is that it eliminates the concern that you may be intruding on someone or photographing them without permission. It also allows for the possibility of asking for a model release, which may be essential if you plan to sell the resulting photos commercially (as opposed to selling them as fine art prints). What you lose in total spontaneity and serendipity, you gain in having time to interact with your subject and take multiple images without fear of offense.

Be careful to maintain the candid, spontaneous aesthetic of street shooters, though. If you start posing or directing your subjects too much you may get fine portraits, but you'll lose a lot of the go-with-the-flow feeling that characterizes the street photography genre.

So, how do you ask permission to take a photograph of someone you don't know? In some cases it can be as easy as gesturing at your camera and pantomiming the act of taking a picture. If your subject is willing, he or she will respond with a smile or a shrug. If not, they will shake their head, turn away, or keep walking. In most cases I find the best approach is just to ask politely. There's no need for a labored explanation. In fact, the more simple your request, the better. "Excuse me, would you mind if I took your picture?" is all it takes. Most people are flattered to be the subject of someone else's attention and will rarely refuse.

Of course, it's only natural for a subject to ask *why* you want to photograph them. The best answer is always short, observant, and flattering. For example:

"I love photographing life in the city. You caught my eye because you look so happy."

"You look stunning in that blue dress. I could never forgive myself if I didn't ask to take your picture."

"I believe that every picture tells a story. To be honest, I'm curious as to what yours might be."

...or whatever else seems appropriate to the situation. Your compliment could just as easily be about their hairstyle, work attire, or anything else that makes your subject feel relaxed and comfortable.

You may also encounter subjects who are in a friendly, chatty mood and want to engage in small talk. By all means, do so: even if you're the shy type, it would be rude to photograph someone and then refuse to spend a few minutes conversing with them. If they express an interest in your work you can direct them to your website. If they want a copy of the photo(s) you took, you can arrange to email them, or whatever other method they prefer. You may discover that talking to your subjects is one of the more enjoyable parts of your day. Not only will you be doing yourself a favor by making your subjects feel comfortable, you will also help spread the notion that street photographers are rather decent folk who are pursuing a harmless, or even occasionally beneficial, pastime.

Only rarely will you encounter someone who gets angry or abusive about being politely approached for a photograph. It's never fun when that happens, but if and when it does, it will almost always be because of *their* issues, not you. Apologize, be on your way, and send them prayers for a better day. As long as your heart is in the right place, there will be plenty of people who not only say yes, but who will be delighted you asked.

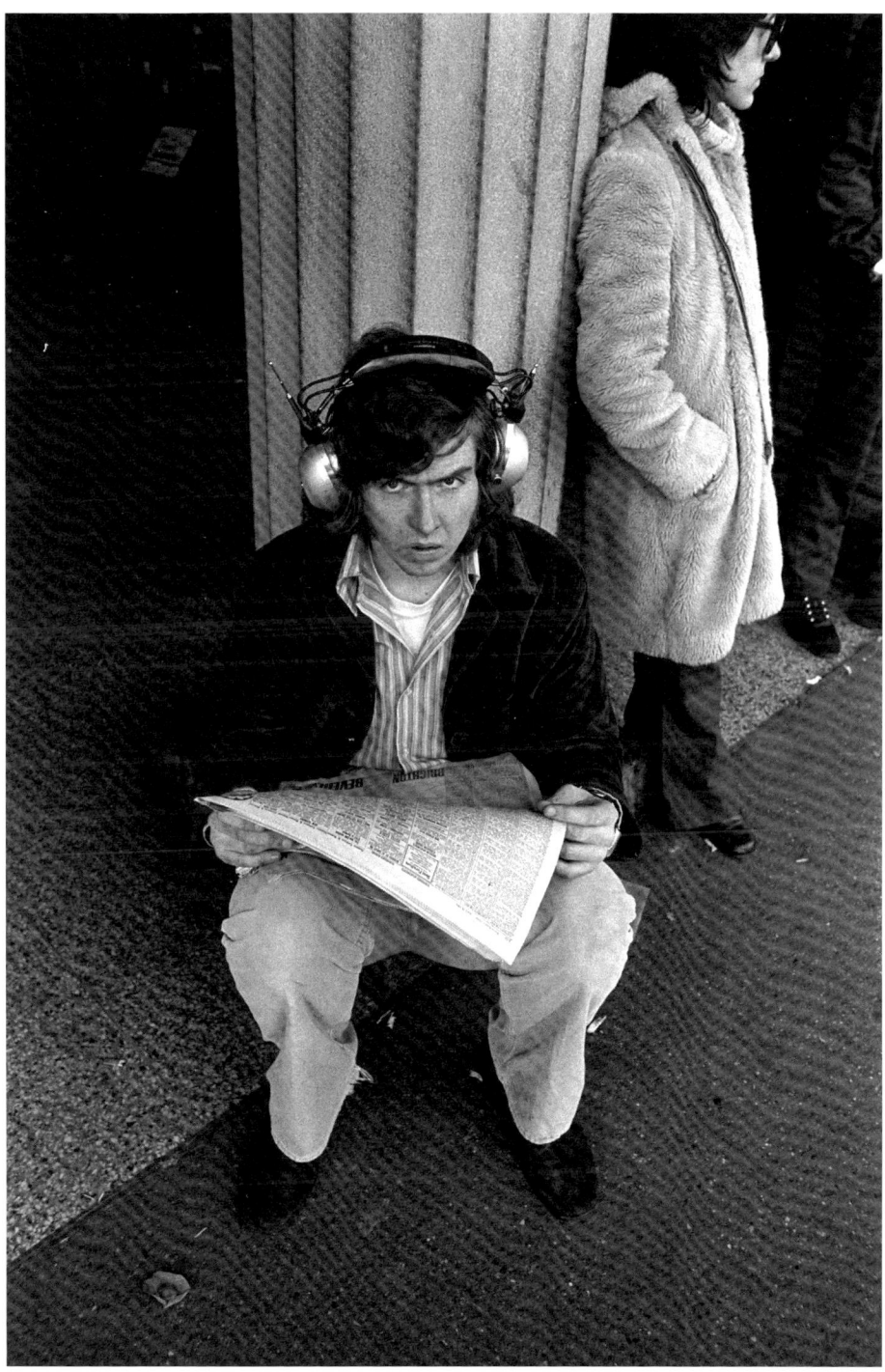

Scowler, Cambridge, MA 1973

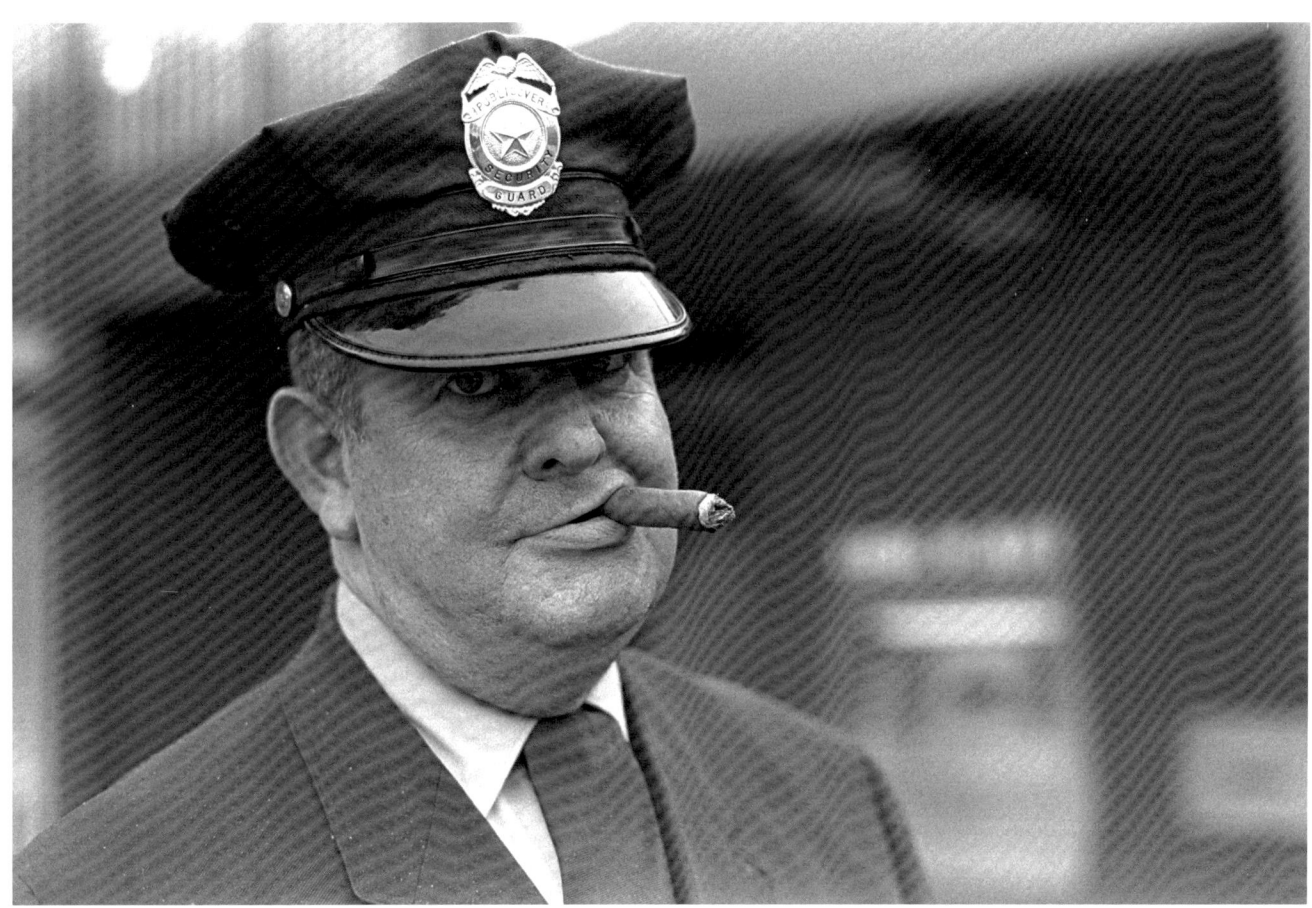

Security Guard, Boston, MA 1974

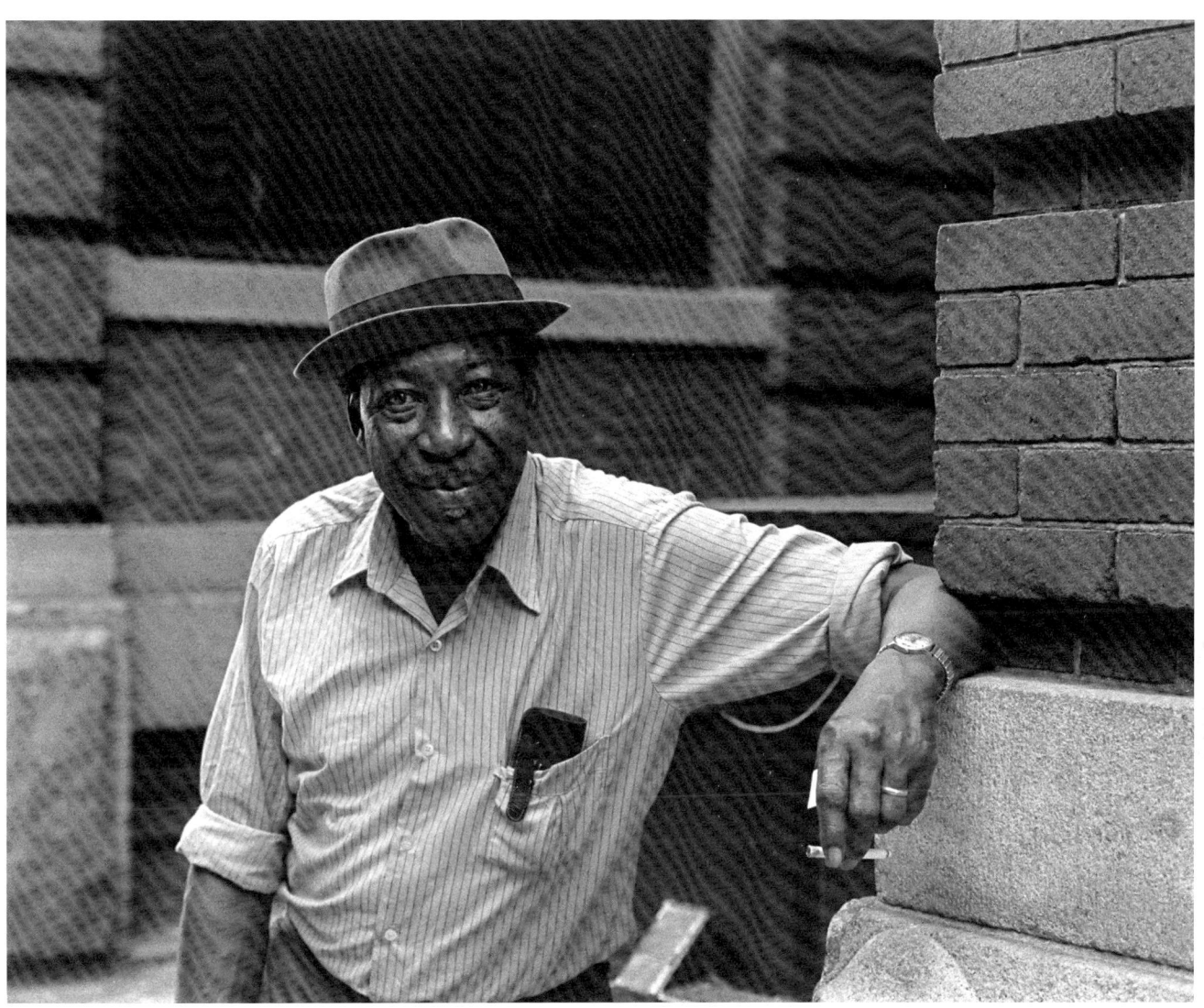

Charming Gent, Atlanta, GA 1972

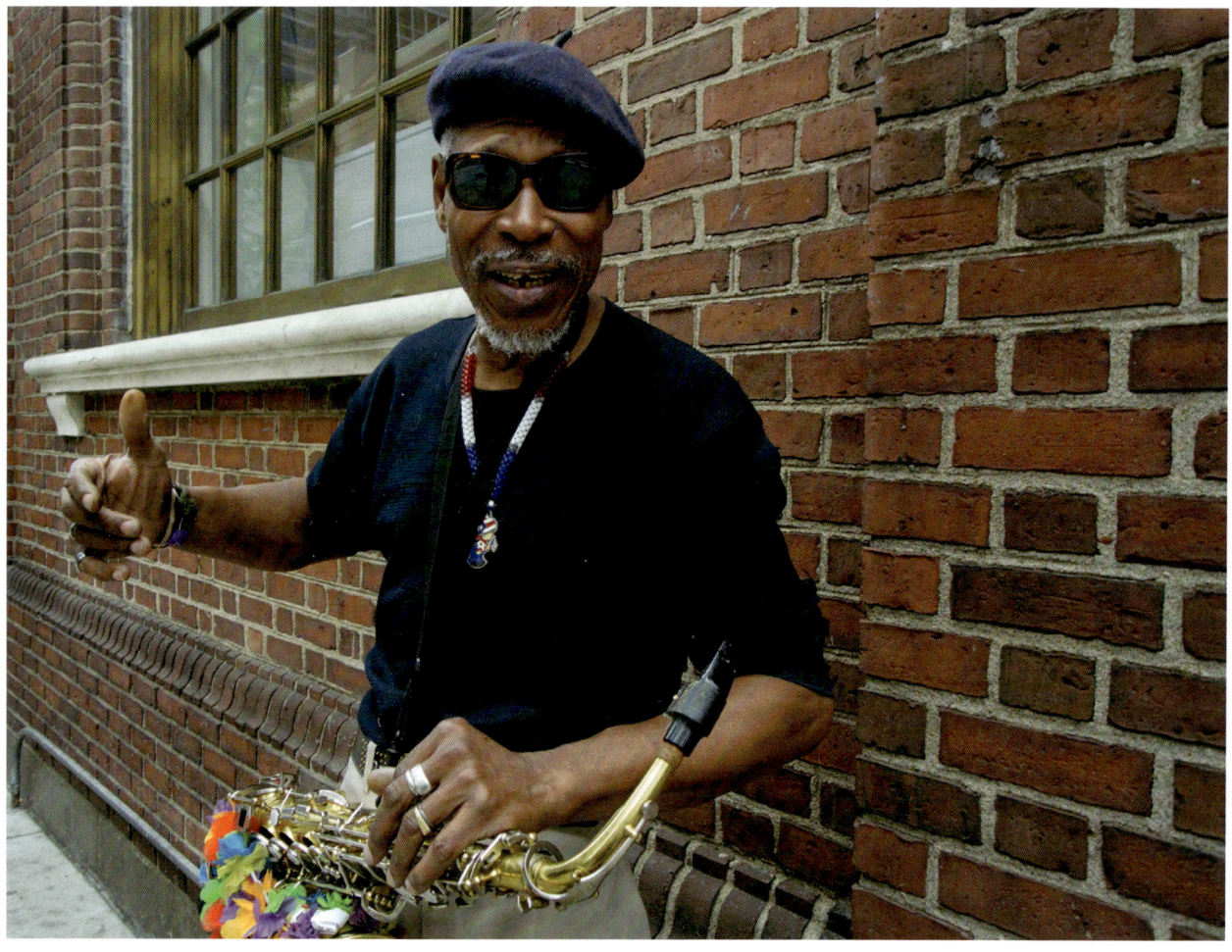

Sax Appeal, Philadelphia, PA 2012

OPPOSITE PAGE:
All-American, Philadelphia, PA 2013

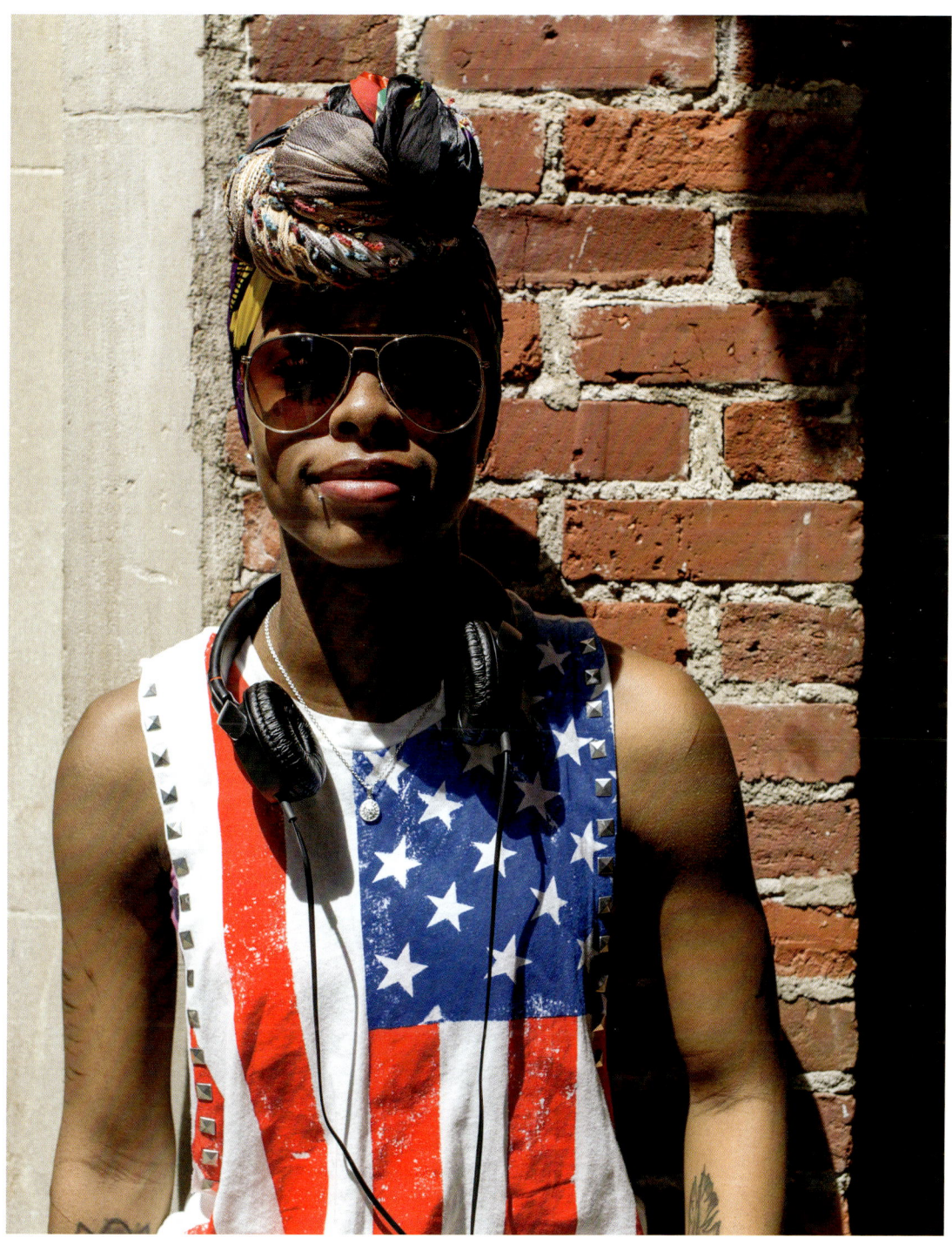

Gallery
of Contributing
Photographers

Master Street Photographers

Henri Cartier-Bresson
Elliot Erwitt
Garry Winogrand

Contemporary Street Photographers

Steve Dierkens
Rinzi Ruiz
Kip Praslowicz

The Masters of Street Photography

It's difficult to advance as an artist without becoming familiar with the work in your field that precedes you. Any blues musician worth his or her salt is intimately familiar with the styles of B.B King, Albert King, Freddie King (none of whom were related, by the way), Etta James, Howlin' Wolf, and more. Anyone who is serious about producing impressionist paintings understands the nuances of the works of impressionist masters such as Monet, Degas, and Renoir. If you're serious about developing your skills as a street photographer, you should become familiar with the methods and styles of the street photography masters.

The photos shown here are examples of Henri Cartier-Bresson's, Elliot Erwitt's, and Garry Winogrand's work. These images are not necessarily the best or best-known photographs by these artists; they are examples of the origins of street photography from the early 20th century. As you look at them, reflect on how much of our culture has changed, and how much has stayed the same.

If you haven't already, it's a good idea to familiarize yourself with the other photographers on the list. Some may intimidate you; others may annoy, confuse, or inspire you—but the lasting impression of their work will be strong. In my opinion, that's as good a description of a master and teacher as any.

While there is no universally agreed-upon list of master street photographers, the works of the following artists is considered exemplary in this genre.

Eugene Atget (1857–1927)
Andre Kertesz (1894–1985)
Walker Evans (1903–1975)
Henri Cartier-Bresson (1908–2004)
Robert Doisneau (1912–1994)
Helen Levitt (1913–2009)
Dianne Arbus (1923–1971)
Saul Leiter (1923–2013)
Robert Frank (1924–
Elliott Erwitt (1928–
Lee Friedlander (1934–
Garry Winogrand (1928–1984)
Joel Meyerowitz (1938–
Martin Parr (1952–
Alex Webb (1952–

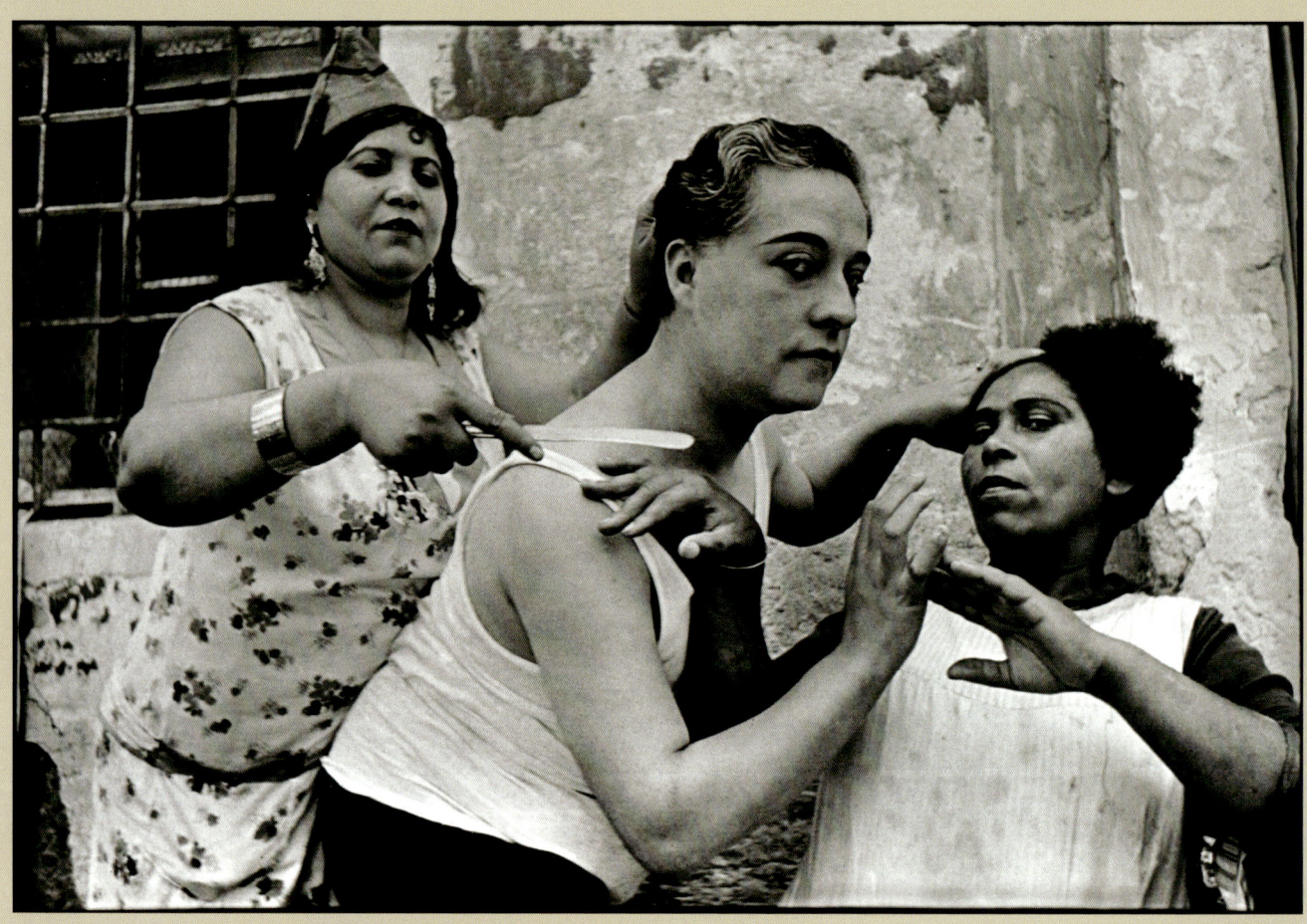

© Henri Cartier-Bresson/Magnum Photos
Valencia Province, Alicante 1933

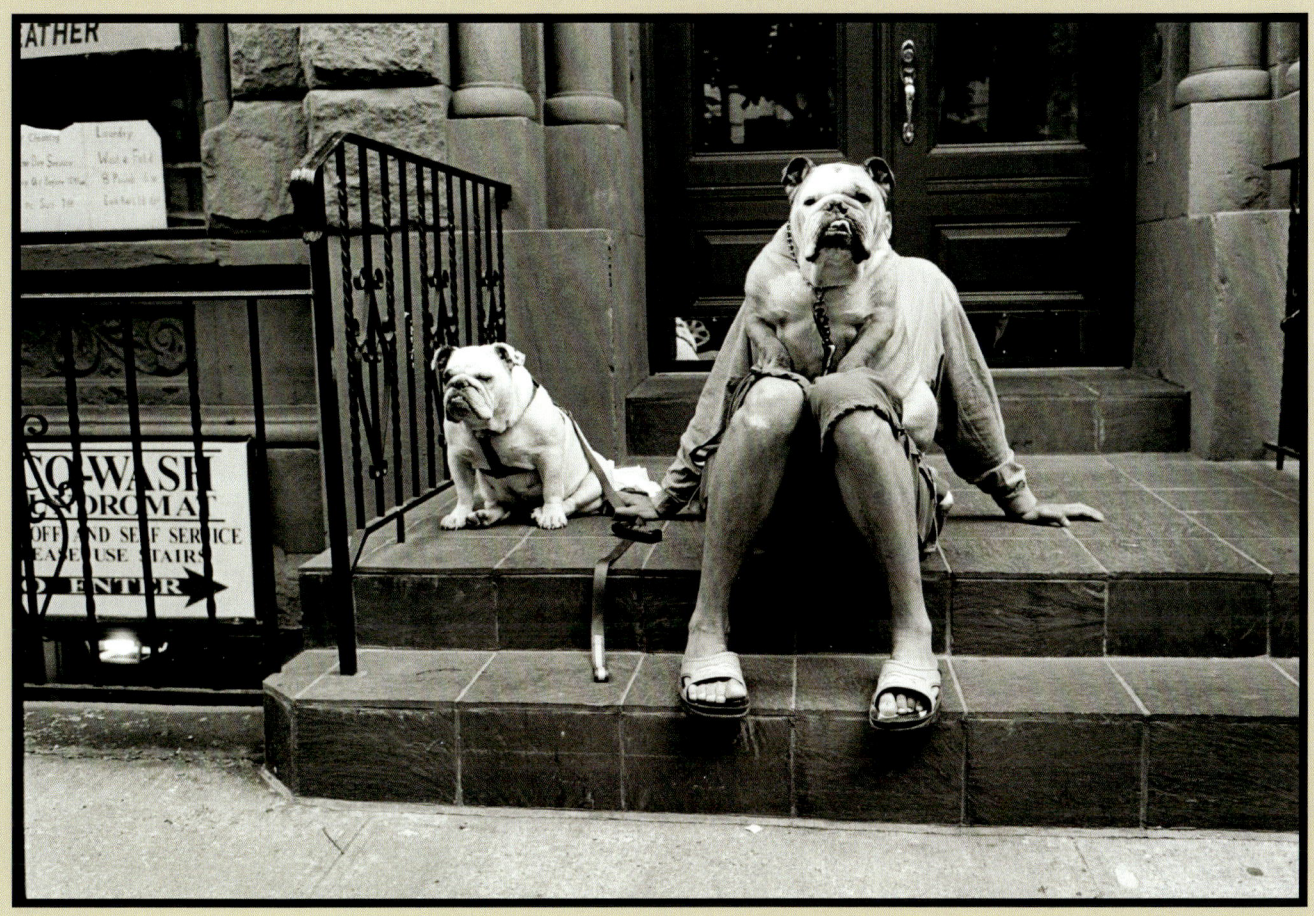

© Elliot Erwitt/Magnum Photos
New York City, NY 2000

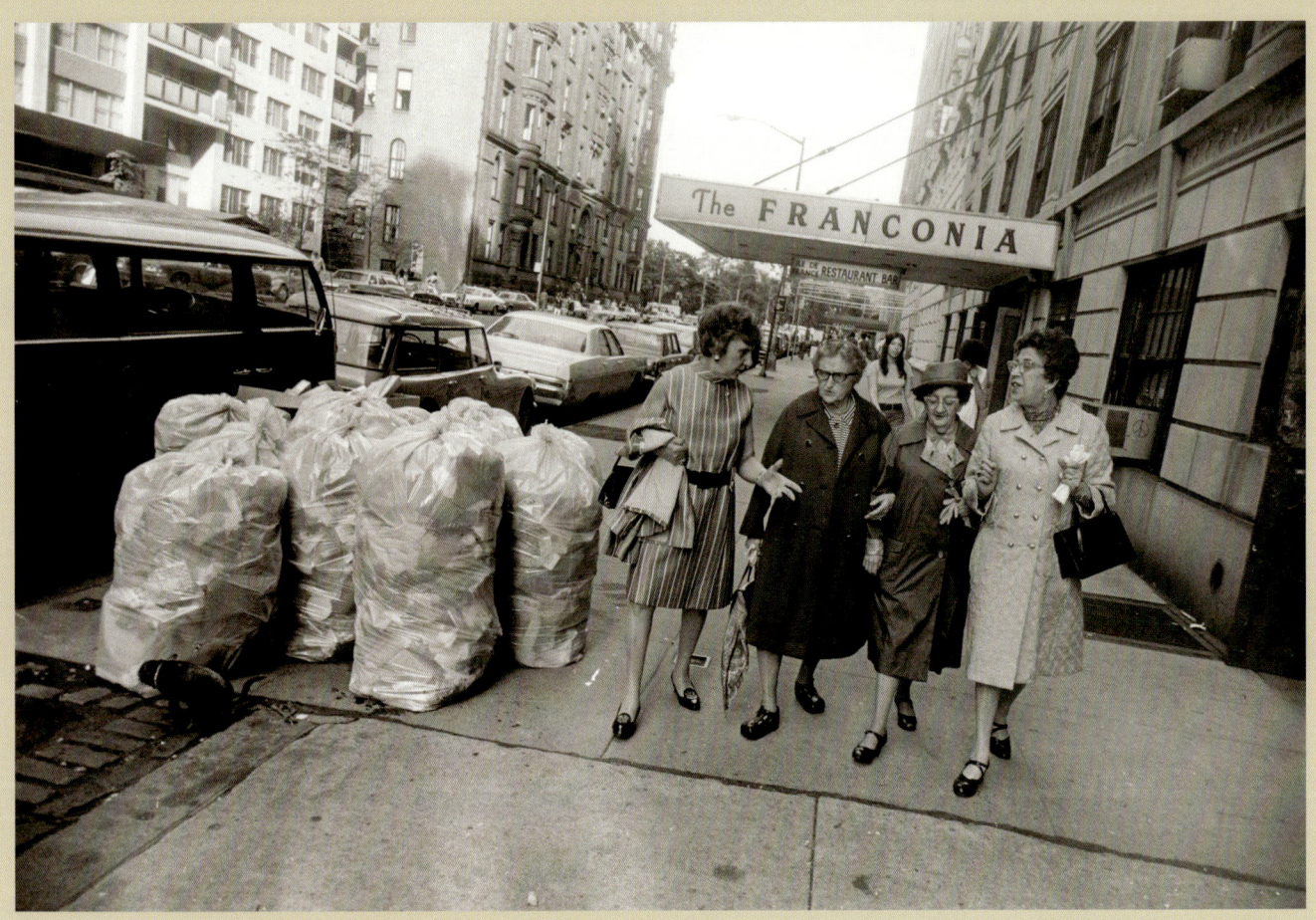

© The Estate of Garry Winogrand, courtesy Fraenkel Gallery, San Francisco
New York City, NY 1970

Contemporary Street Photographers

As much as I love the photographs I've selected to illustrate my own work in the genre of street photography, my images ultimately represent only my approach to the art. They show the places I've been to, the subjects I'm most interested in, the way I like to shoot, and the way I like my images to look. My images do not represent the best nor the only way to shoot. Your work should reflect the places *you've* been to, the subjects *you're* most interested in, the way *you* like to shoot, and how you like *your* images to look.

The following images are samples from three contemporary street photographers with unique styles and points of view. I chose to include their images because I appreciate their aesthetics, and I wanted to show a diversity of street photography styles. I think you'll enjoy their work, too.

Steve Dierkens (www.stevedierkens.be) is a Belgian photographer who has a well-developed talent for capturing colorfully odd, absurd, or even cartoonish moments of everyday urban life.

Rinzi Ruiz (www.streetzen.tumblr.com) is equally adept at shooting images in both black-and-white and in color. His images emphasize deep shadows, low-key tones, isolated figures, and lurid colors to convey a sense of mystery, wonder, unease, and irony.

Kip Praslowicz (www.kpraslowicz.com), who shoots in both black-and-white and color, produces images that have a quiet subtlety, ambiguity, and intensity. His images invite us to linger over every detail to find deeper insight into the message of the photograph.

I invite you to visit these artists' websites to see more of their work. Other contemporary street photography websites worth visiting include:

- **Street Photographers** (http://www.street-photographers.com/)
- **iNPUBLiC** (http://www.in-public.com/)
- **Urban Picnic** (http://www.urbanpicnic-streetphotography.com/)

These websites offer amazing images from like-minded photographers from around the world. You'll also find a supportive community, and perhaps even a venue for your own work.

Steve Dierkens

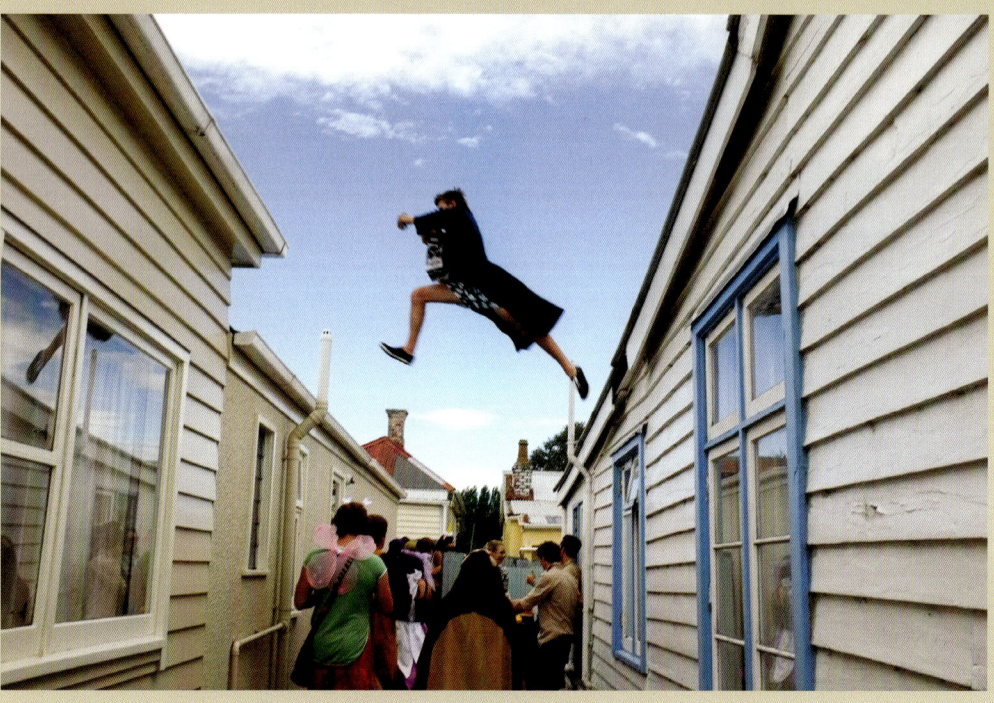

© Steve Dierkens, 2012
Dunedin, New Zealand 2012

Next to paragliding, pursuing the art of street photography is my favorite pastime. I like to roam the streets and other public places on a hunt for humorous, absurd, or ambiguous scenes and situations to photograph. It's necessary to be totally focused, or you might miss out on something special. Street photography is all about reacting quickly and anticipating what might happen next. It pays off to always carry a camera with you, even when you go to the grocery store around the corner. You never know! Photographic opportunities just present themselves to you—for example, something or somebody in the street might grab your attention. It can be beneficial to stay with the subject, hang around a bit, try to relate it to other elements in the environment, and wait for the right moment. Being patient is important when photographing, but there's also a tiny bit of luck involved. Sometimes a detail you didn't notice while photographing a scene turns out to be a key factor in the picture. To me, a compact and non-obtrusive (digital) rangefinder camera with a fixed 35mm equivalent lens works best for street photography. The fact that there is no zoom available on the camera forces you to get in close. The difficult part of street photography is to become invisible as a photographer and shoot in a candid way.

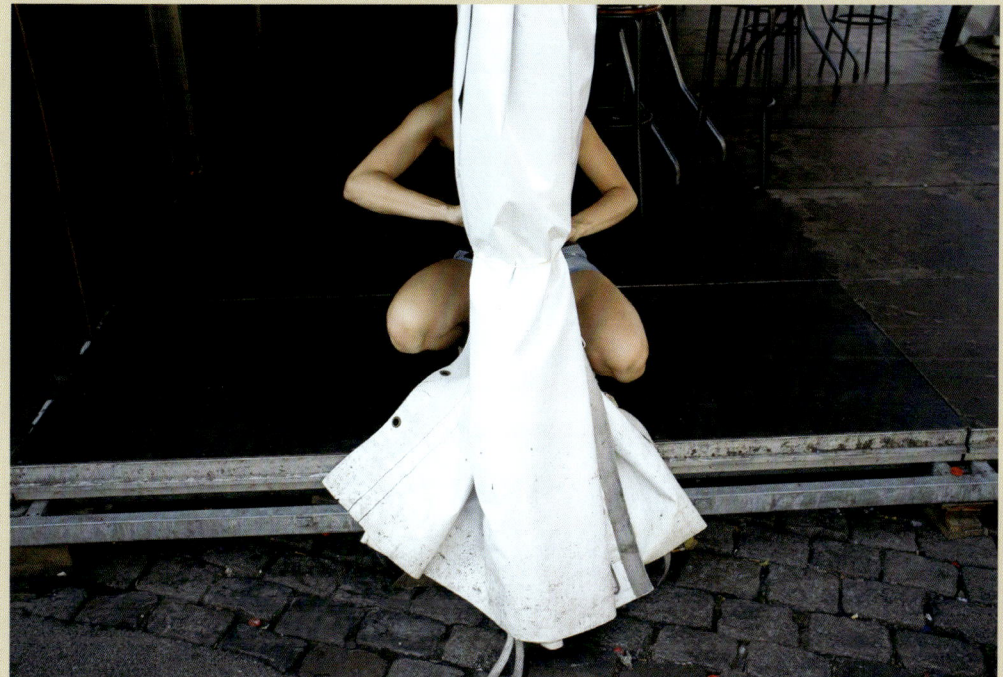

© Steve Dierkens, 2014
Ghent, Belgium 2014

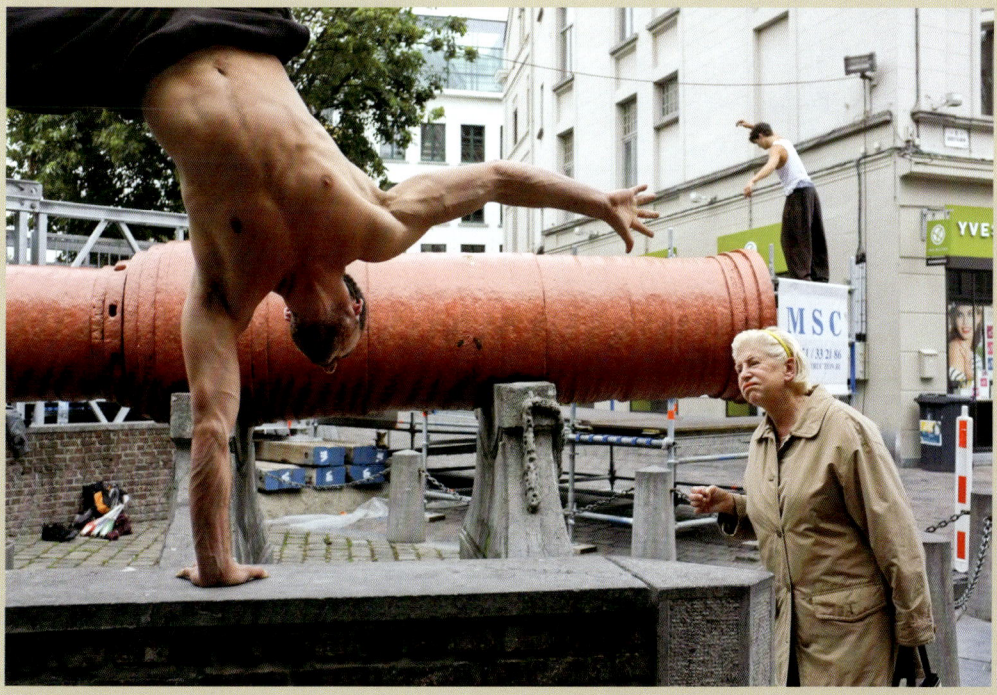

© Steve Dierkens 2013
Ghent, Belgium 2013

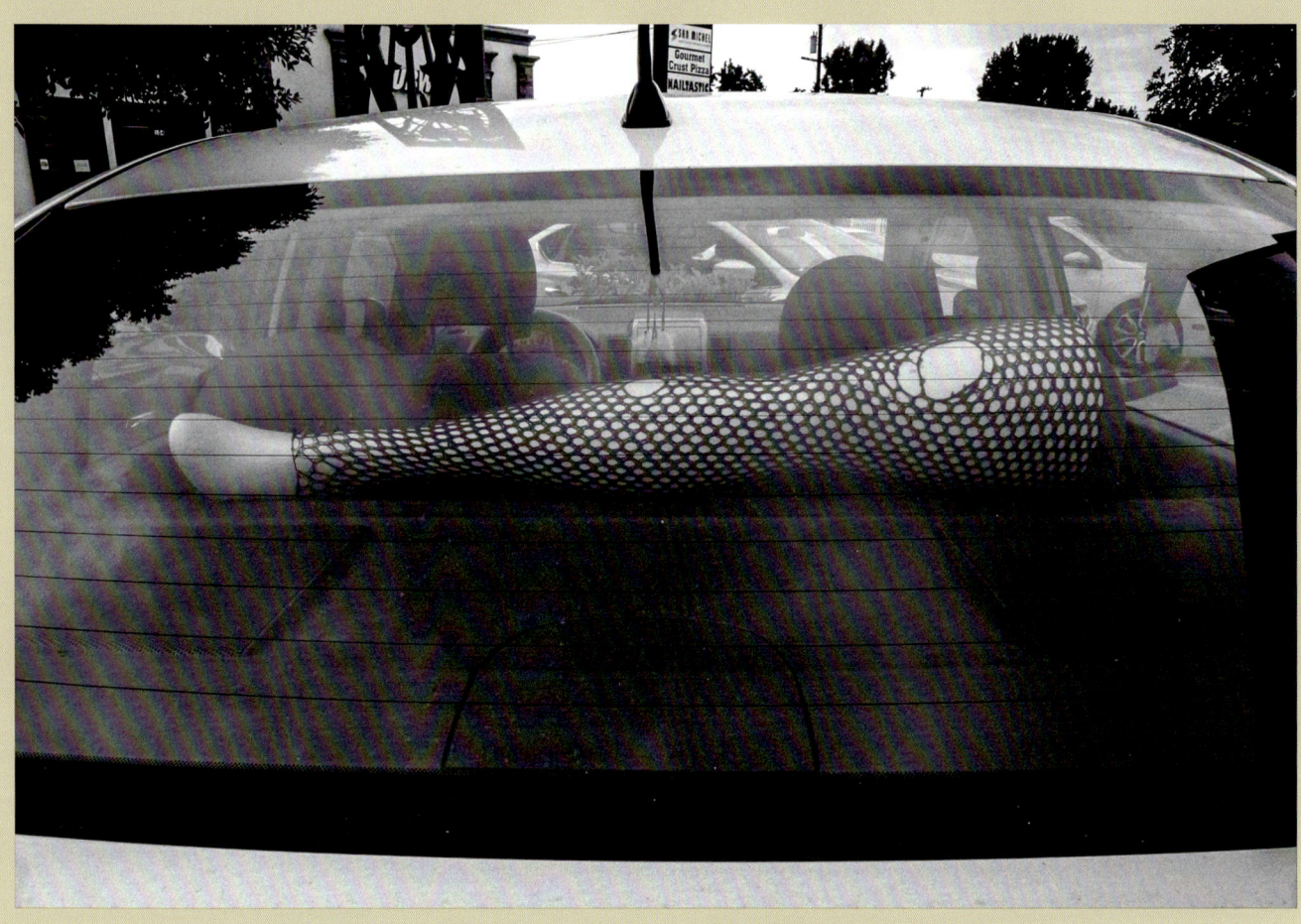

© Rinzi Ruiz 2014
Burbank, CA 2014

Usually I drive to downtown LA to walk around and shoot, but sometimes I find interesting subjects while running errands locally. I was making a quick stop to get coffee when I noticed this mannequin leg in the car. It's not something I see very often, especially in the residential area where I live, so I wanted to get the shot. Since I have a camera with me all the time, I was able to take the picture.

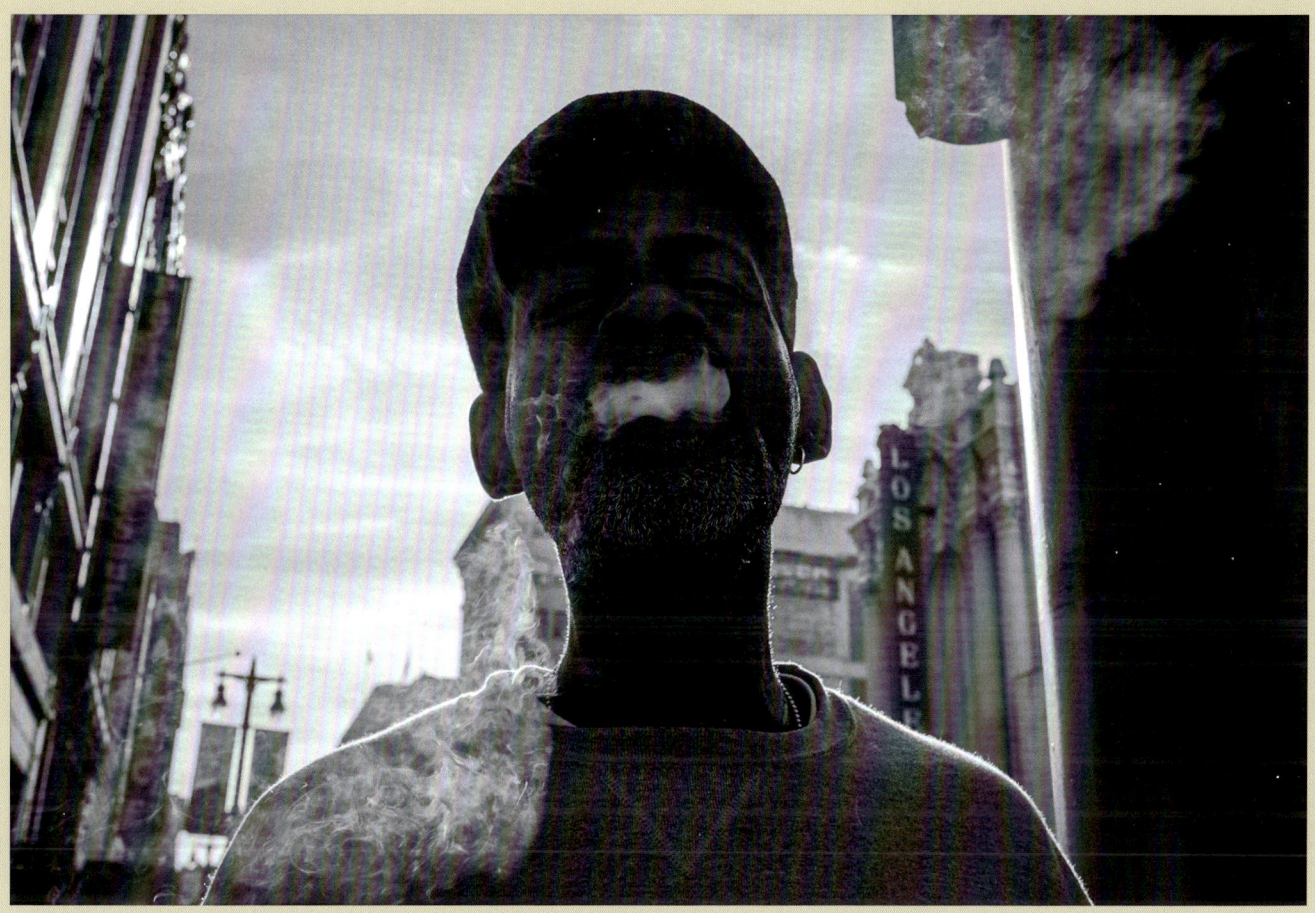

© Rinzi Ruiz 2014
Los Angeles, CA 2014

I saw this man walking toward me from a distance. What caught my attention was the amount of smoke he was producing. I got low as he got closer, and took a few shots of him as he exhaled smoke. I smiled and greeted him afterwards. It was a brief and positive interaction. He was curious to see how the pictures turned out, so I showed him. He complimented the image, we shook hands, and we both went on our way.

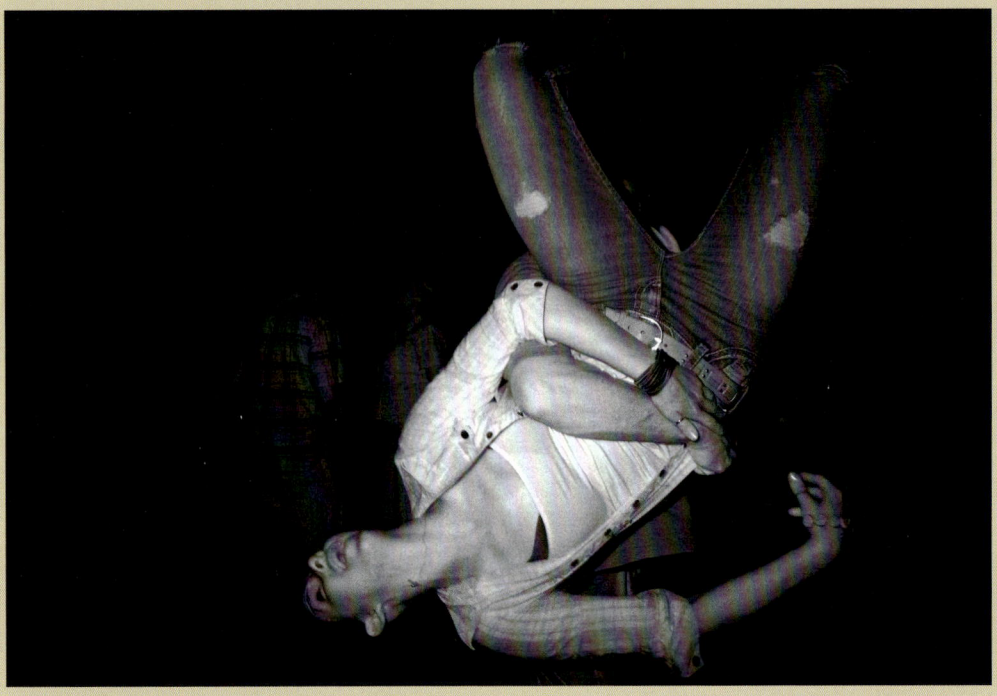

© *Kip Praslowicz 2011*
A Woman Flips, *Rex Bar, Duluth, MN 2011*

A core foundation of traditional street photography comes from the pursuit of capturing examples of the unexpected in human behavior and society. To successfully capture these moments, I feel like the act of street photography is closer to a sport than the more deliberate visual arts, such as painting or sculpture. Street photography requires the need to be completely at ease with using your gear, and being ready to put yourself into the position to snap a photo in a heartbeat is an important skill (one which paid off to make this photo). This image was taken on a Thursday night—a band was playing in front of a small crowd, and one couple used the open floor space to bust out some more advanced dance moves.

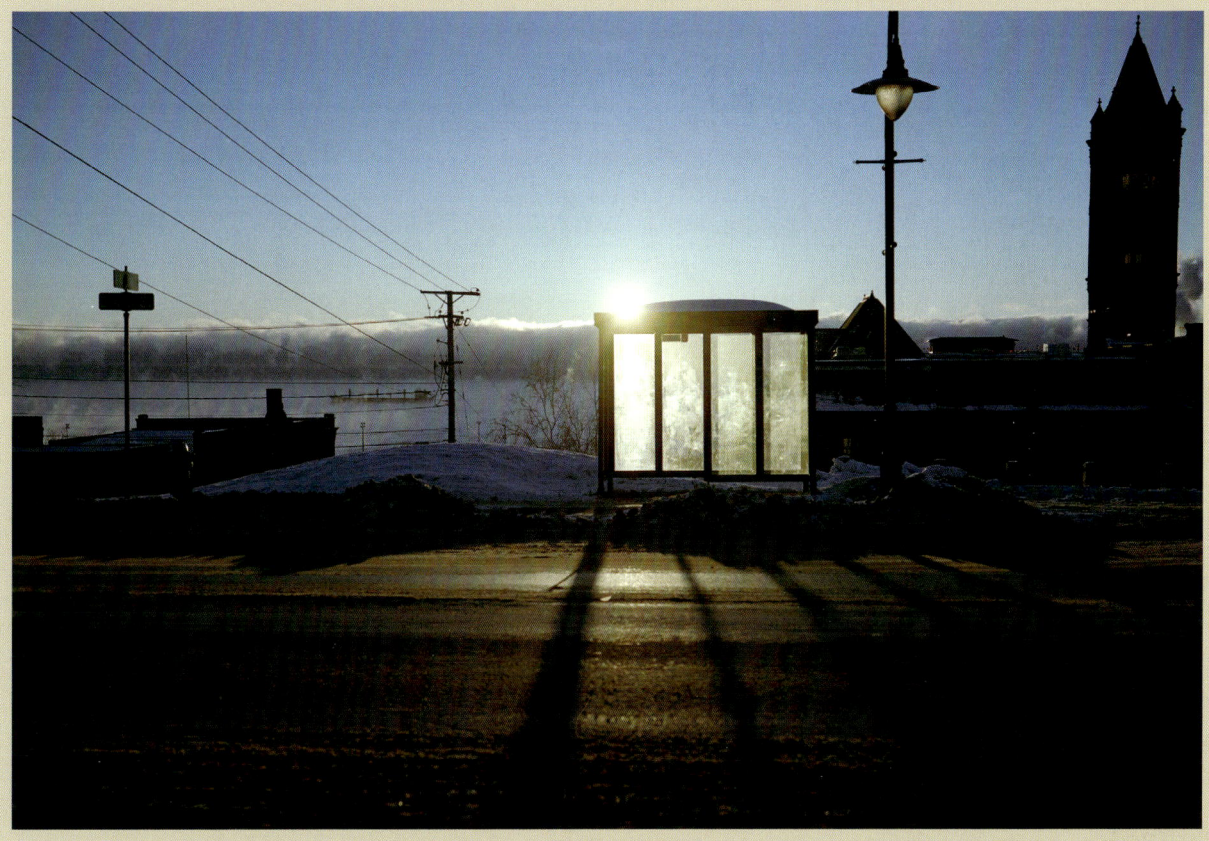

© Kip Praslowicz 2010
Bus Stop, *Duluth, MN 2010*

While actually depicting humans is the typical theme of street photography, I believe the genre to be more about humanity as a whole:
not just the behavior of individuals in public, but also our constructs
and how we manipulate and use the space around us. While this
photo lacks actual human figures, the sun backlighting the bus stop
illuminates the smudges on the glass left behind by the many people
who have used the shelter to hide from the harsh elements raging in
the background.

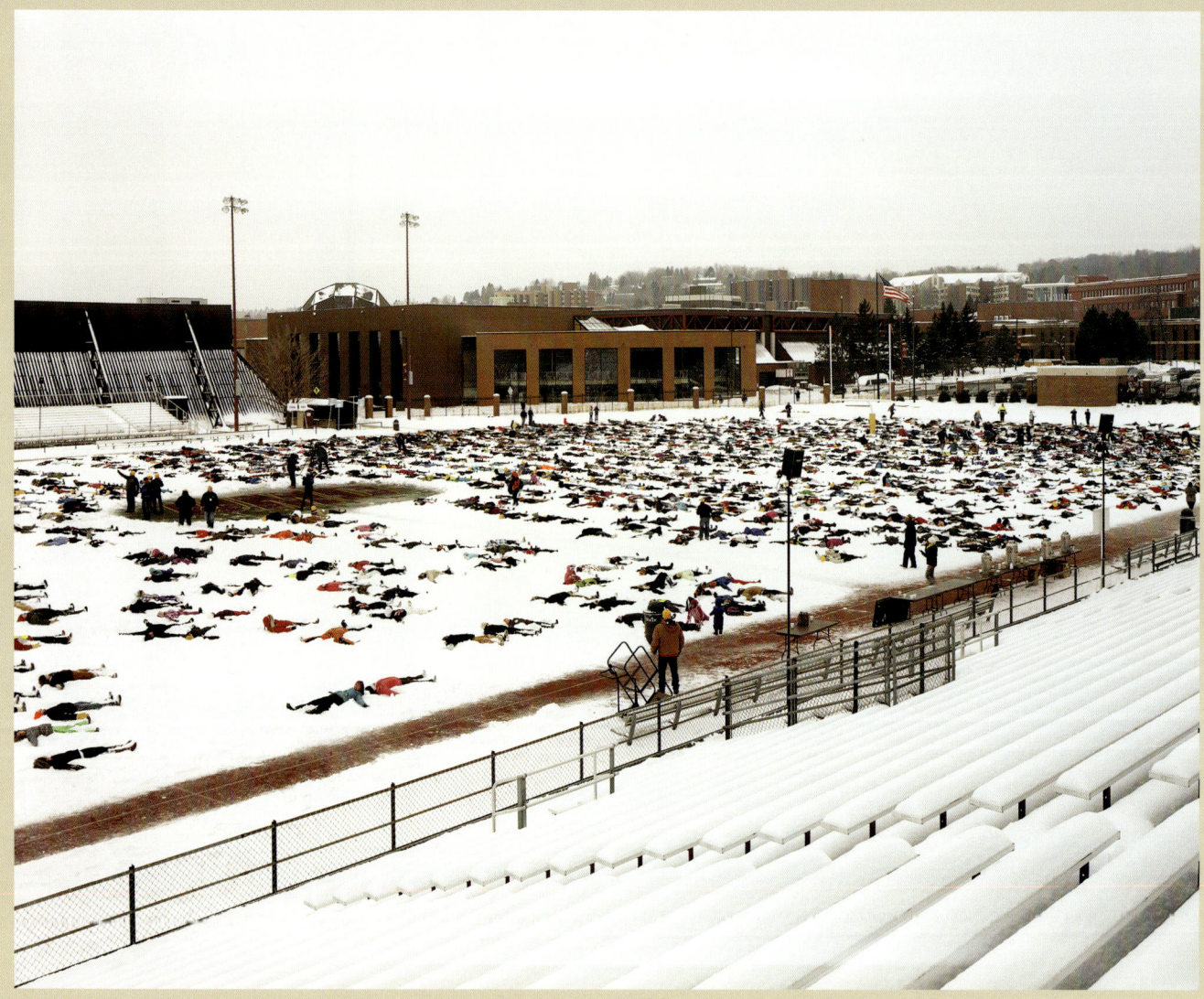

© Kip Praslowicz 2013
**World Record Attempt At Snow Angels.
7086 People Short,** *Duluth, MN 2013*

These next two images are an example of how I've been approaching street photography for the past few years. Gone are the handheld rangefinder cameras and the attempt to be unseen. Instead, I use a large 8x10 camera, and I have zero hope of trying to be stealthy. The goal is to intentionally compose a scene like a landscape photographer would, except I try to anticipate where interesting human activity will unfold. Then I wait for just the right scene to unfold before making a single exposure. This style is an attempt to approach street photography with more deliberation, like that used in the art of painting.

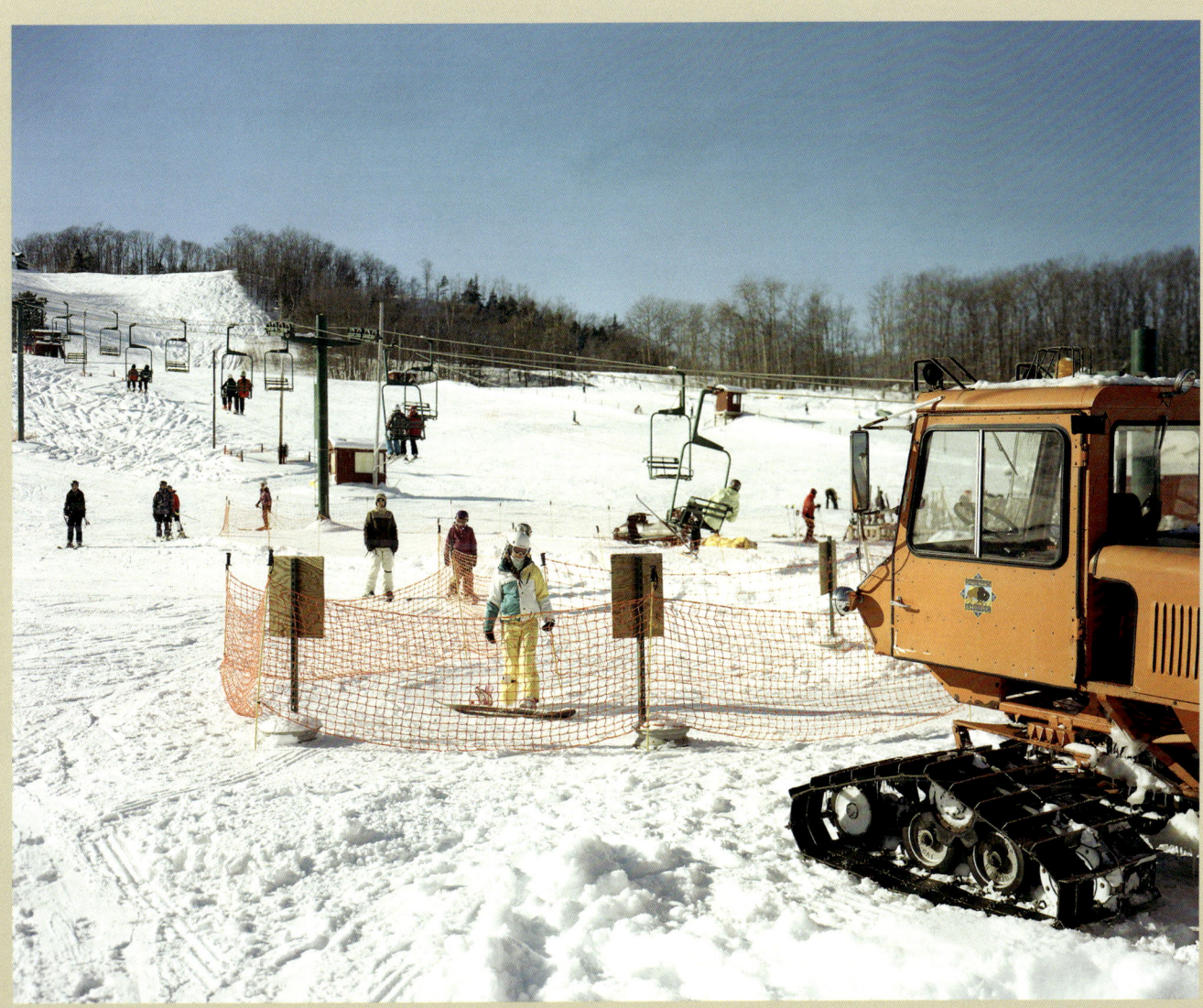

© Kip Praslowicz 2014
Mt. Ashway, Bayfield, WI 2014

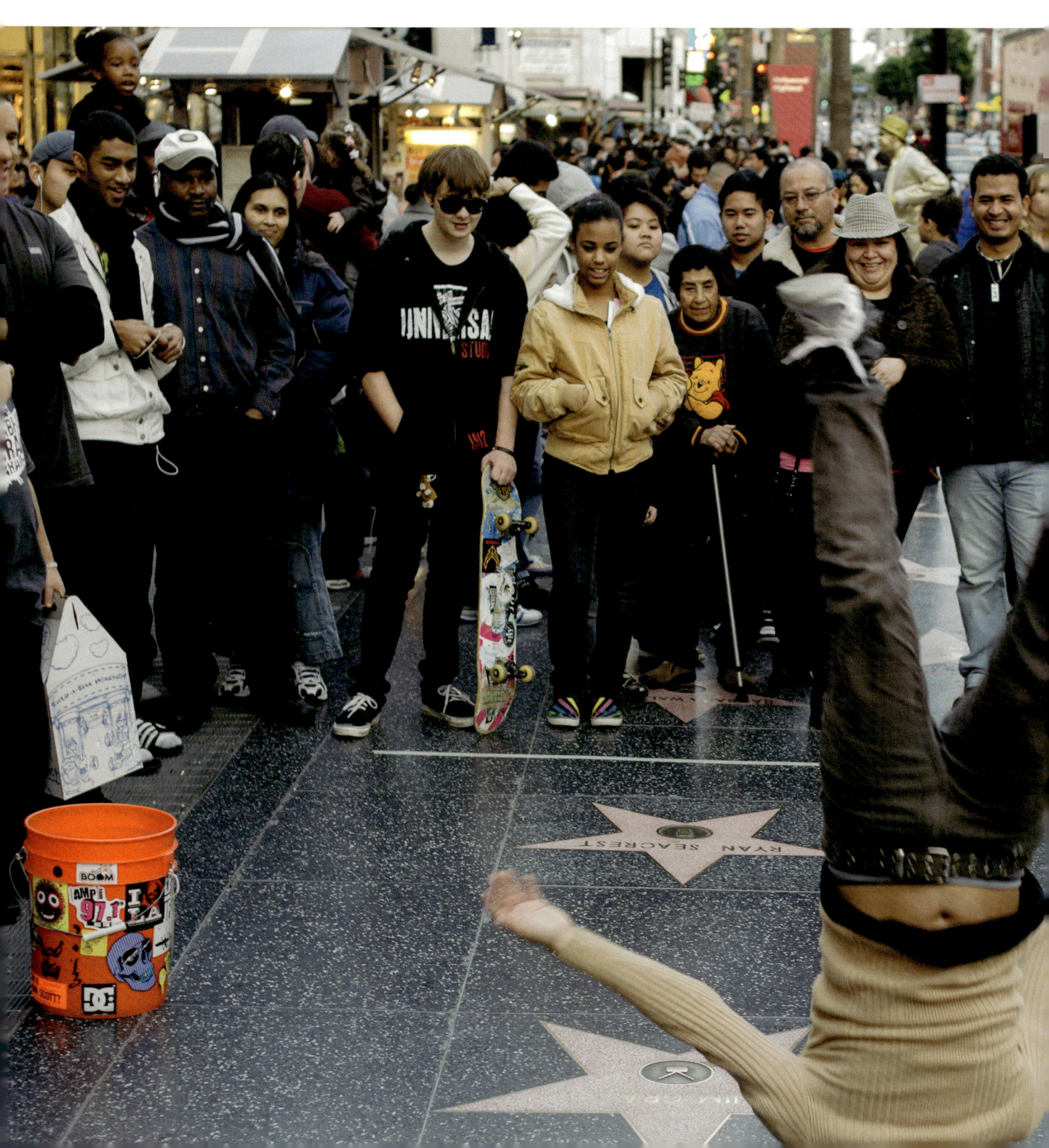

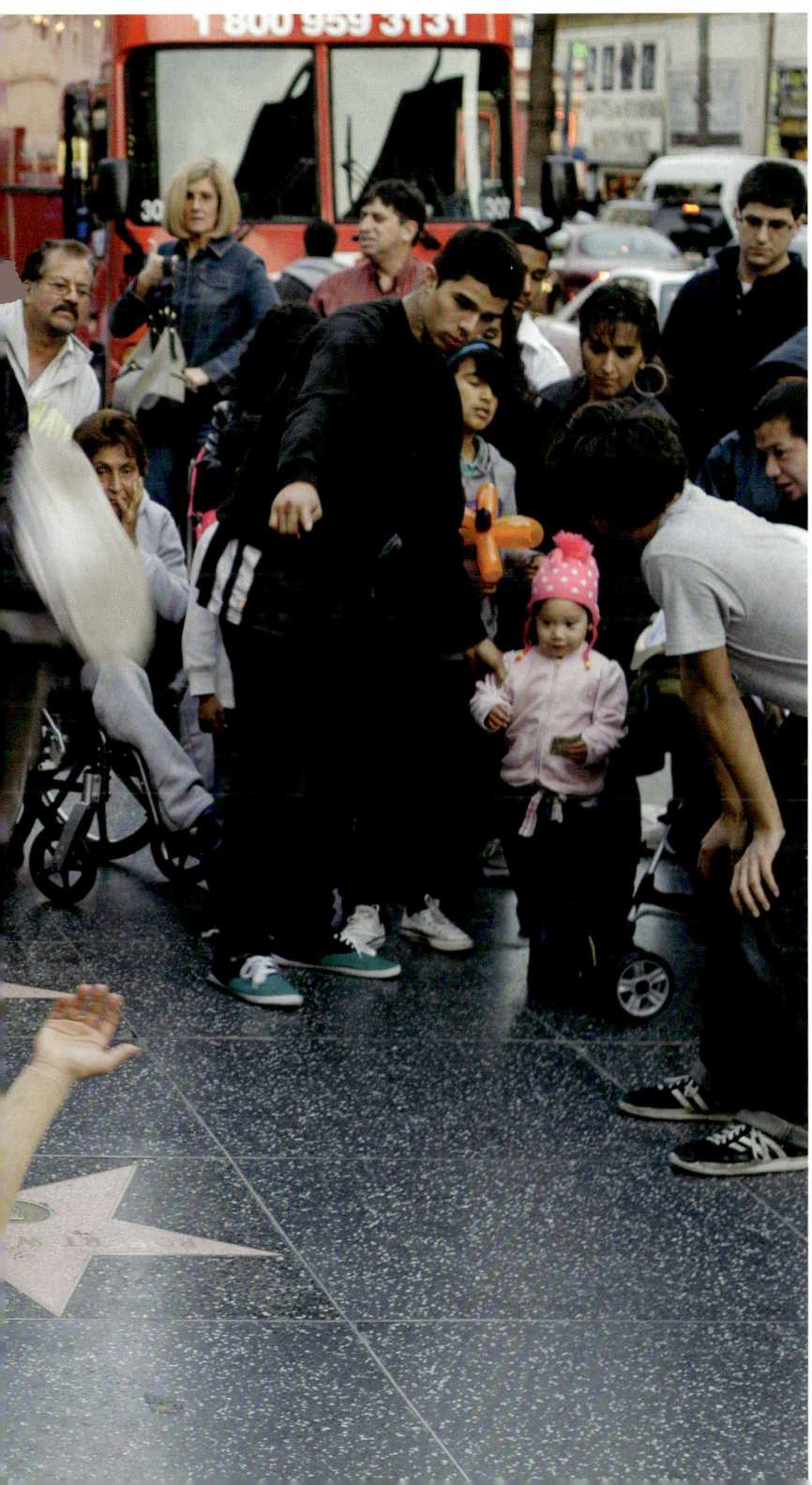

Chapter 4

Locations and Events

When it comes to buying a home or a place of business, only three things matter: location, location, and location. This applies equally well to street photography. Some locations are fertile grounds for street photography; others are not. The wilderness may be the perfect place to photograph landscapes, wildlife, and mushrooms, but it's not the best place to capture the bustle of the urban environment.

That being said, there are a lot more places to practice street photography than streets and sidewalks. *Street photography* is a term that, as indicated by the subtitle of this book, generally applies to candid photography in public places. These public places don't have to be in large cities, or even in cities at all. You can apply a street shooter's sensibility to many situations. This is true even if you prefer to document *evidence* of humanity rather than humanity itself. What follows is a list of promising locations for street photography and the types of subjects you can expect to find in each one. This list is not all-inclusive— there may be other possibilities I haven't mentioned—but hopefully it will inspire you to venture forth and document the wide variety of public spaces available to you.

Bright Lights, Big City

Street photography as a distinct genre began in major urban centers such as Paris, New York, and London—cities with dense concentrations of people. Not only were the great buildings and grand boulevards captivating subjects, but also the streets were filled with multitudes of people from all walks of life going about their daily activities.

Today's major cities are still an ideal location for street photography because they offer many people, places, and opportunities for candid photographs. If you happen to live in a major city, you probably have a good idea of what those opportunities are. It should go without saying that if your goal is to photograph people in an urban environment, you need to shoot where and when people are on the streets. (If you're less interested in people and more interested in documenting the urban landscape, you should do the opposite.)

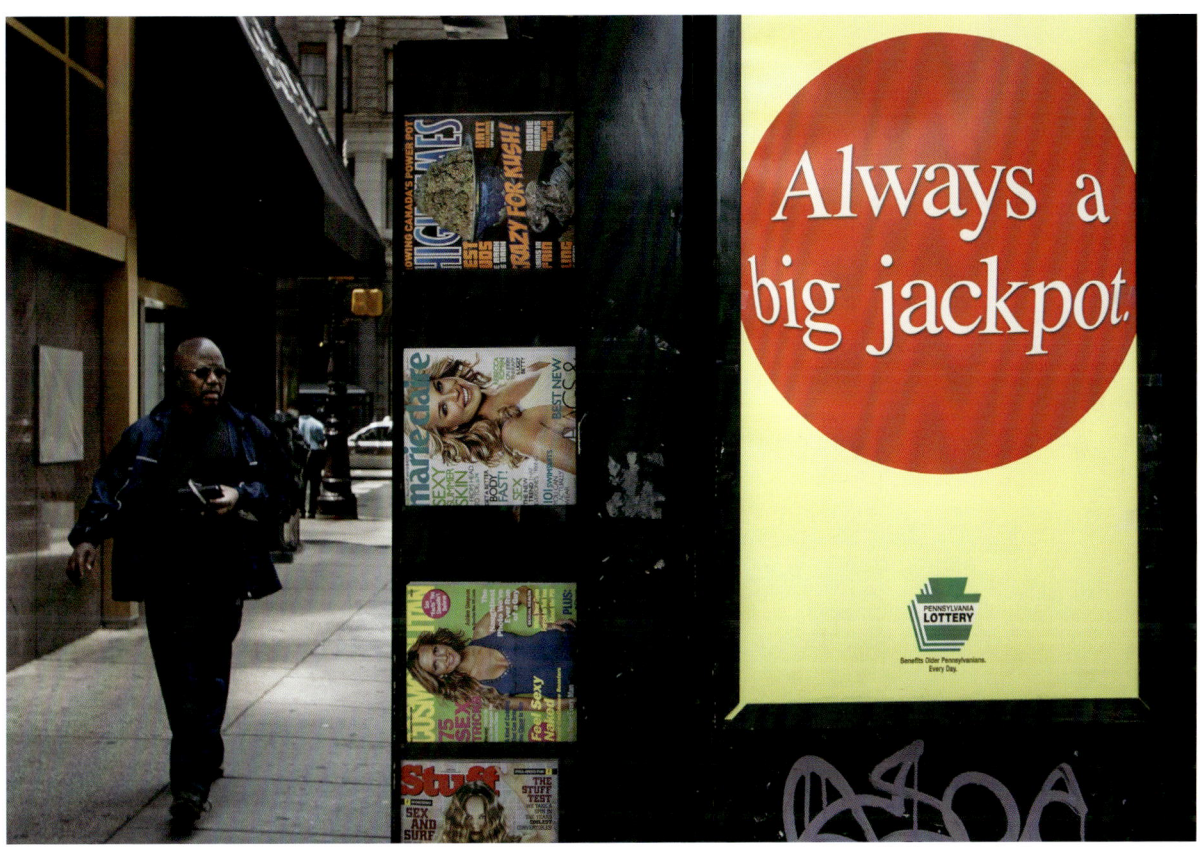

Big Jackpot, Philadelphia, PA 2013

Busy Streets and Neighborhoods

Whether it's Broadway, Broad Street, Hollywood Boulevard, or Champs-Élysées, every city has its main drags: the major streets where people walk and congregate. Some streets will be dominated by office workers; others by shoppers, tourists, college students, immigrants, or the working poor. If you know your city well, you can probably already picture the streets and neighborhoods I'm talking about. If you're unfamiliar with a city, you're sure to discover its character and rhythms as you explore the streets. A busy metropolis may have dozens of these bustling neighborhoods; a small town may have only one or two. If you're looking for people in public places for reasons other than a special event, this is where you're most likely to find them.

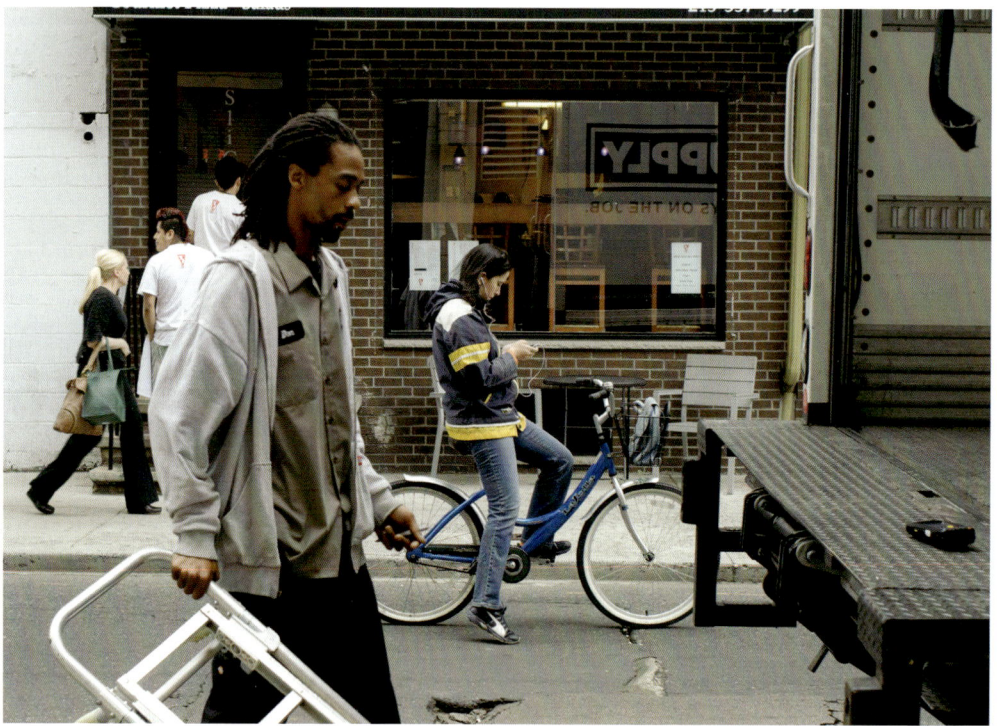

Deliveries, Philadelphia, PA 2012

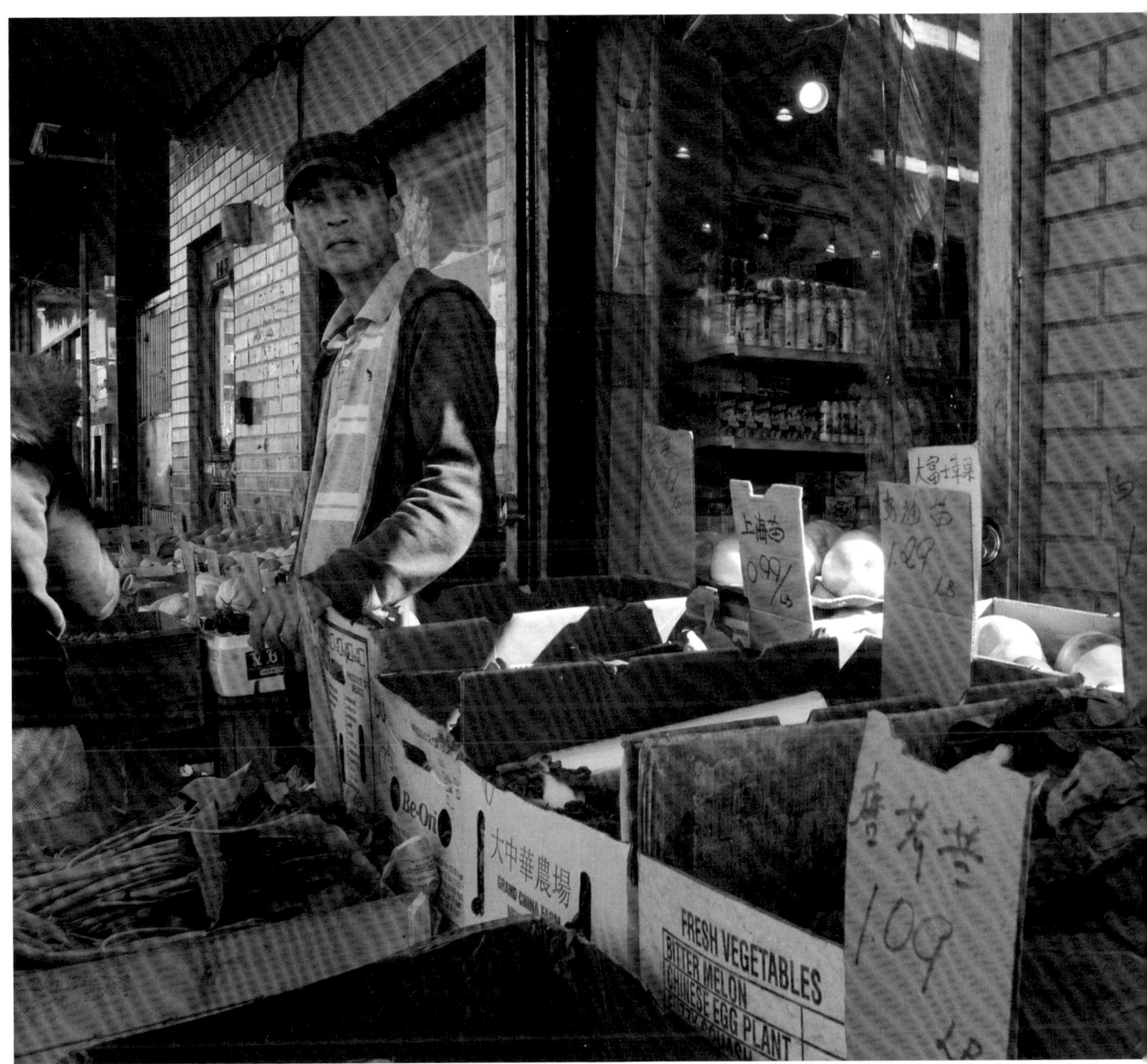

Chinese Grocer, Philadelphia, PA 2011

Large Office Complexes

These complexes have large numbers of office workers and visitors who enter and exit, especially in the mornings, lunch hour, and late afternoon.

Public Squares

These attract people who go to see others and be seen, smoke a cigarette, eat a snack, relax, and enjoy the air.

Pedestrian Malls

These attract a crowd similar to those at public squares; the difference being that pedestrian malls are often bordered by small shops and cafés, and therefore attract more shoppers and diners.

Colleges and Universities

The areas surrounding colleges and universities will have not only students, but the types of clothing, food, and youth-orientated businesses that attract students.

Tourist Attractions

Any place that attracts large numbers of tourists is a natural location to find subjects who are probably taking lots of pictures themselves, and therefore not paying attention to you and your activities.

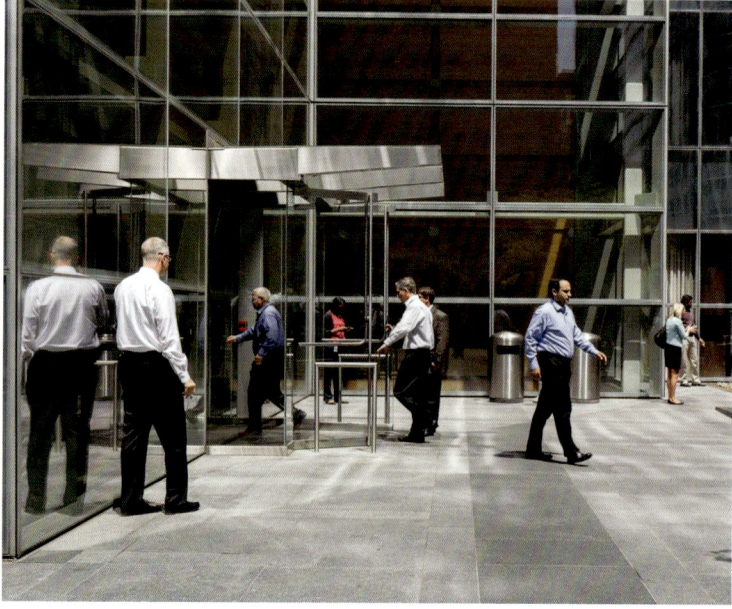

Comcast Lunch Break,
Philadelphia, PA 2014

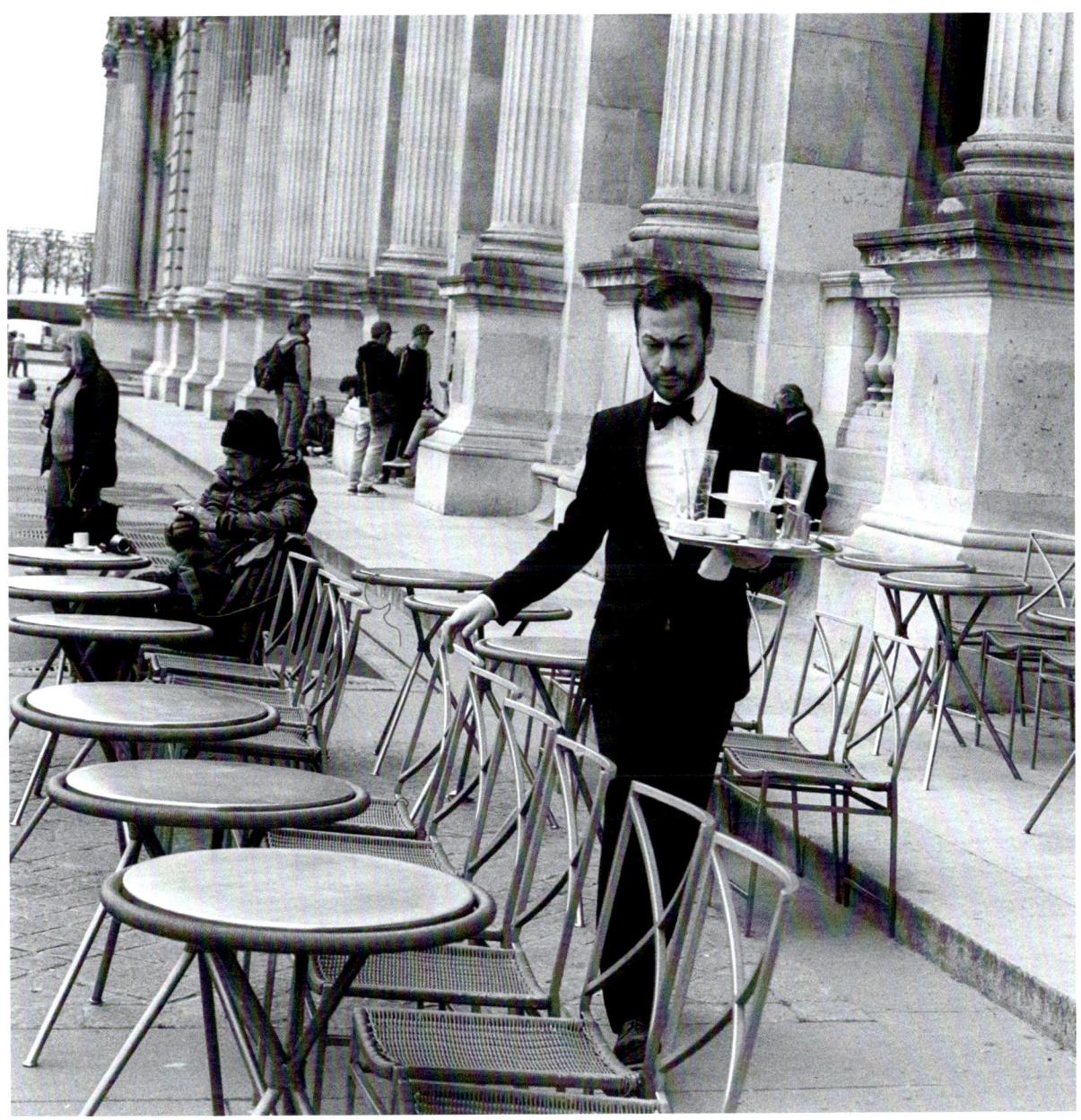

Waiter, Musée du Louvre, Paris 2013

Train Stations, Bus Terminals, and Airports

These locations are often packed with people of all ages and ethnicities, in constant motion, on their way from one place to another. Unfortunately, because of concerns over perceived "terrorist motives," photography in such locations is often discouraged or forbidden. Be careful not to arouse attention, and if asked to desist, comply.

Subway Trains and Stations

In addition to all of the qualities of train stations and airports, subway trains offer you the added advantage of being able to photograph relatively stationary subjects while you ride. The catch is that you, too, are captive, at least until the next subway stop—so be extra careful not to antagonize anyone while photographing.

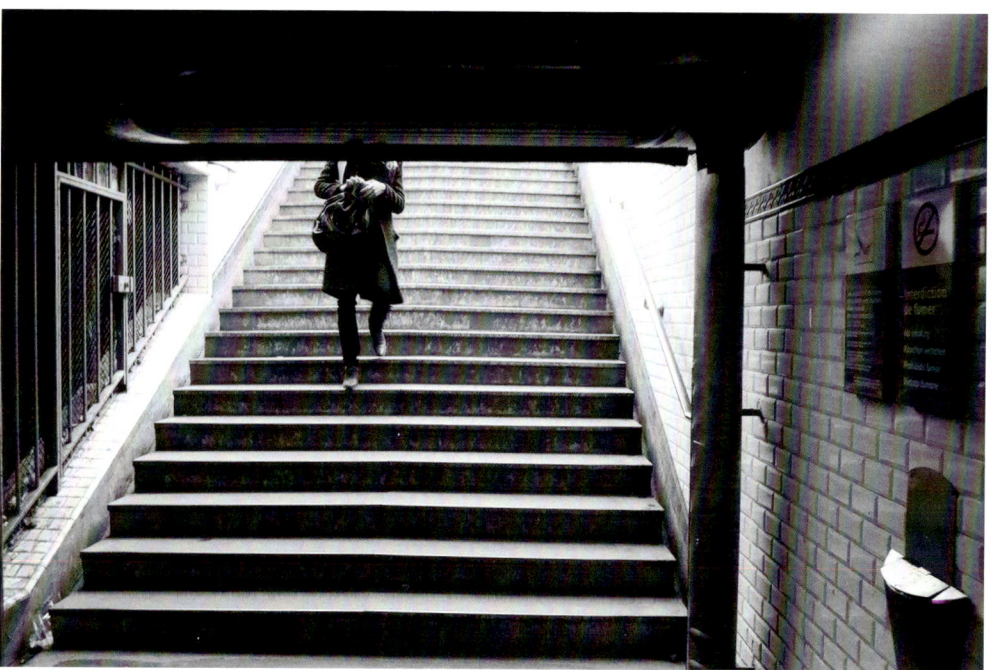

Paris Metro, Paris 2013

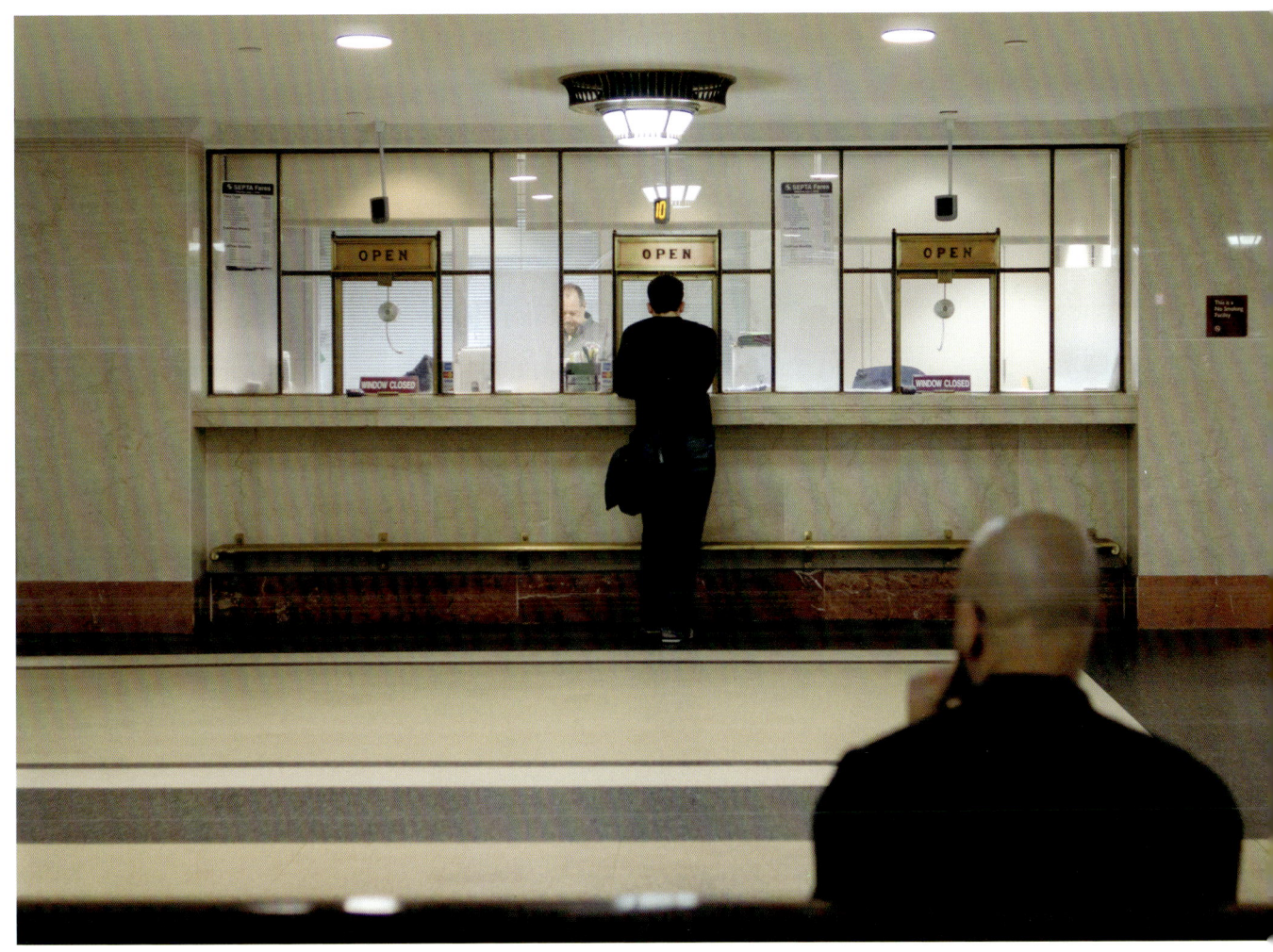

Suburban Station, Philadelphia, PA 2011

Museums

Museums offer not only people to photograph, but interesting exhibits as well. Photography is generally permitted, as long as you don't use a tripod or flash lighting.

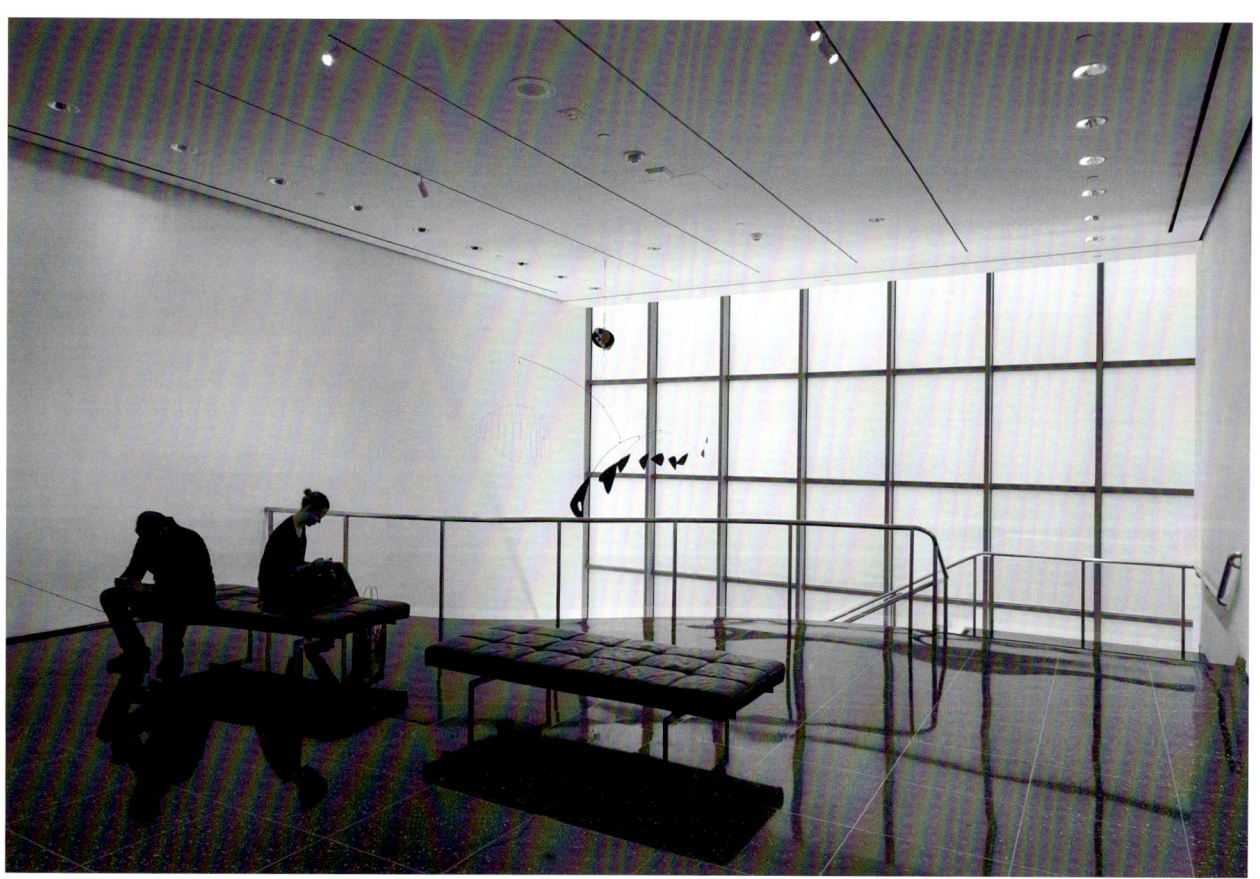

MOMA Atrium, New York, NY 2014

Parks and Gardens

Major cities usually have large, multi-acre parks where urban dwellers gather to enjoy trees, lakes, fountains, and open spaces. You'll find people riding bikes, walking their dogs, playing sports, picnicking, and relaxing.

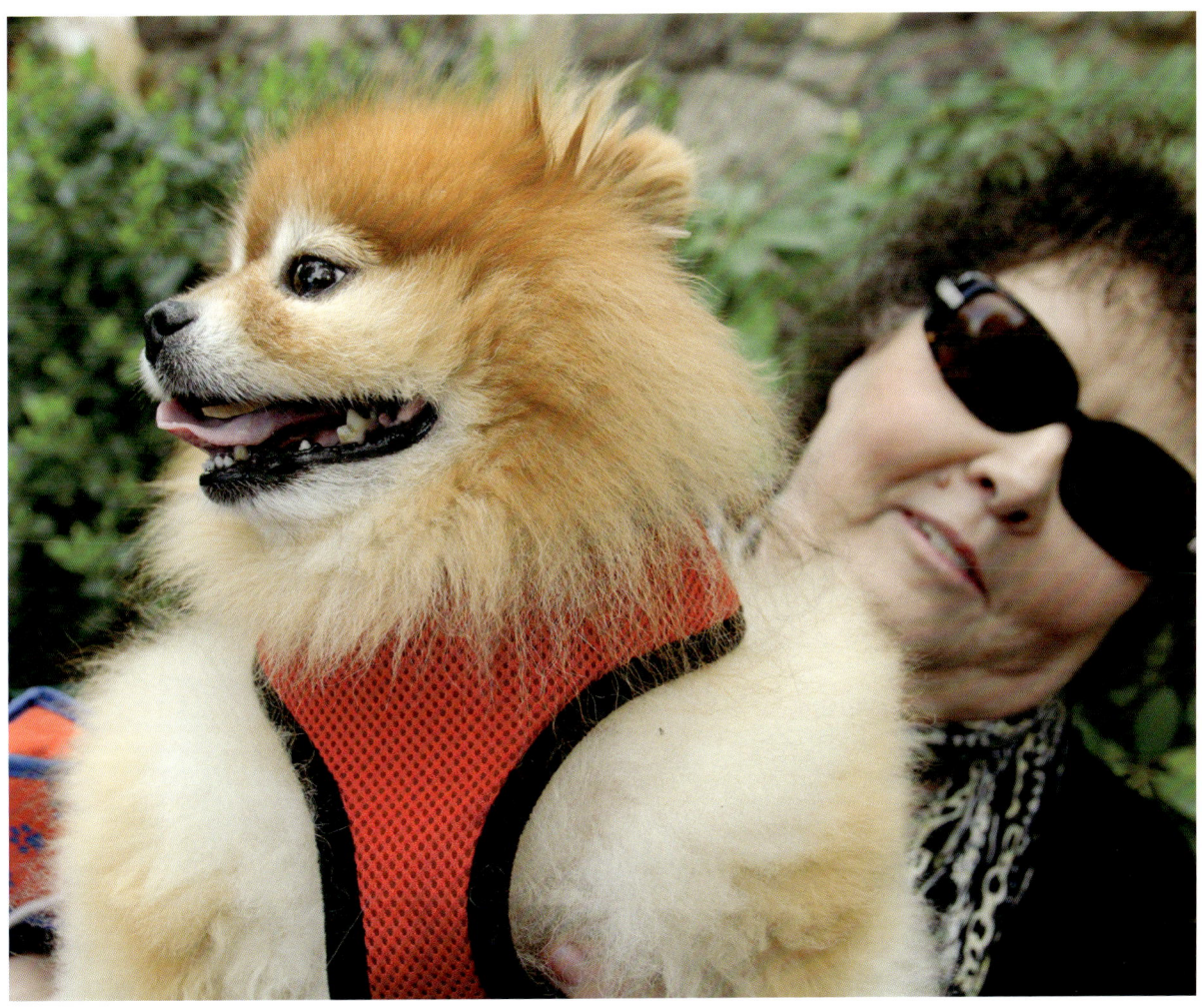

Dog with Vest, Philadelphia, PA 2012

Open-Air and Flea Markets

These types of markets tend to be more common in European, Asian, or Latin American cities, but most large U.S. cities have them as well. Wherever you find them, they are naturally colorful and attract a diverse cross-section of society, from the vendors to the customers.

Keep in mind that not all cities are the same. You'll find more and better opportunities for photographs in cities such as New York, Chicago, Paris, London, Tokyo, and Beijing, where millions of people are concentrated into a relatively small geographic area. It's also nice when a city has a strong public transportation system, because it minimizes automobile traffic, and more people will be out on the streets.

In contrast, western U.S. cities such as Los Angeles, Phoenix, Houston, and Dallas, which also have millions of people, are much more spread out and decentralized into large suburbs. Public transportation is minimal, which increases automobile traffic and decreases pedestrian traffic. This is not to say that such cities are hopeless causes, but be aware that prime locations for street photography are fewer and farther in between.

If you don't live near a big city or simply don't care for them, there are other places you can shoot. In fact, you could build a solid portfolio by shooting in just one of the following locations:

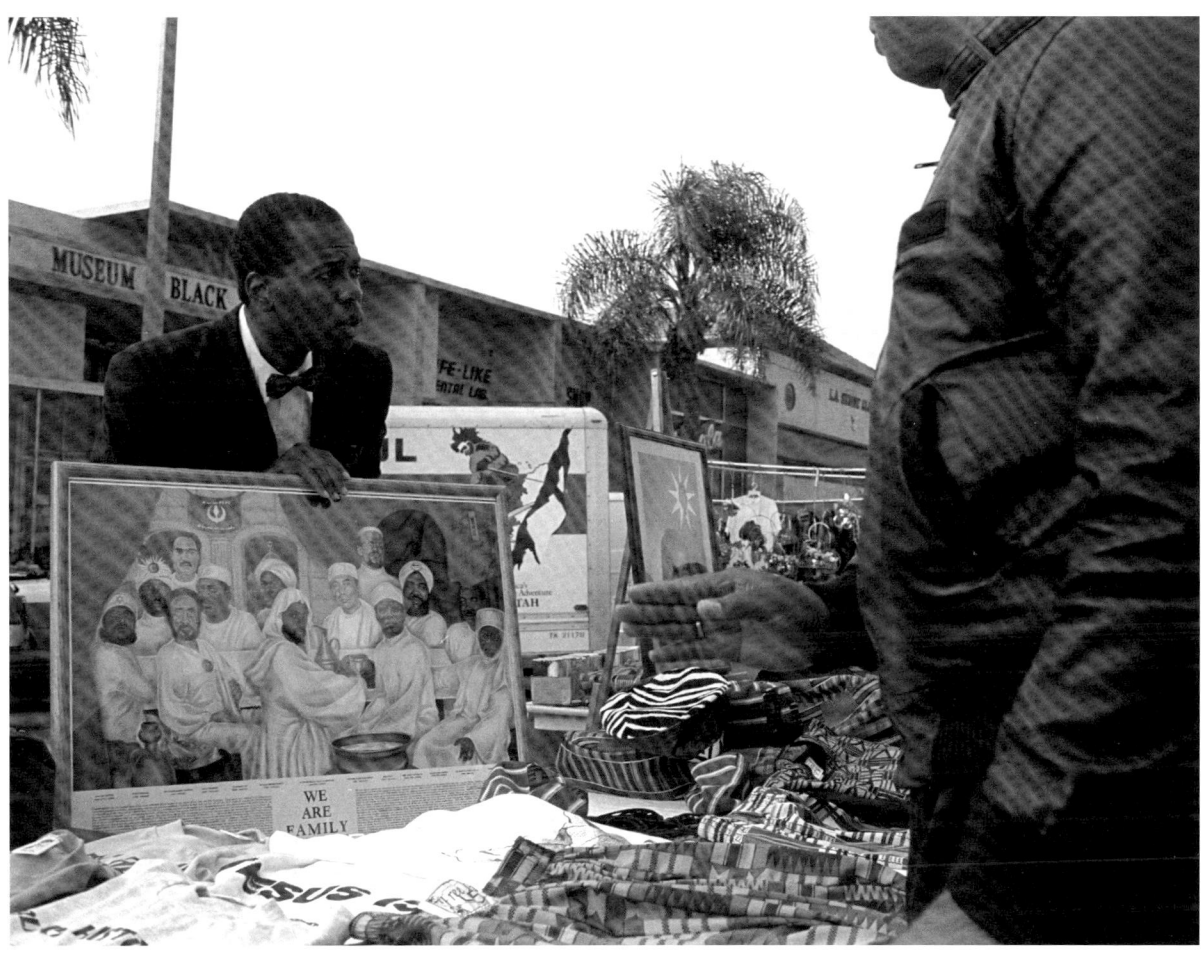

African-American Flea Market, Los Angeles, CA 1984

Beaches and Boardwalks

During warm summer months people flock to public beaches, boardwalks, and riverbanks in droves. Some beaches are mainly for swimming and sunbathing, in which case you have to be careful not to be perceived as a voyeur.

Other beaches have boardwalks, bike paths, and arcades that attract street performers, as well as hundreds of other people with cameras. In either case, as long as you aren't attracting undue attention or making a pest of yourself, you can shoot all day without worrying about upsetting anyone.

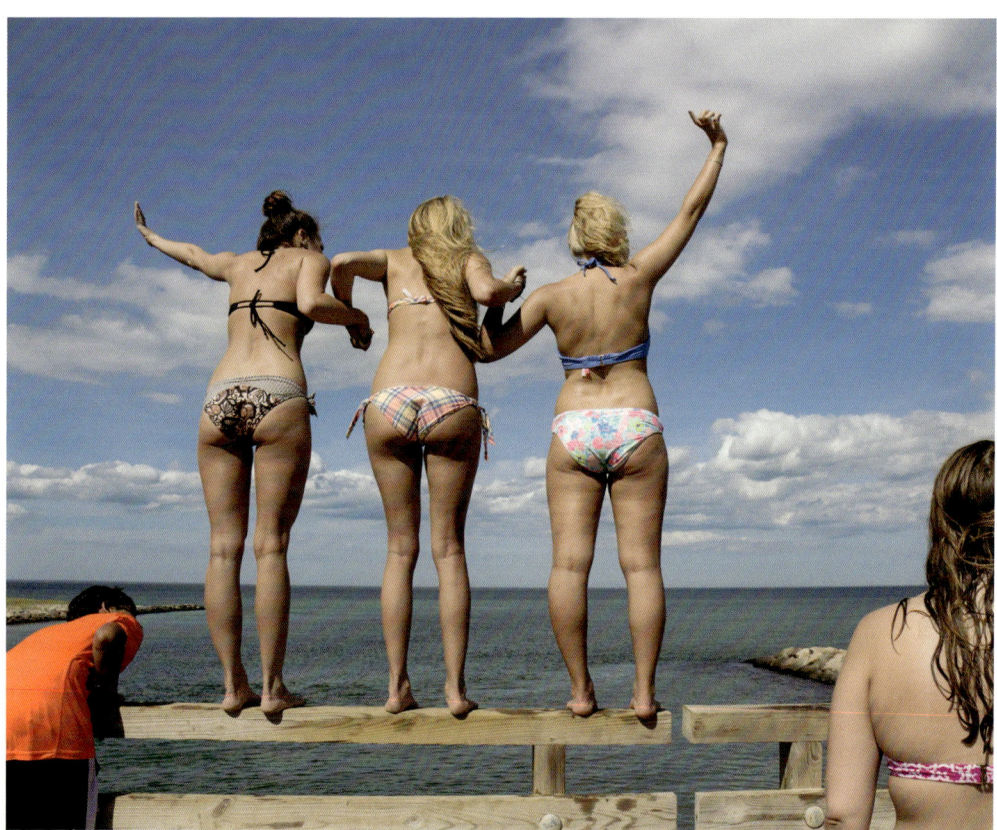

Girls Jumping From Bridge, Martha's Vineyard, MA 2014

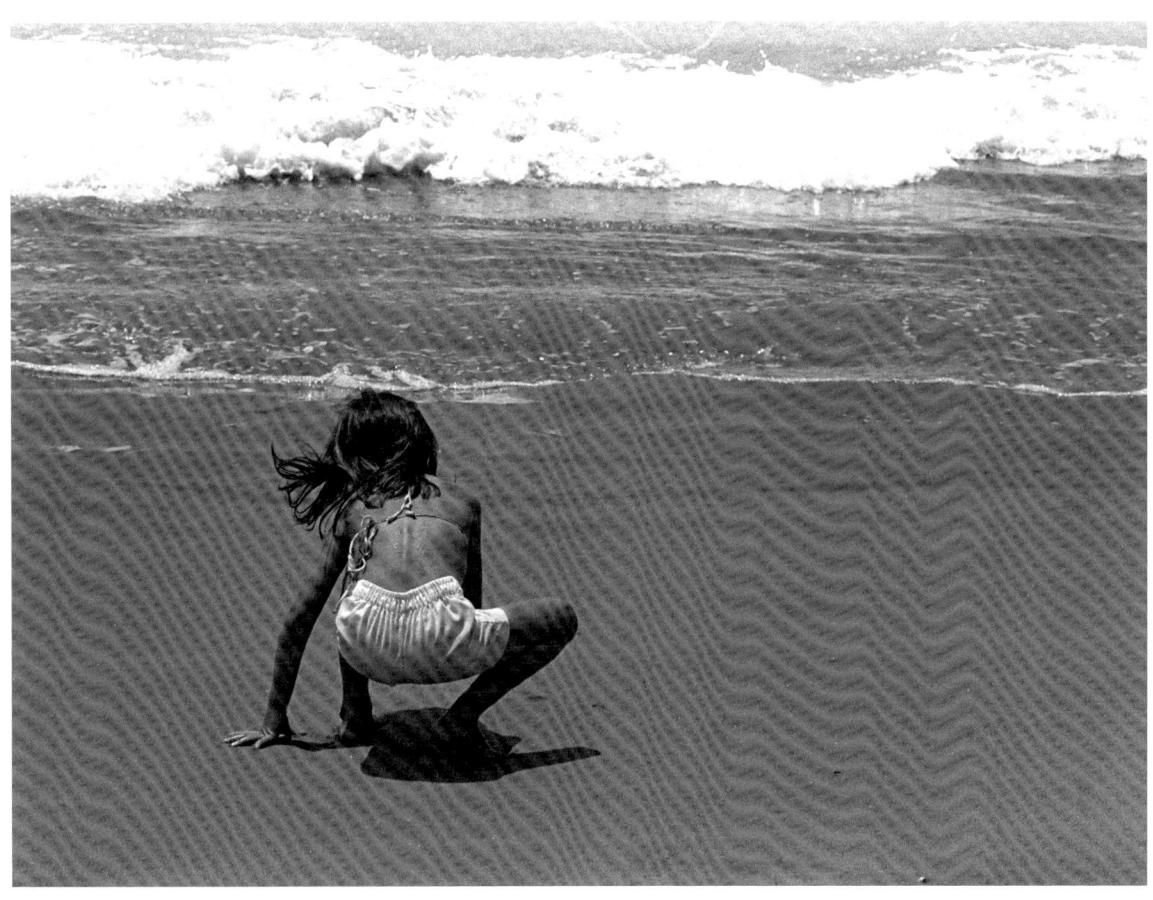

Girl Watching Waves, Santa Monica, CA 1979

Amusement Parks

Amusement parks attract crowds similar to those at beaches and boardwalks. The difference is that the crowds tend to skew younger because they are so popular with families and teenagers. They (the amusement parks, not the families and teens) tend to have a commercialized, prefabricated look to them, but depending on your vision this could be an advantage. A definite downside is that most require paid admission and can be pricey, so they're generally not the sort of place you'd visit on a whim.

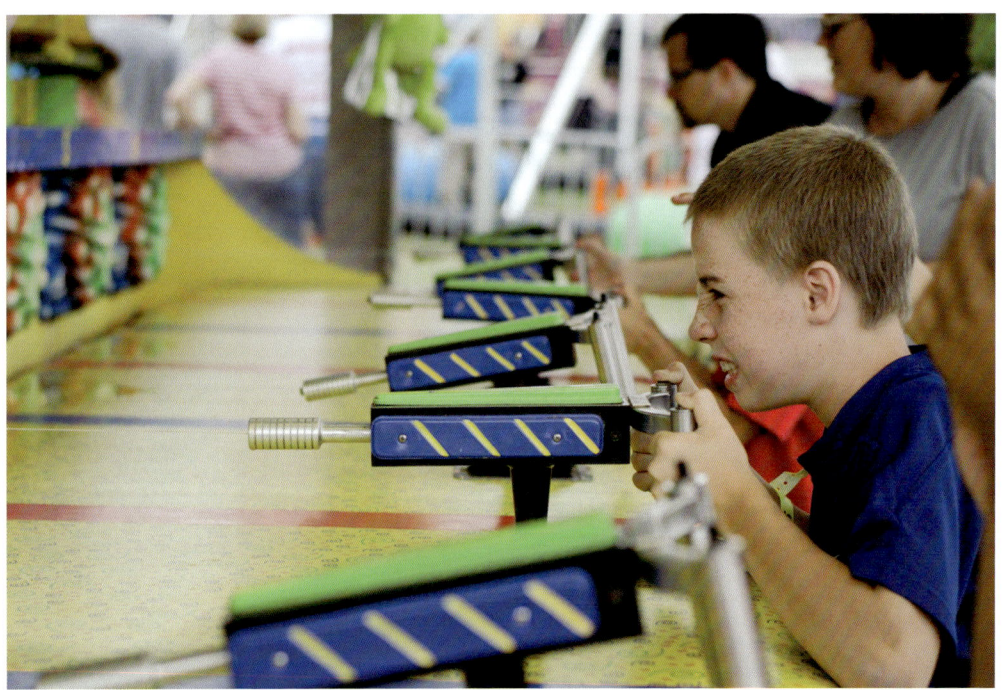

Intense Carnival Emotion, Abington, PA 2012

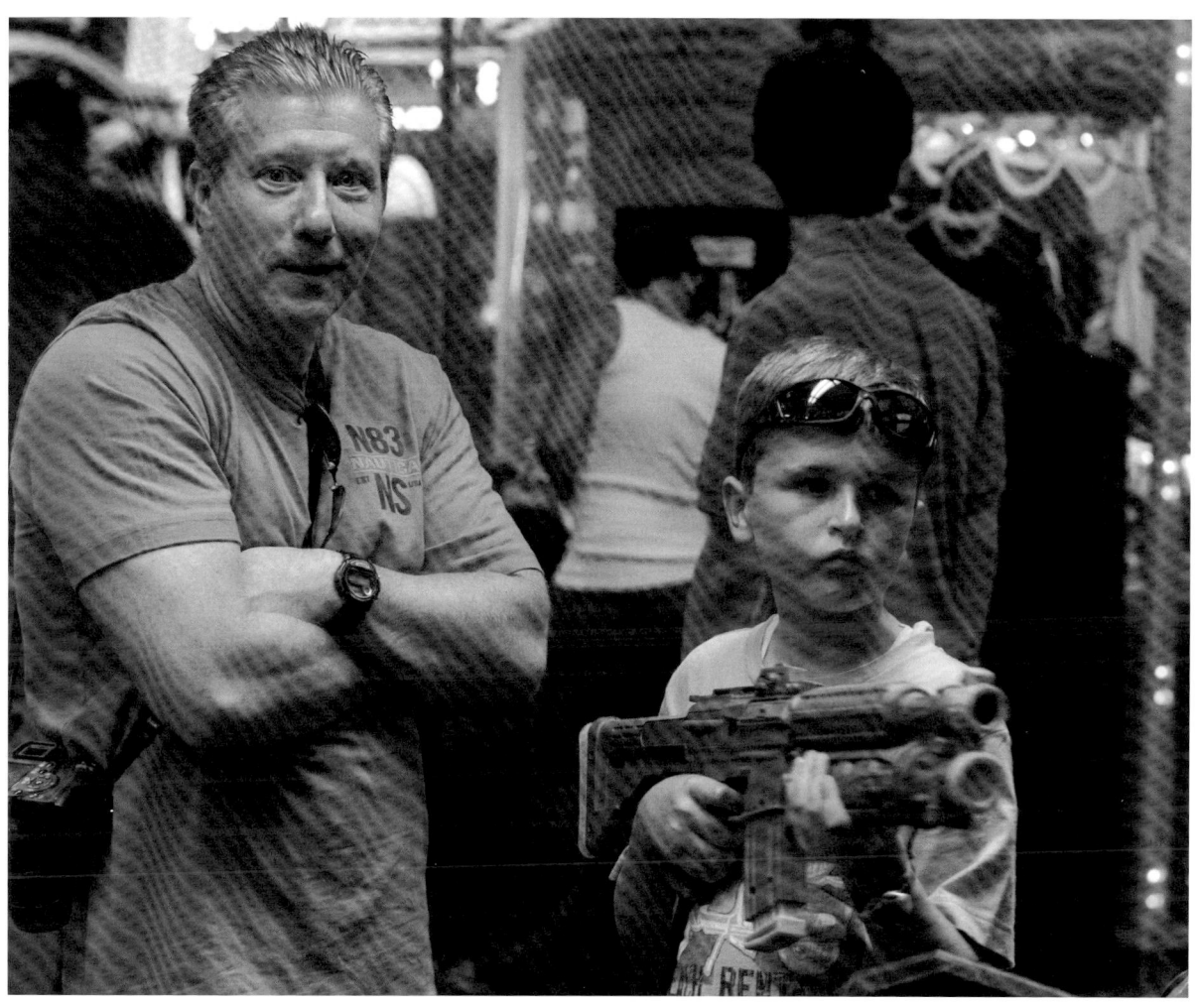

Boardwalk Arcade Scene, Wilmington, NC 2013

Events

Big cities, beach, and amusement parks are by no means the only or even the best places to practice street photography, and even if they were, not everyone is fortunate enough to live close to these types of places. However, wherever you live, you can take advantage of events that attract crowds. The best examples include:

Parades

Parades attract large crowds of spectators. You may be just as interested in photographing the spectators as the parade. Keep in mind, however, that it's generally easier to photograph people who are standing on the side of the street opposite to you. People standing on your side of the street will be facing the parade, which makes it difficult to get far enough in front of them to photograph their faces straight on. You'll often have to settle for side views.

Rallies and Demonstrations

Political rallies and demonstrations draw crowds of fervent supporters. They can also draw crowds of people who are just as fervently opposed to the stated cause, as well as police officers and security guards who are there to preserve order, and onlookers who are caught somewhere in between. People participate in rallies and demonstrations for the specific purpose of being seen in public, so they are hardly surprised to see photographers documenting the event.

Although this can make for great street theatre and dramatic images, it requires you to be alert, aware of your surroundings, and careful not to be perceived as a threat to the parties involved. When in doubt, ask before you begin taking photographs and be very open about your activities. Furtiveness can easily be mistaken for having suspicious motives. Stop when asked or if the mood turns angry and aggressive.

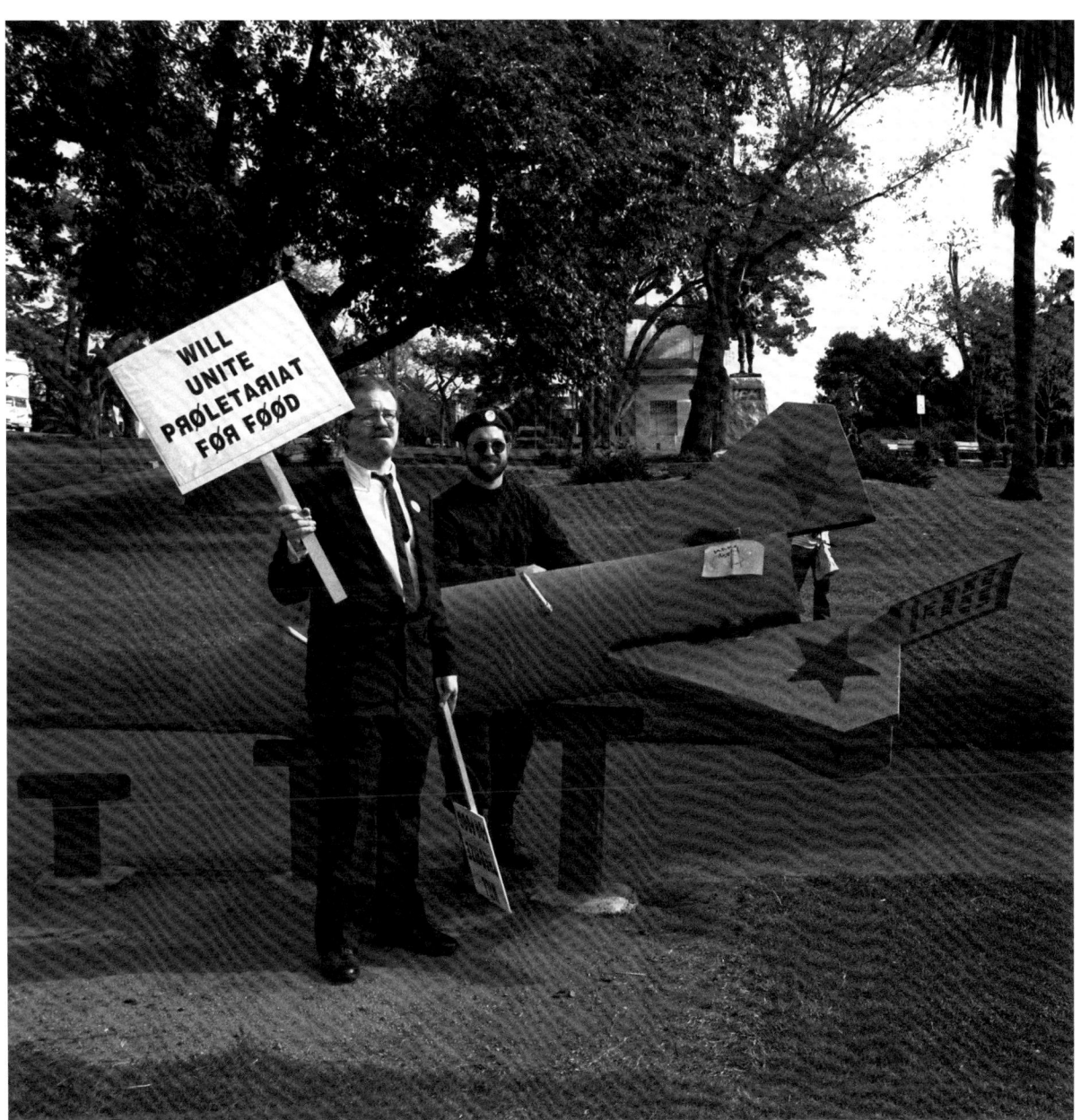

Will Unite Proletariat, Pasadena, CA 1982

Fairs and Carnivals

Fairs and carnivals are most common in the mid-to-late summer. They attract crowds similar to those at amusement parks, but with more individual, quirky character. For example, these events tend to have sub-events such as pie-eating contests, magic shows, skits, and bands. The attendees are often participants in these events. Either way, everyone is having a fine time and could not care less about someone taking pictures of the festivities.

Outdoor Music Festivals

The types of people you will see at a music festival is largely determined by the type(s) of music featured. Classical and jazz will generally attract a more calm and mature crowd. Rap and rock attract younger, more energetic, uninhibited listeners, though a lot of this depends on the ages of the performers. The latter type of music is much better for street photography, especially if there are lots of other activities and side stages that encourage spectators to walk around, dance, and express themselves. One caveat is to be alert to spectators who are drunk or high on drugs—some people become unpredictable, irrational, and aggressive when under the influence.

With so many choices of places and events to photograph, it's to be expected that some will interest you more than others. It's important to determine what type of street photography inspires you the most in order to hone your particular style. If you're photographing people simply because they happen to be in the same place at the same time as you, you're just going through the motions of street photography without developing your aesthetic. That's fine in the beginning, when you're starting out and trying to discover what locations and subjects interest you the most, but for your work to have greater meaning and value over time, you will eventually need to establish a deeper connection to the locations where you choose to photograph. Many street photographers become so familiar with a chosen location that they know exactly where and when they plan to visit, down to the month, day, and hour. They know what camera and lens they will use and where and when the light is best. You can do the same—this will allow you to photograph subjects that interest and inspire you the most, and develop your photographic aesthetic.

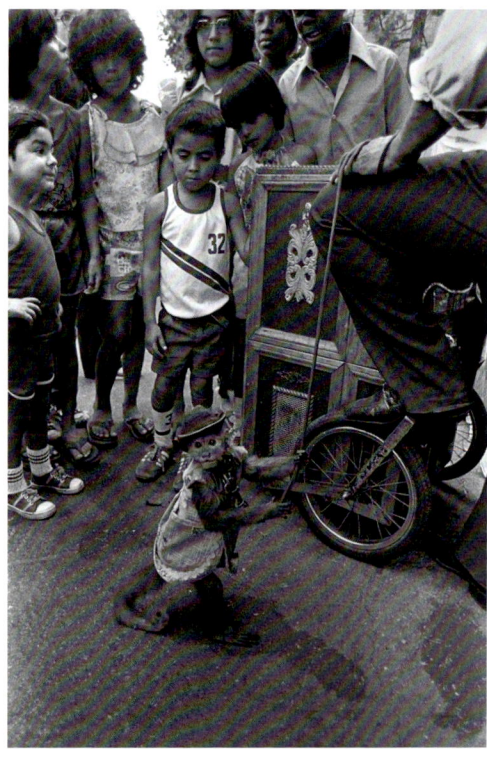

Kids Watching Monkey, Los Angeles County Fair, Los Angeles, CA 1979

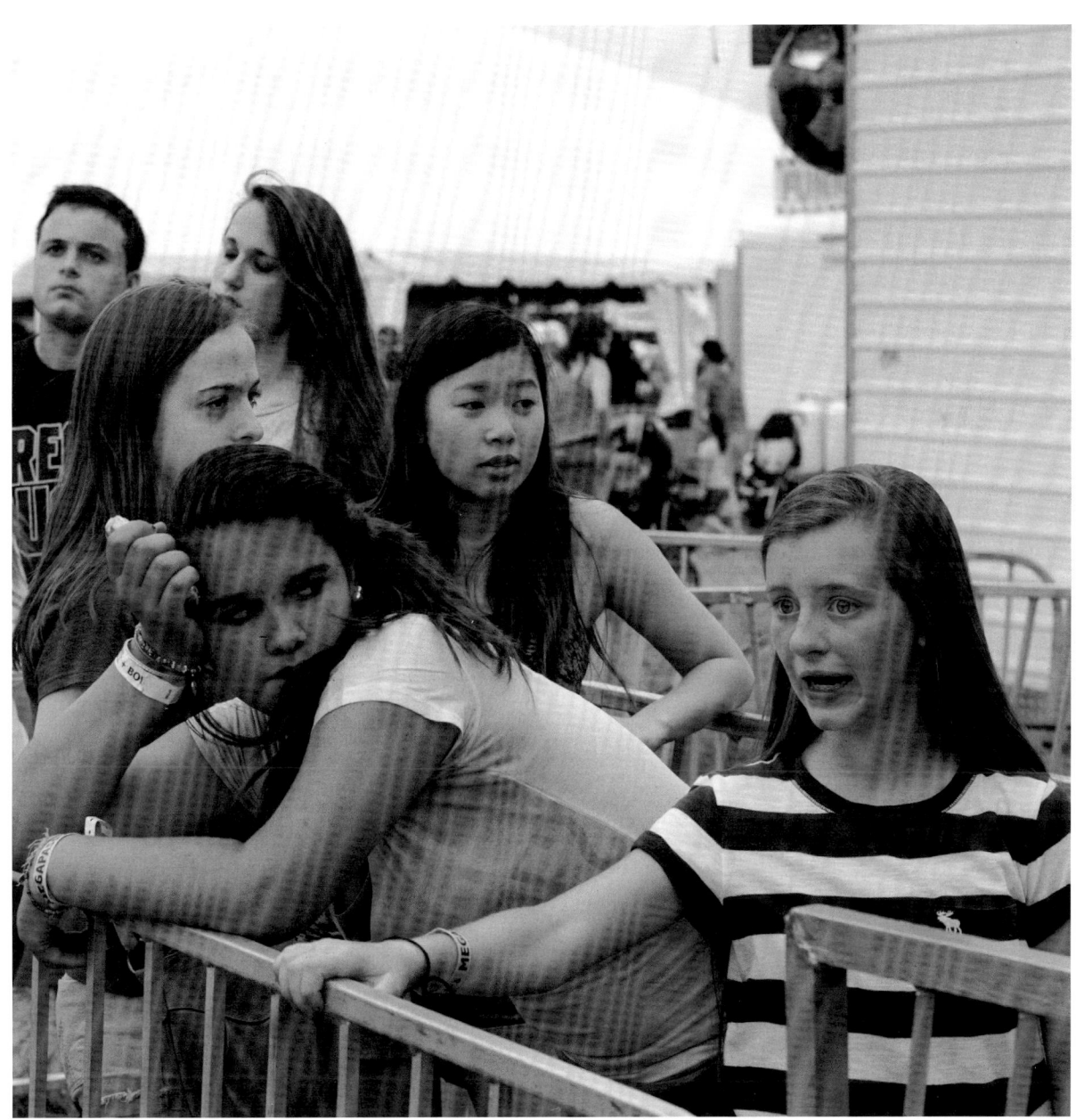

Teens Waiting for Amusement, Abington, PA 2012

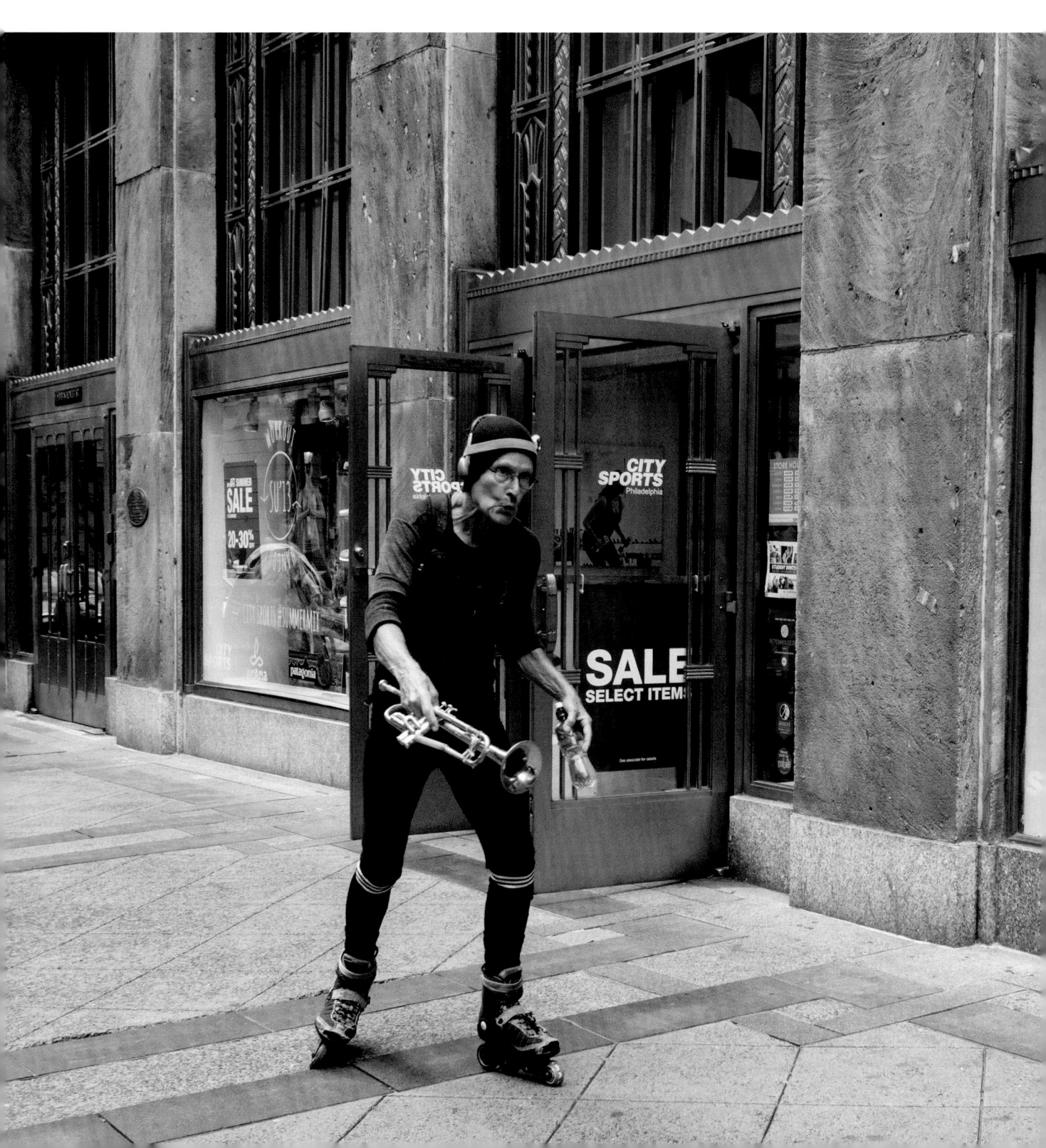

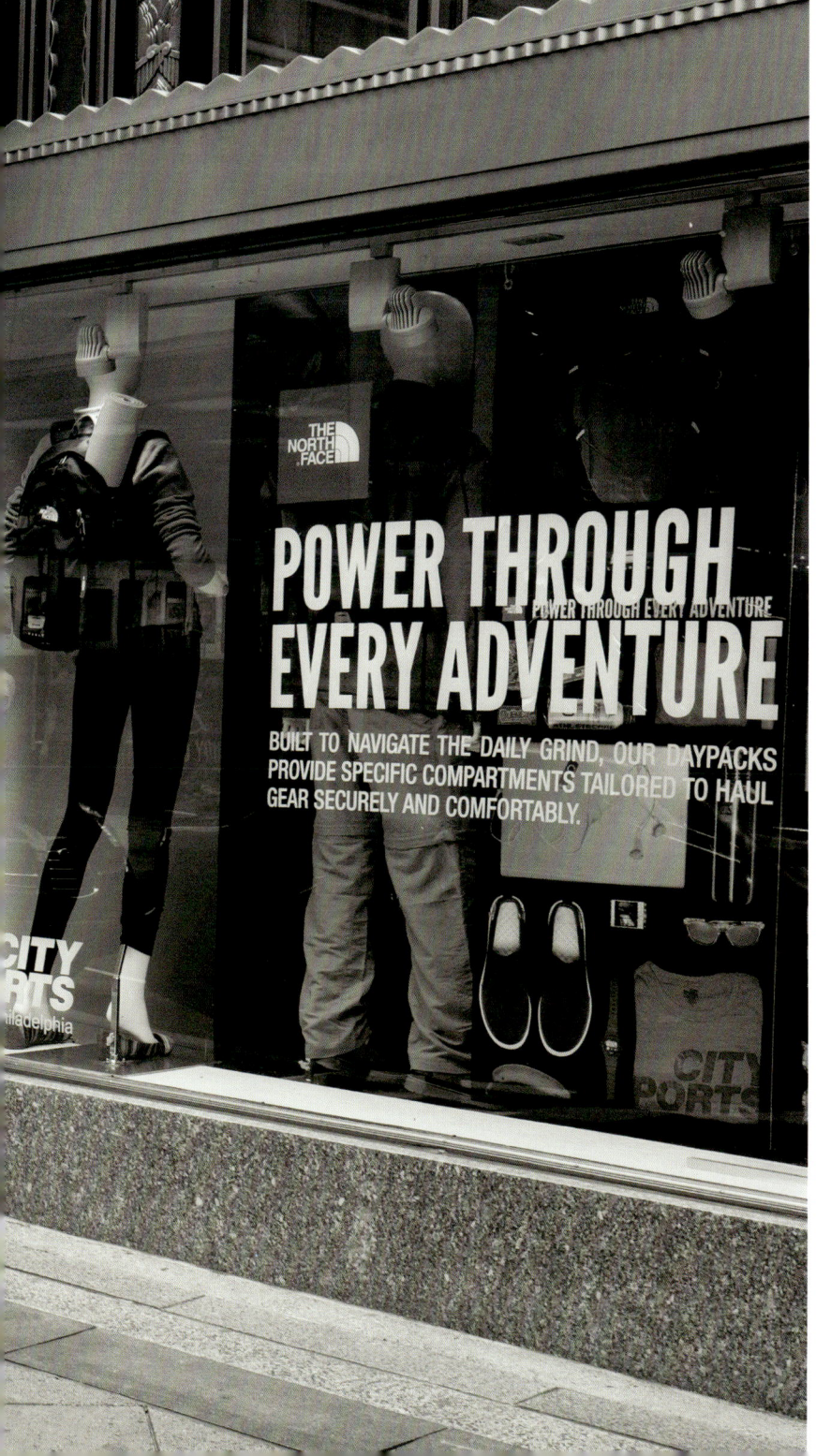

Chapter 5

Styles of Street Photography

One of the most common misperceptions about street photography is that it all looks alike. If you're at all familiar with the work of the best street photographers, it's obvious that there is an amazing amount of stylistic freedom and variation in this photographic genre. One photographer's images can be dramatically different from another's, even when they are literally photographing the same streets at the same time.

On the other hand, it's also true that most of the street photos you can find on the Internet are unadventurous and conventional. If you suspect that *your* images fall into this category, this chapter will supply ideas for reenergizing your work by giving it meaning and direction. I won't tell you what to do and how to do it; instead, I intend to open your eyes and your mind to possibilities. We will look at examples of what's been done before, what's being done today, and think about what could be done tomorrow. Who knows? You may develop a style that's unique. You have a lot to gain and little to lose from experimenting.

What Is Style?

Before we get too far into this subject, let's agree on what we mean by *style*. One definition is "a working method or approach." Some photographers have a very discreet and stealthy style of photographing their subjects. Others are more direct, even confrontational. Some are contemplative, others impulsive. This type of style will be determined in large part by your personality. We all tend to develop a system of shooting that's most compatible with who we are, our outlook on life,

what we're most comfortable with, and what we're trying to accomplish.

The definition of *style* in terms of an artistic aesthetic is "the consistent visual characteristics that identify and distinguish your work." Call it your visual signature if you like. The way your photographs look is a form of self-expression that observers can use to gain insight into your personality and what interests you. This is the type of style I intend to focus on.

> Street photography itself is considered a genre rather than a style. A *genre* refers to a category of artistic endeavor. For example, "blues" is a musical *genre*, while "Chicago blues" is a musical *style*. Other genres of photography include landscape, wildlife, sports, still life, portraiture, and so on.

Style Has Value

A stylized approach to shooting is one distinguishing factor that separates the street photographer from the documentarian or photojournalist. The documentarian or photojournalist is expected to maintain a measured objectivity toward subjects and events, but the street photographer is free to make an artistic statement. All options are on the table: you can be a Surrealist, Expressionist, cynic, optimist, iconoclast—whatever floats your boat.

A consistent style will also help distinguish your work from that of other street photographers. This is particularly useful if you're shooting with a digital camera (like most photographers these days).

Straight-from-the-camera digital images have a homogenous quality: bright colors, accurate white balance, sharp focus, long tonal scale, minimal granularity or noise. That's fine if that's what you like. If you'd like something more unusual and adventurous, there are multiple ways to achieve something different and uncommon.

The need or desire to distinguish yourself from others is particularly important if you're entertaining the idea of submitting portfolios to selective galleries, either physical or online. Their primary objective is to showcase work that is somehow exceptional. What, after all, would be the point of showcasing work that anyone could have done and that does little to excite the viewer's interest?

How to Develop a Style

Developing a distinctive style takes study, time, and effort. You may be tempted to accelerate this process, perhaps by mimicking the style of some master you admire. There's nothing wrong with this. Mimicry can provide useful firsthand insights into a master's working methods to achieve similar results. Too much mimicry, however, will cause your work to be obviously derivative and clichéd. While it is a good learning exercise, mimicry is ultimately a dead end in terms of developing your own style. There are limitless possibilities if you originate, but only limited possibilities if you duplicate.

Another common way to distinguish your digital images from others is to post-process them. You can use software to make it look like you were using a particular type of film, processing technique, or "art filter." The trick is knowing how to do it without drawing

undue attention to the fact that the image has been processed. The look you choose has to be compatible with your subject matter, personality, and message. If you use too heavy a hand or indulge in whatever effect happens to be the flavor of the moment, the results won't be authentic and engaging examples of your style; instead they will be a lot of over cooked images.

The time-tested way to develop an authentic style is to invest time, study the masters of *any* visual art (including painting), and shoot a lot. Practically all of the masters of street photography were trained in the visual arts. Many worked as photojournalists, fashion photographers, filmmakers, or in similar professional fields. Their styles were the result of conscious choices they made about whose work and ideas influenced them. They made deliberate decisions about how, when, and why to take a different approach. Most importantly, they knew what they wanted to say with their work and how they wanted to say it.

Because so much of style is based on your personal choices and preferences, the most that I or anyone else can do is be open to possibilities. It's up to you to look inward and discover what moves you. If you see photographs you like with a style that you aspire to achieve, feel free to try it on for size. The point isn't to copy it exactly. (Why would you? You're trying to develop a *personal* style, right?) The point is to learn what you like and want to adopt as your own versus what you don't like and prefer to toss out.

Don't be afraid to experiment. Adjust the way you shoot to suit your skill level. Combine styles and techniques in ways you find appealing. Keep at it long and rigorously enough and your work will eventually take on a visual coherence and consistency that may surprise even you.

The Elements of Photographic Style

Style is ultimately a reflection of the choices you make. You choose what camera and lenses to use, when and where to shoot, your subjects, what exposure settings to use, when to release the shutter, and so on. The more conscious and selective you are about these choices, the more distinctive your style is likely to be. The following is an exploration of the choices available to you: the elements of style. Give thought to which options and choices appeal to you most, and whether or not you're even making conscious choices at all. Is your style a product of intent or default? There are no right or wrong choices; there are only choices that support a coherent vision and those that don't.

Camera Choice

The camera you use influences your style to the extent that it optimizes or limits the way you can work and the results you're looking for. Cameras that have a large sensor or have large film formats provide a richness of tone, color, and detail that's hard to replicate with small-format cameras. The downside is that such cameras tend to be large and heavy, which makes them more difficult to carry for long periods of time. These types of cameras lend themselves more to relatively static subjects.

At the opposite end of the spectrum are small pocket-size cameras. What you give up in richness of detail and the ability to create prints in large sizes, you gain in having an inconspicuous, unintimidating camera that is easy to carry anywhere and use at a moment's notice—sometimes without even raising it to your eye. If you like to travel light and be ready to capture an image in the blink of an eye, you probably prefer a pocket-size camera.

There are, of course, intermediate-size cameras that provide various degrees of compromise between these two extremes. It's important that whatever camera you use doesn't cramp your style (as in "working method"). As long as you're able to do what you need to do with minimal effort and inconvenience, you're using the right equipment.

Lens Choice

A photographer who is shooting for a client or for a specific purpose is obligated to use the lenses best suited for that project. If you're doing sports or wildlife photography, you're going to need a telephoto lens or two. If you're doing low-light photography, you're going to need fast lenses. As I mention in the Techniques chapter, most street photography is done with wide-to-normal focal length lenses. You may discover that the environments you shoot in and your method of shooting favor wide-angle lenses over normal lenses, or vice versa. The lens you use is an integral part of how your photographs will look. Don't fight it; embrace it. The better you get at previsualizing how your images will look with certain lenses, the better prepared you can be for taking those shots. The fewer distractions you have to deal with on the streets (what focal length is this zoom set to?

Do I need to move closer or further away?), the better your ability to seize photographic opportunities when they appear.

Color vs. Black-and-White

There are street photographers who shoot exclusively in color simply because it's the default mode on their camera. Others shoot exclusively in black-and-white because it's the classic look for street photography, so they assume it's the way *their* photographs should look. There is nothing wrong with choosing one or the other, but your images will be a lot stronger if your choice is motivated by something more than conformity or default settings. You should be striving for a specific mode of expression. For example, you can use contrasting, complementary, or selective colors as compositional elements. You can use a background of desaturated or neutral color to draw the viewer's eye to one or two bright, saturated colors. You can alter the color balance to make the overall mood look warmer or cooler.

You have similar options with black-and-white photography. You can heighten or reduce the contrast between tones. You can use color contrast filtration adjustments to make specific areas lighter or darker. You can use black-and-white simply to strip your images of the distractions and complications of color.

There is no need to shoot exclusively in one or the other. Each option has its strengths, weaknesses, and challenges. I personally use both, depending on what looks best for a particular image. That said, I group my black-and-white images separately from my color images so that each portfolio or body of work has a coherent look.

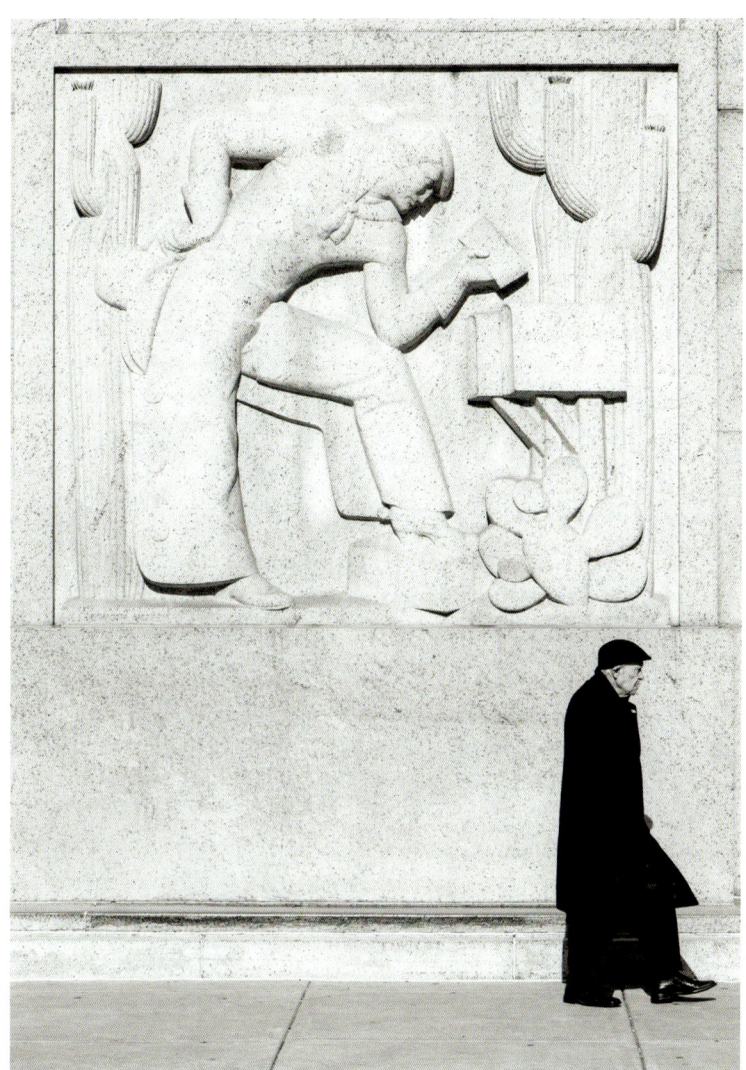

Left Foot Forward, Philadelphia, PA 2011

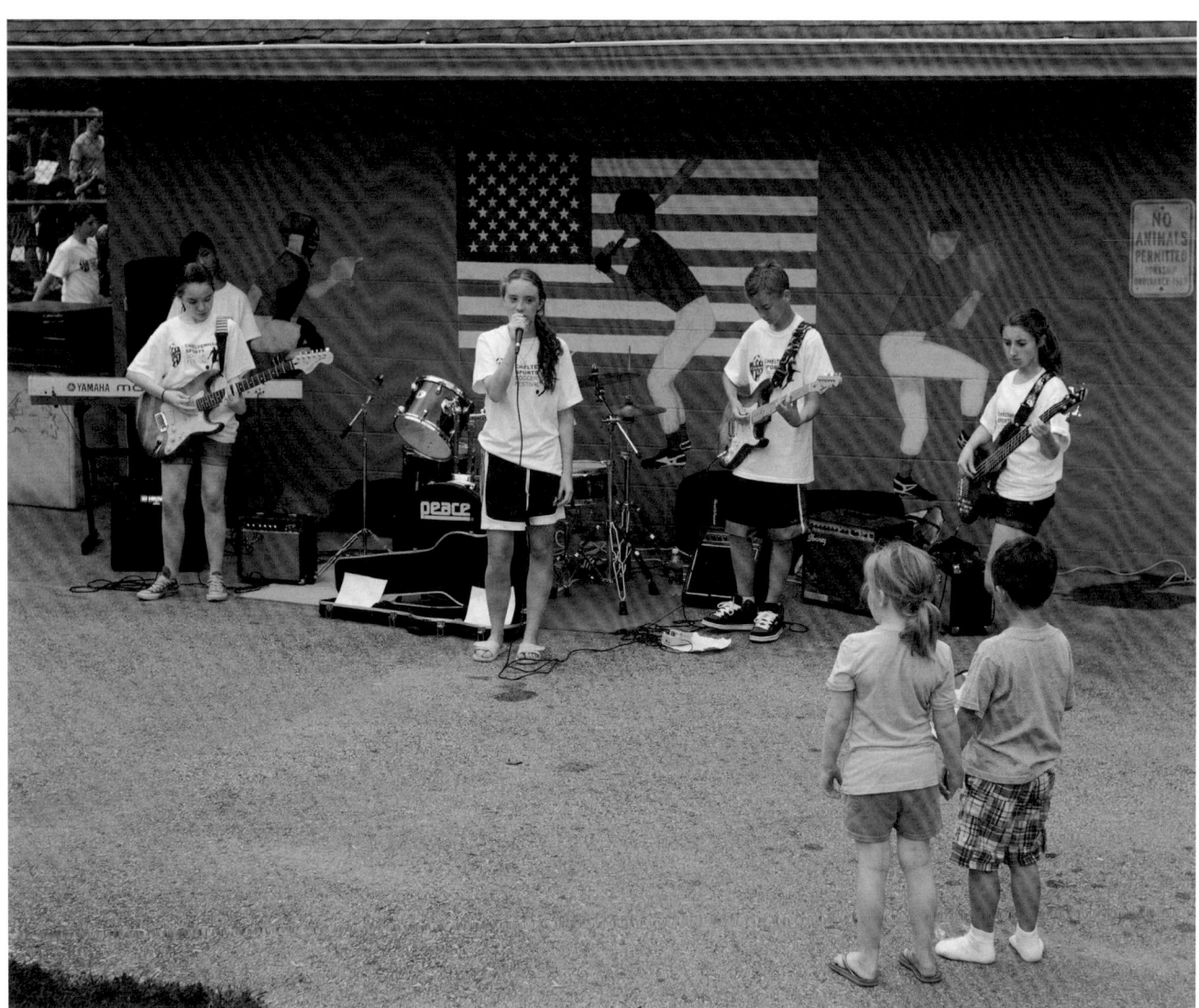

Rock & Roll Home Run, Woodland Little League Complex,
Cheltenham, PA 2011

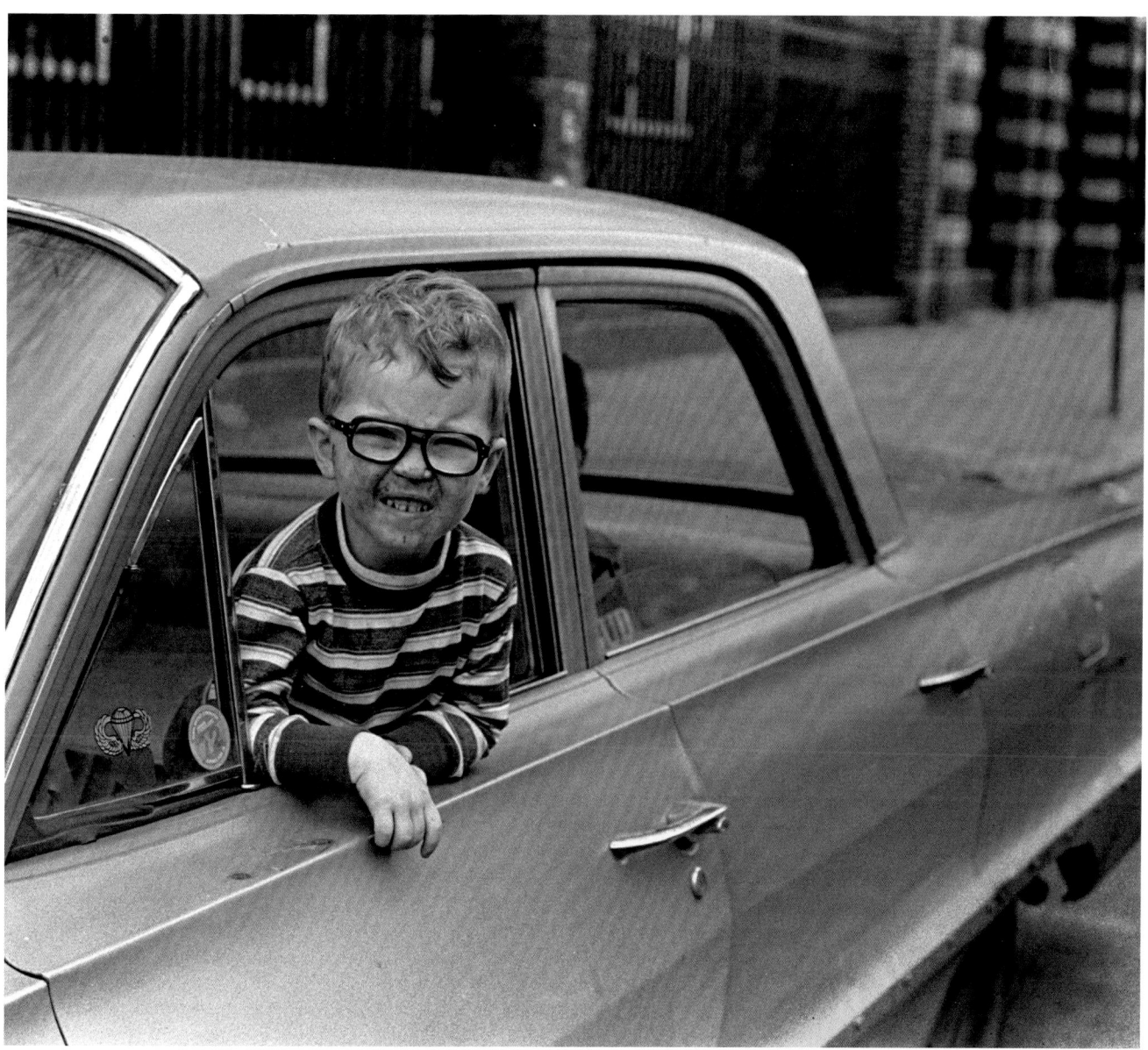

Kid in Car, Harvard Square, MA 1972

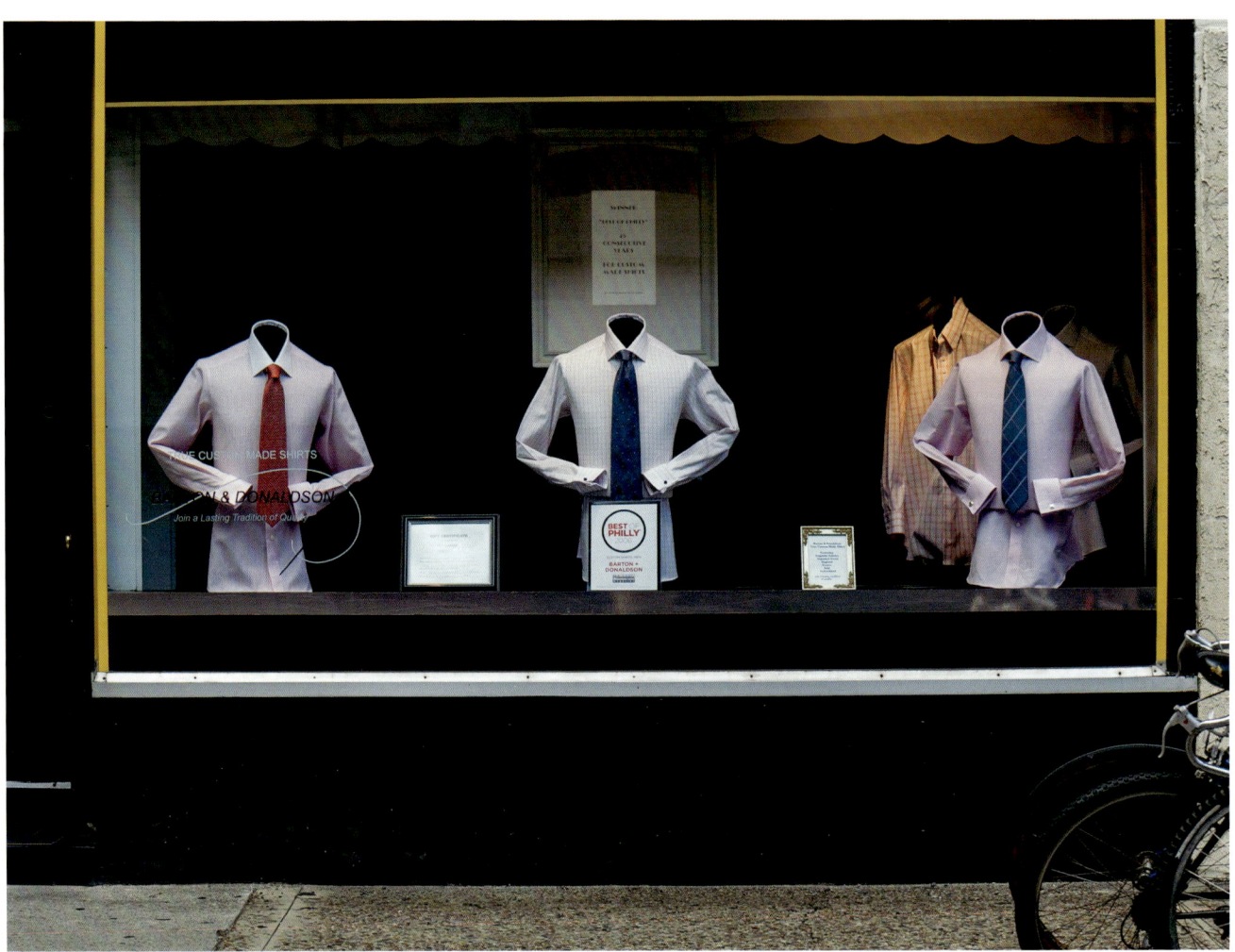

Colorful Shirts, Philadelphia, PA 2011

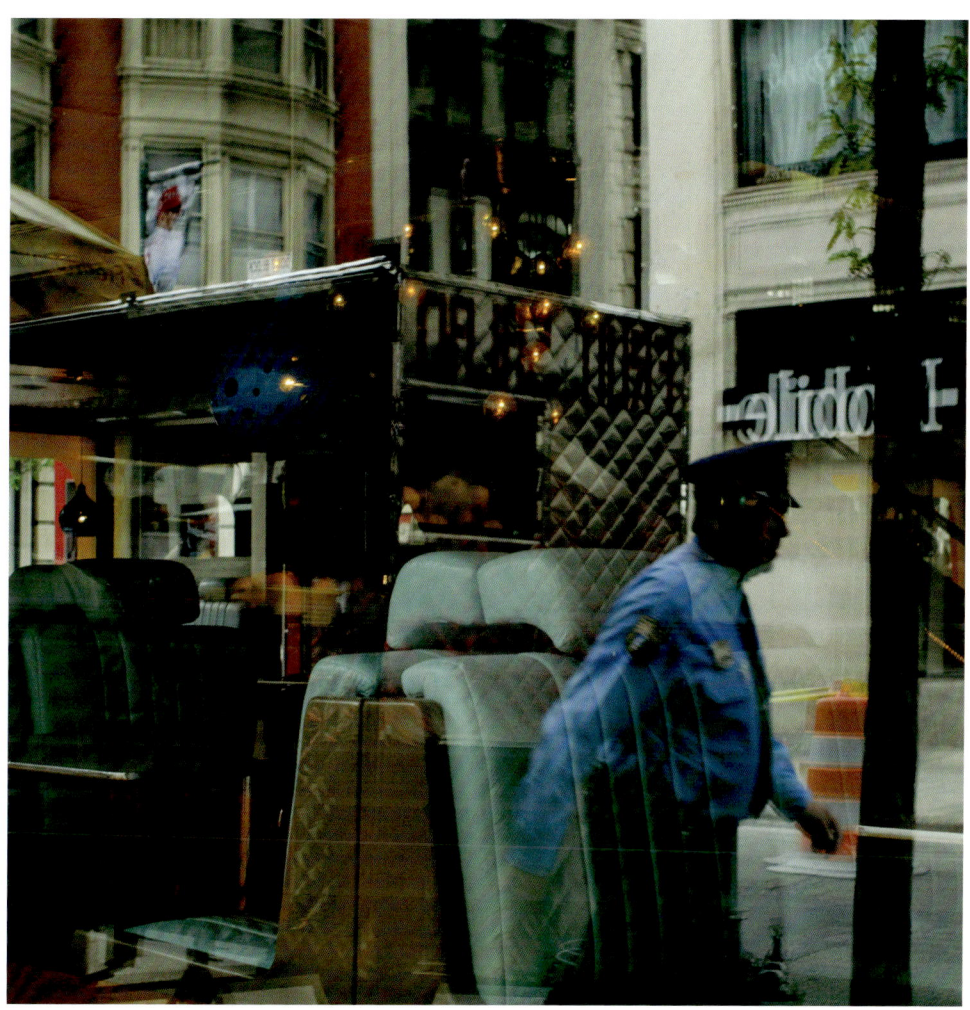

Street Reflections, Philadelphia, PA 2012

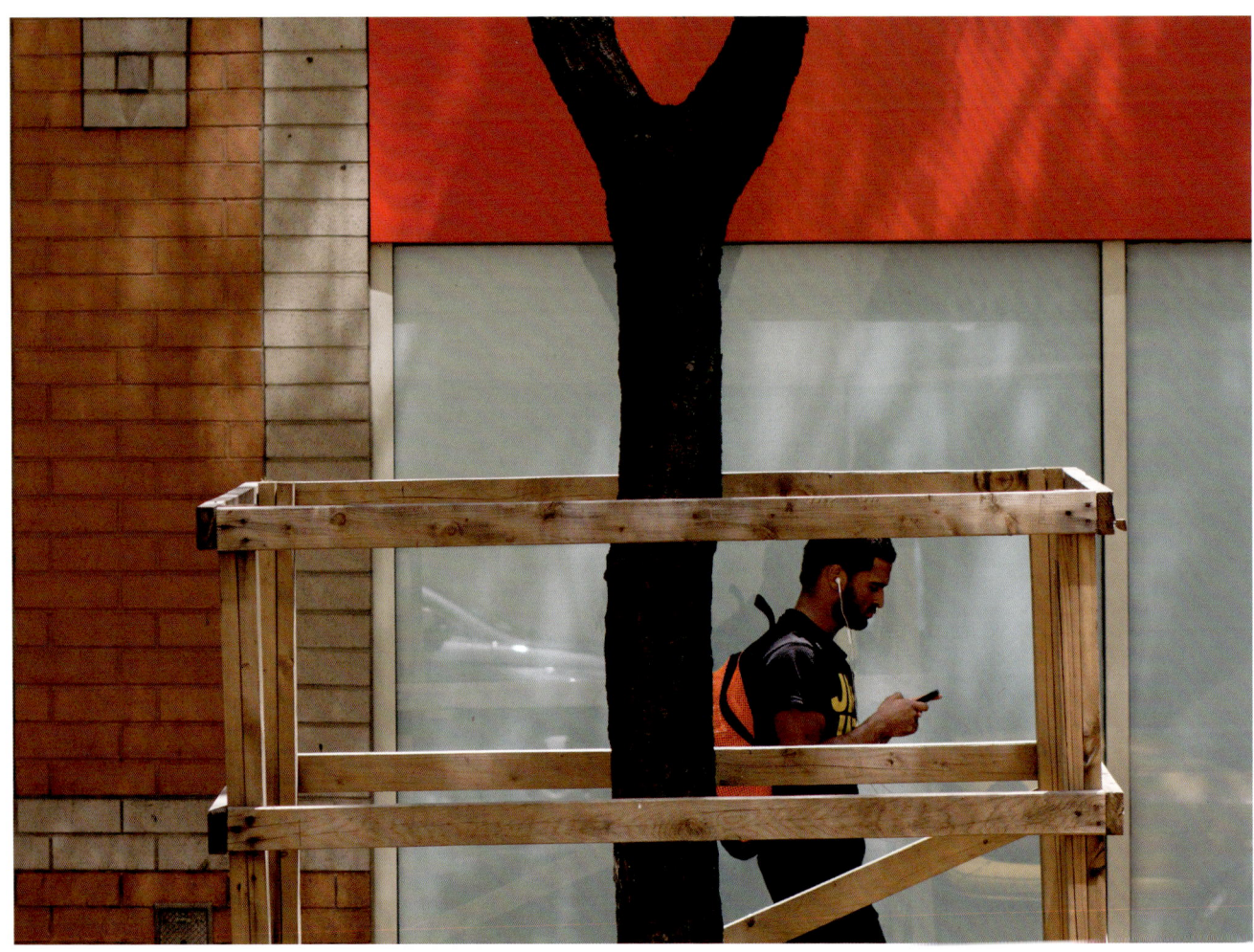

Boxed In, New York, NY 2013

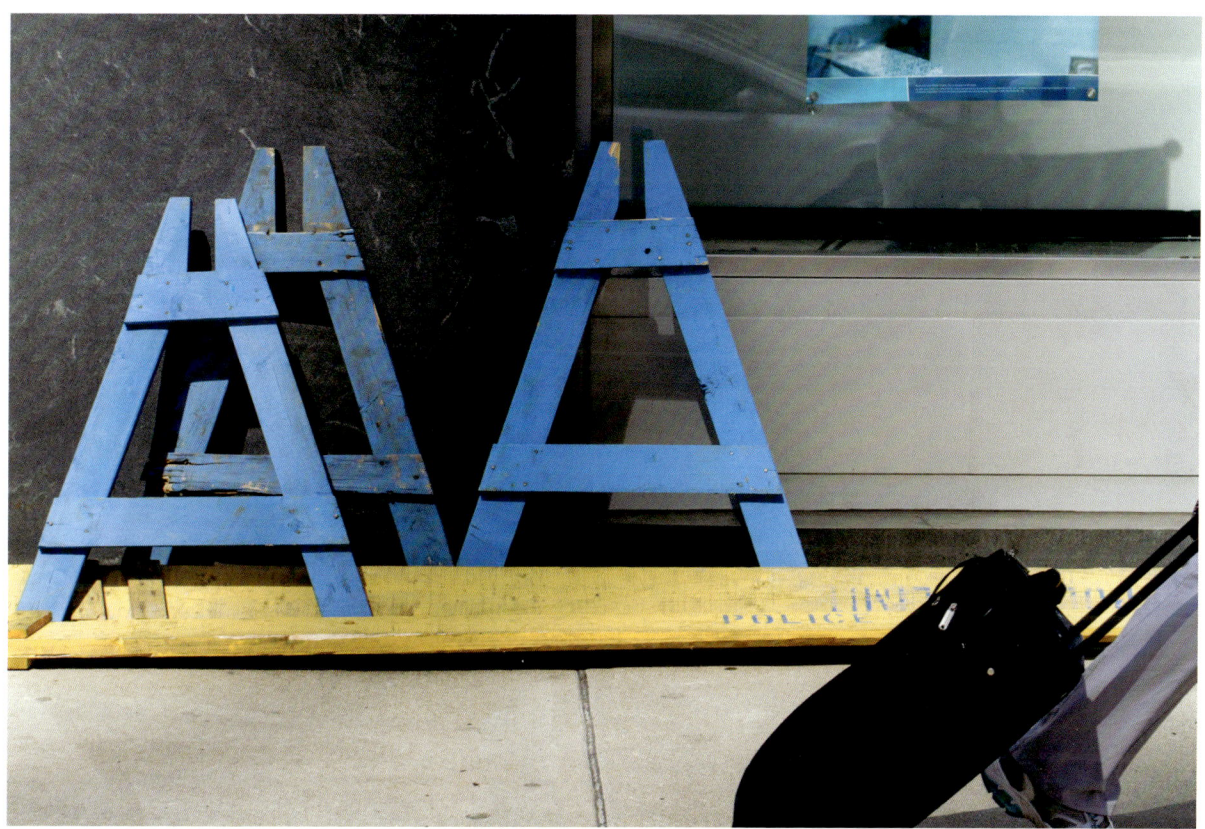

Blue Sawhorses, Philadelphia, PA 2010

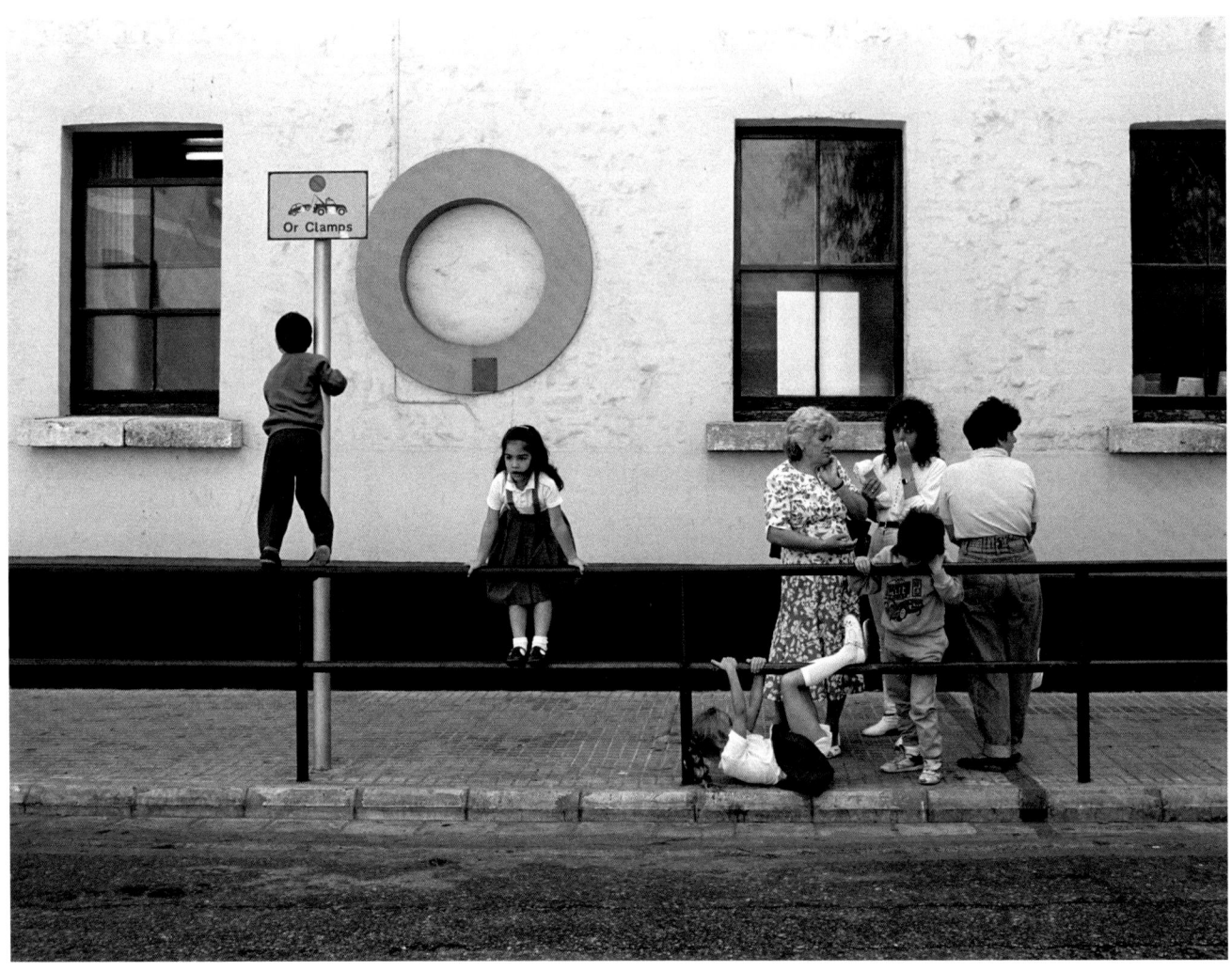

After School Scene, Rock of Gibralter, 1982

Film vs. Digital

One of the reasons many street photographers prefer to use film rather than digital cameras is because of the particular look of film images. No matter how well various film emulators may mimic the look of film, film has a distinctly different look from digital. For starters, every film emulsion has a different look. Print films look different from slide films. Kodak films look different from Fuji films. High-speed black-and-white films look different from slow-speed, fine-grained films, especially if you develop and print them yourself. You can enhance the film grain to add texture and grit to your images or subdue it to enhance tone and luminosity.

There are, of course, just as many good reasons to shoot digitally, including speed, flexibility, minimal cost per image, and ability to review images on the spot. Just be careful not to be so seduced by the ease of automation that you default to point-and-shoot mode and forget to make conscious choices.

Lighting Dynamics

With few exceptions, street photography is shot in available light. It therefore stands to reason that the look of your street photos will be greatly influenced by the quality of light available to you. If you live and shoot in an area where the sun is almost always hidden behind clouds or tall buildings, your images will have a very different look from someone who lives where overcast days and tall buildings are rare.

Of course, you still have choices. If you live in a city of tall buildings and concrete canyons, you might be constantly on the hunt for those special moments when the light cuts through the gap between buildings or reflects off of a glass tower to create a spotlight effect. If you live where direct sunlight is almost always available, you might prefer to shoot in the early morning or late afternoon to capture moments when the sun is low in the sky, shadows are long, and backlight effects are dramatic. You might even try adopting the techniques of **Bruce Gilden** or **Martin Parr**. Gilden, who shoots in black-and-white, uses a handheld flash unit attached to his camera as a way to separate his subjects from the unlit background. Parr, who shoots in color, uses on-camera flash mainly to fill in dark shadows and add snap to otherwise dull lighting.

OPPOSITE PAGE:
Woman in Glowing Red Blouse, Philadelphia, PA 2013

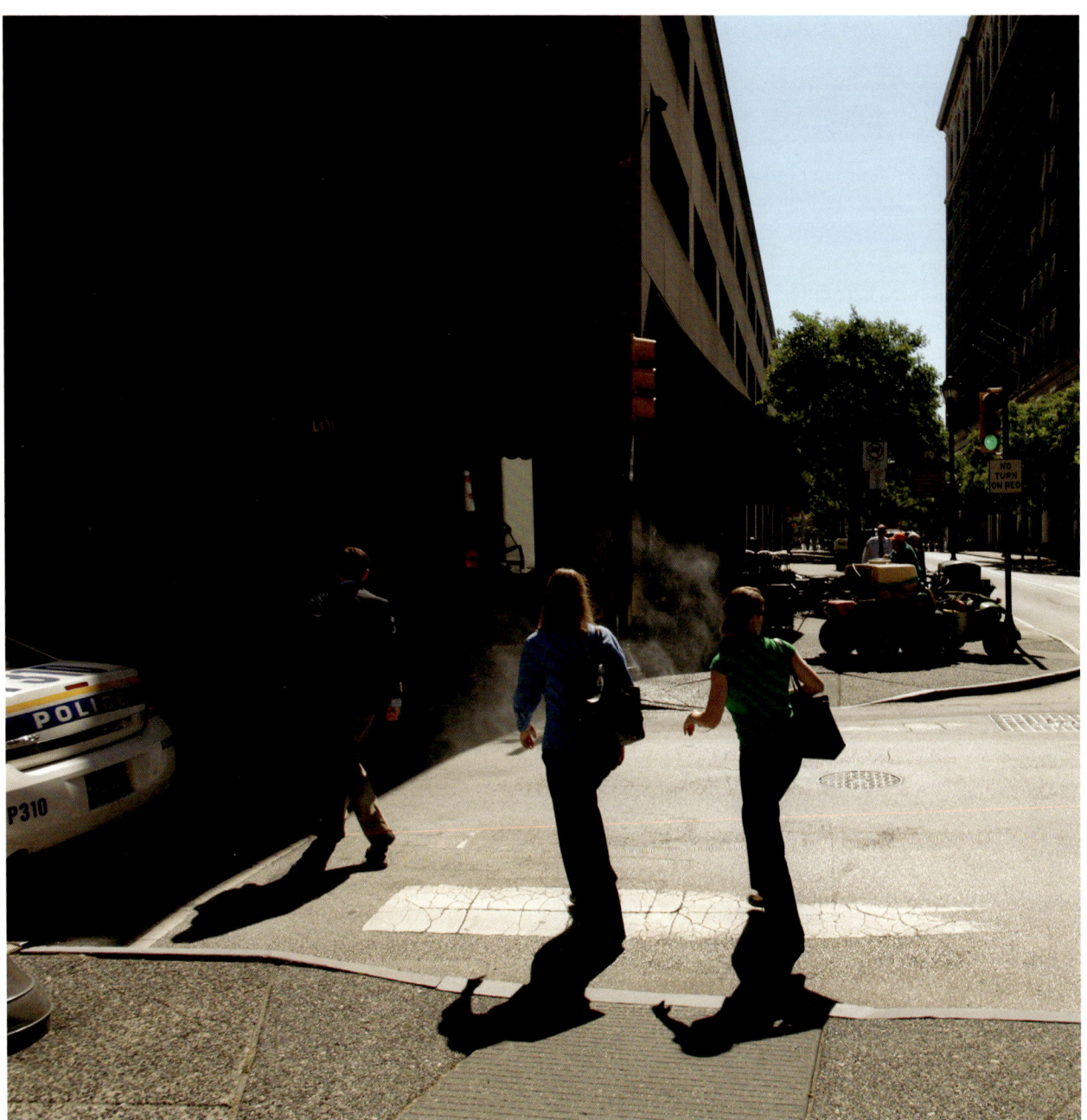

Three Silhouettes, Philadelphia, PA 2010

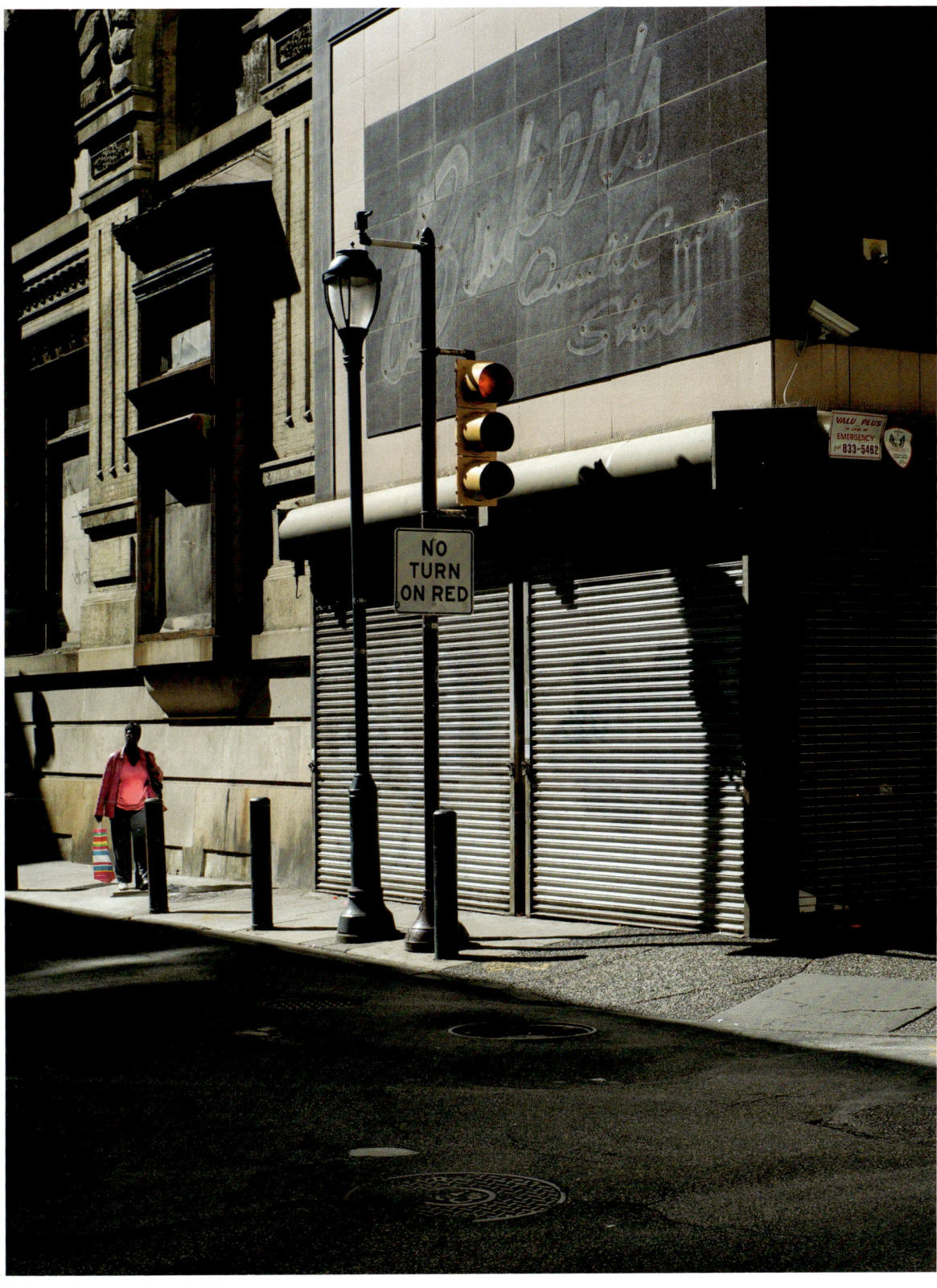

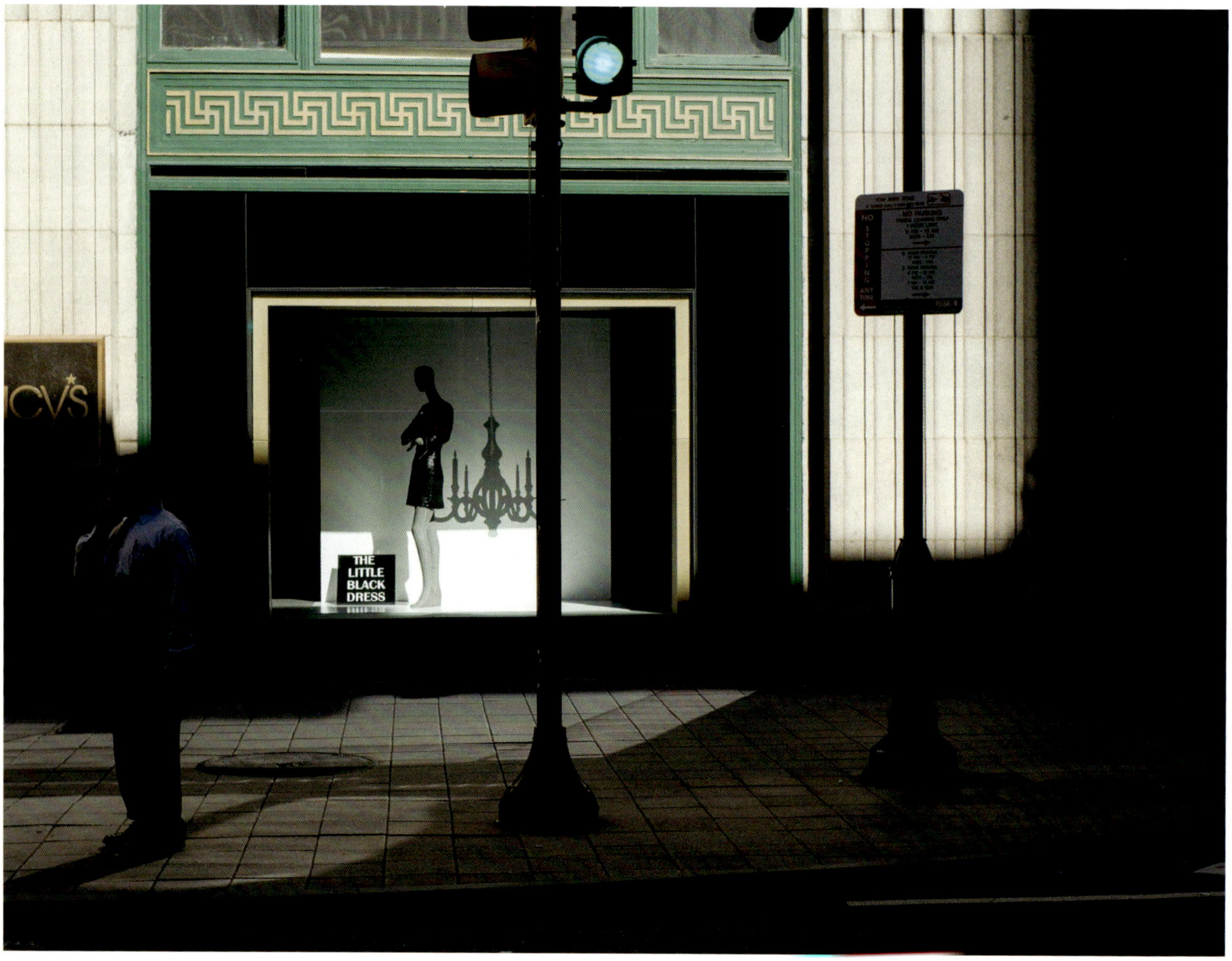

The Little Black Dress, Philadelphia, PA 2011

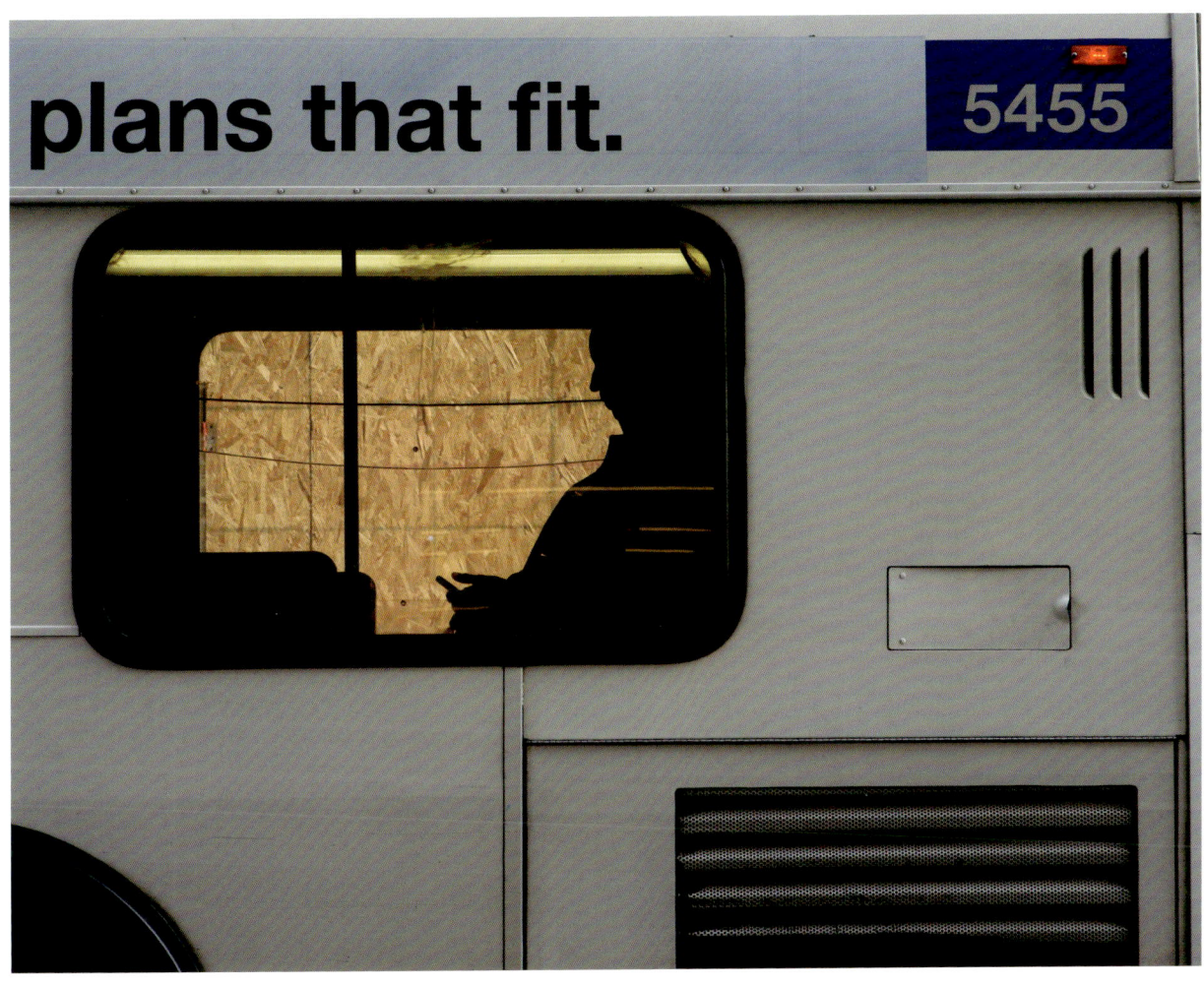

Hitchcock Silhouette, Philadelphia, PA 2011

Static vs. Spontaneous

In general, street photography places a high value on capturing those specific gestures, expressions, or compositions that define a split second in time. Those aspects separate memorable photos from forgettable ones. There are, nevertheless, varying degrees of spontaneity. There may be a particular day of the year or time of day when the light forms a particular pattern of shadows unavailable at any other time. Perhaps it's a rare cloud formation, a rainbow, or a reflection on only one of a dozen windows. Some photographers have an innate feeling for these types of moments, while others have a sense for the exact 1/250th of a second in which to press the shutter. Either way, if your images prompt viewers to linger, gaze deeply, and marvel at your ability to separate the marvelous from the mundane, you're obviously on to something—keep it up!

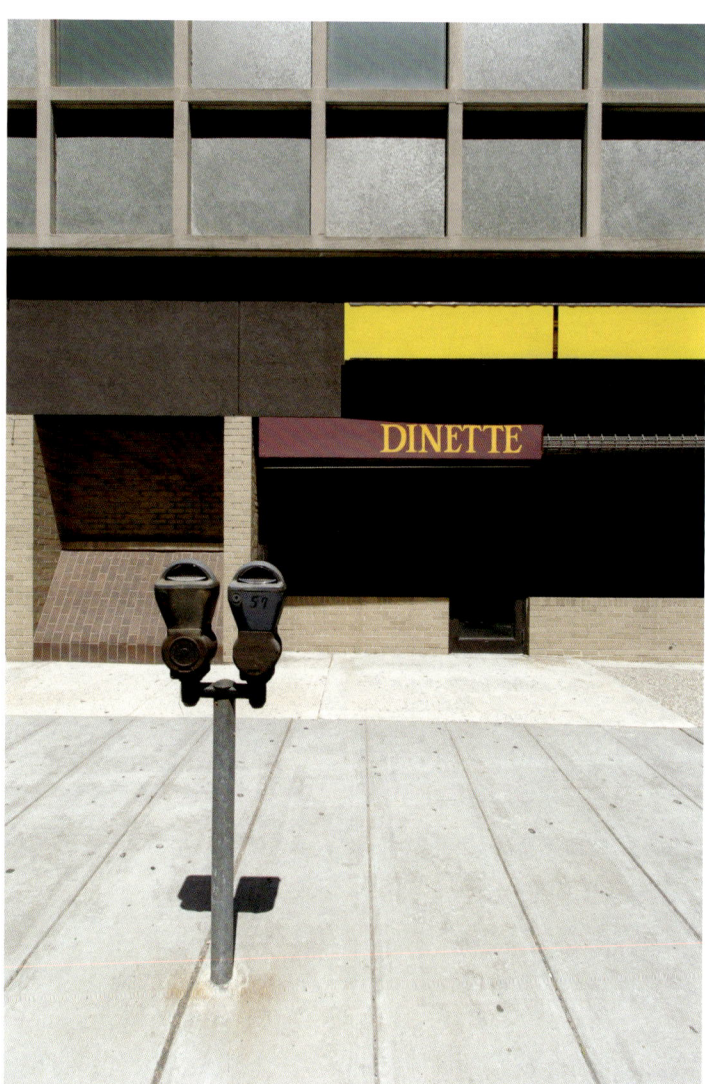

Dinette, Philadelphia, PA 2009

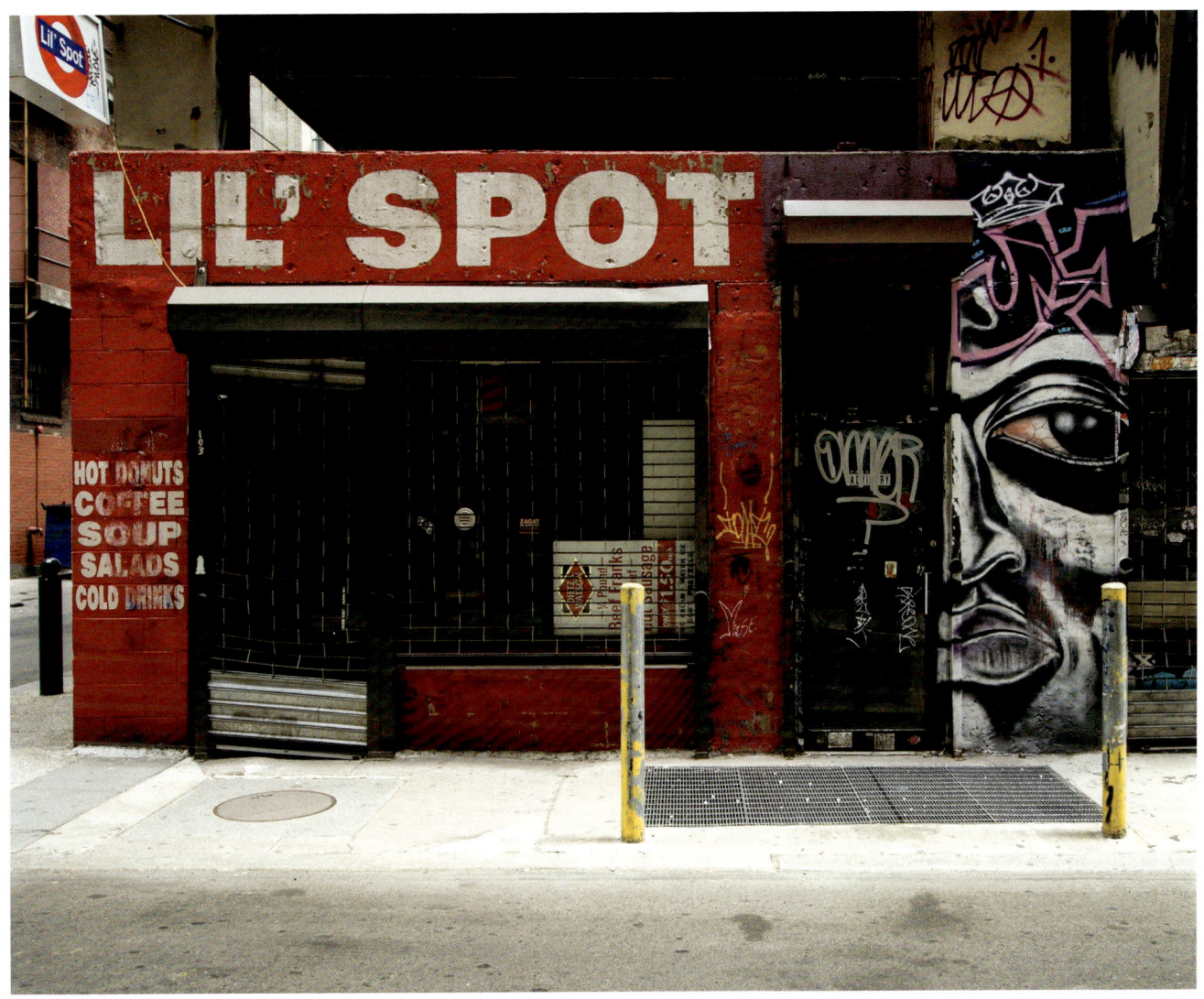

Lil' Spot, Philadelphia, PA 2008

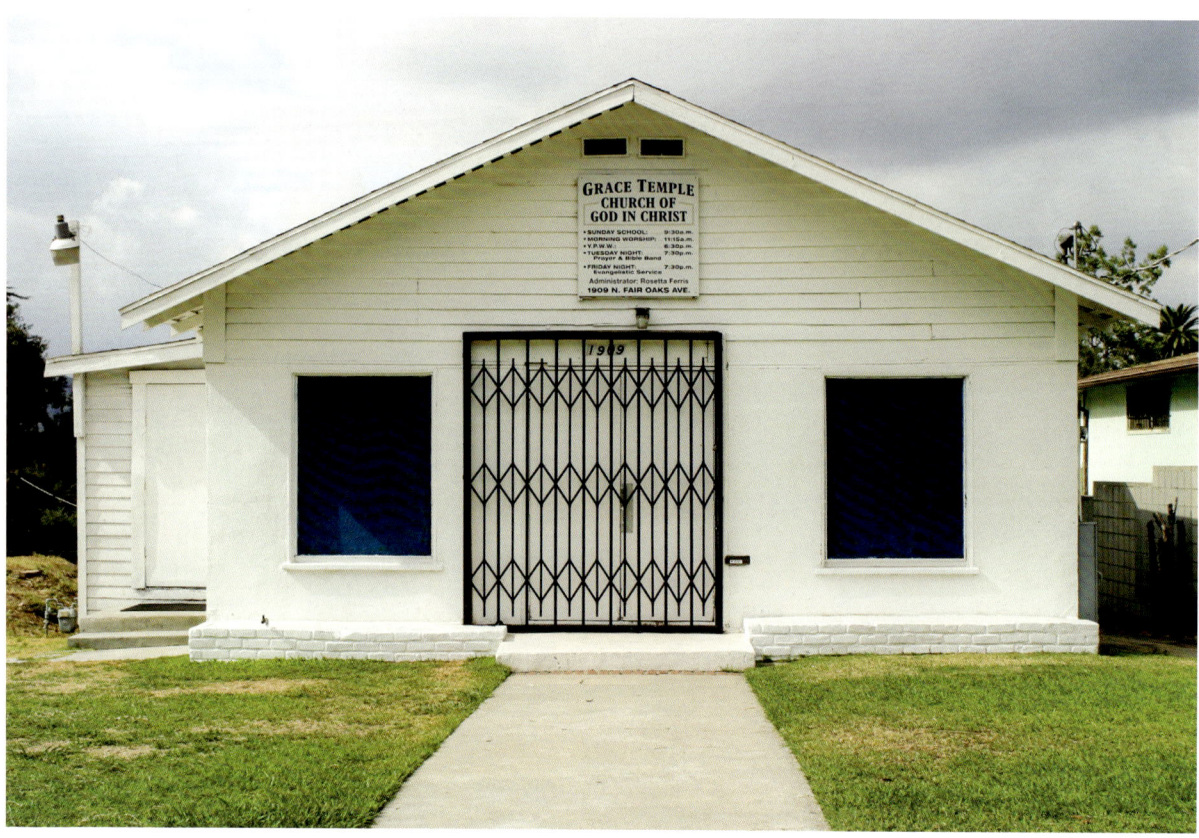

Gated Church, Altadena, CA 2009

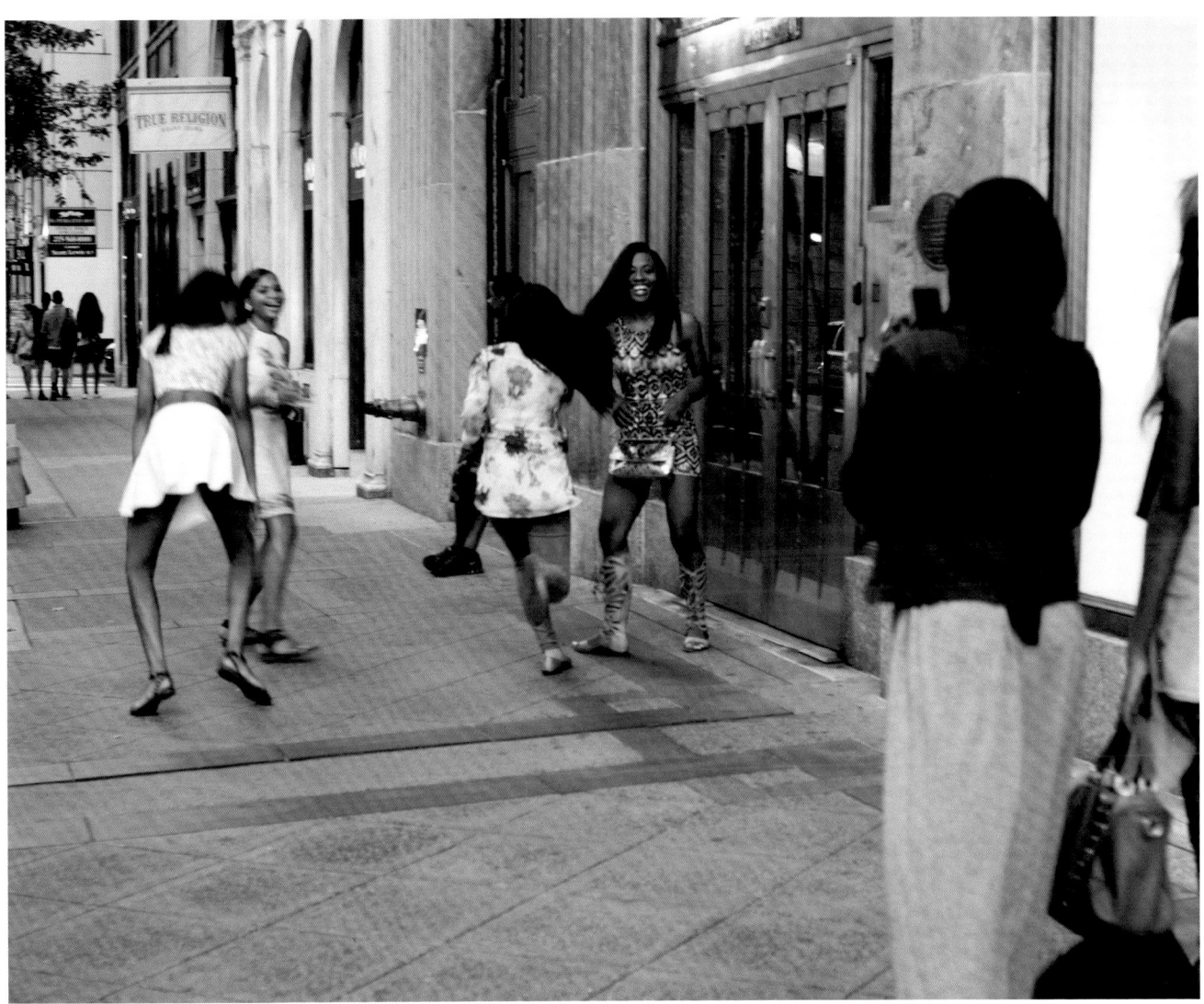

Dancing Girls, Philadelphia, PA 2014

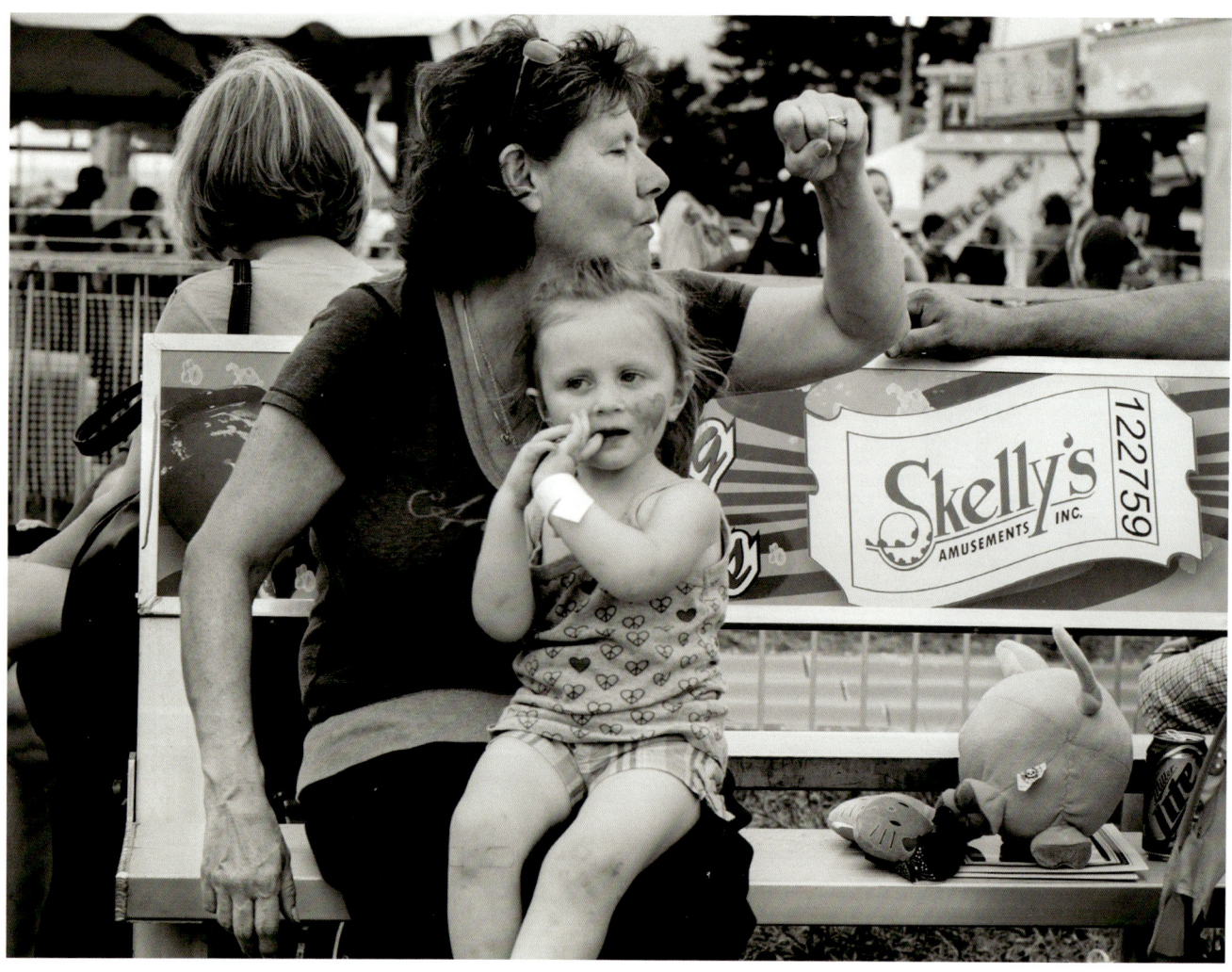

Skelley's, Abington, PA 2012

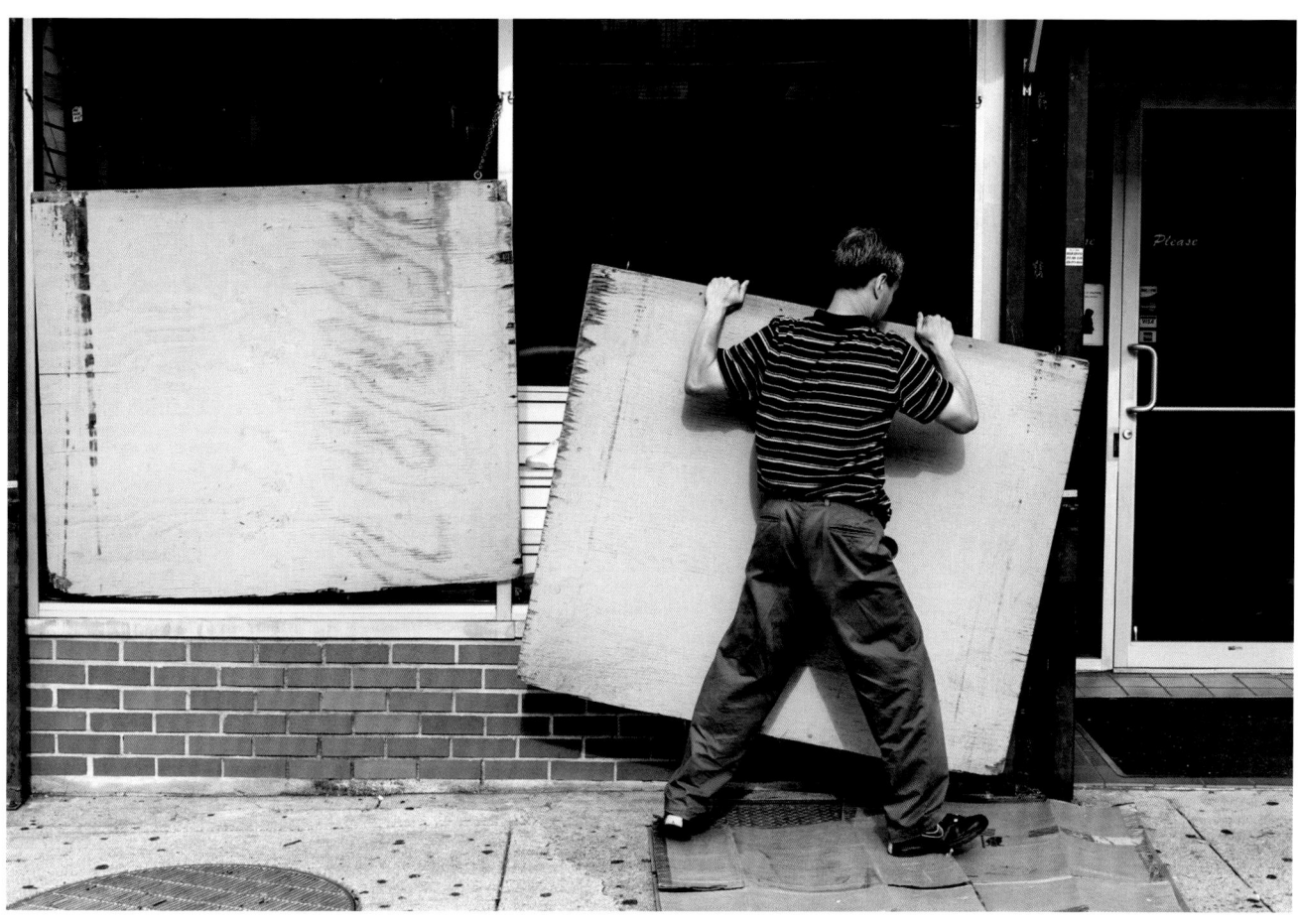

Moving Plywood, Philadelphia, PA 2013

People vs. Artifacts

It's worth remembering that classic street photographers such as **Eugene Atget** and **Walker Evans** built their reputations mainly on photographs of buildings, bridges, monuments, and other artifacts. They even used view cameras, which require a heavy tripod. In Atget's case, the film emulsions were so slow and the exposures so long that any moving objects in his photographs were rendered invisible or appeared as ghostly blurs.

The reason such images are considered "street photography" is that, unlike traditional architectural photography, the goal was not to ennoble a structure for the sake of its designer or funder, but rather to portray it in the context of the street. Some structures look out of place with their neighbors and harken back to earlier times. Some look only days away from demolition, while others offer new and optimistic visions for the future. Some are elegant, others squat and ugly. These qualities aren't necessarily inherent in the buildings themselves; they are all in how you photograph them.

Buildings, monuments, and other artifacts seem so solid and permanent that you may feel no particular value or urgency in photographing them. You may think, "What's the hurry? That building has been there for 20 years. It will be there tomorrow." However, even landmark buildings and businesses disappear everyday. Berlin used to have a wall that separated east from west. New York used to have two World Trade Center towers.

This isn't to say that you're obligated to photograph structures and artifacts if you have no interest in them; it's just a reminder that buildings can be just as ephemeral as anything else you encounter on the street. If you feel inspired to photograph a storefront church with an amusing saying-of-the-week posted on a billboard, or a pink car parked in front of a lime green building, go for it. You may never get a second chance.

Point of View

The choices you make about what types of subjects to photograph, as well as how and when to photograph them, can express a consistent point of view that is separate from that of the subjects themselves. Depending on when you click the shutter, you can make people look happy, hostile, haughty, or humble. You can emphasize what someone has in common with other human beings or what sets them apart. If there is humor in a photograph, you can make your subject appear in on the joke or the butt of it. It's all dependent on what you're attuned to and when you choose to click the shutter.

Let's take **Elliott Erwitt** for example. Although a photojournalist by profession, Erwitt is best known for his black-and-white

Bottle in the Sky,
Philadelphia, PA 2007

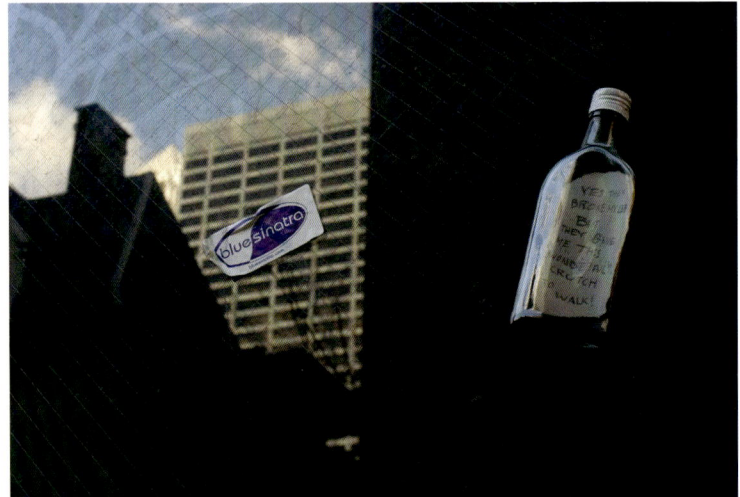

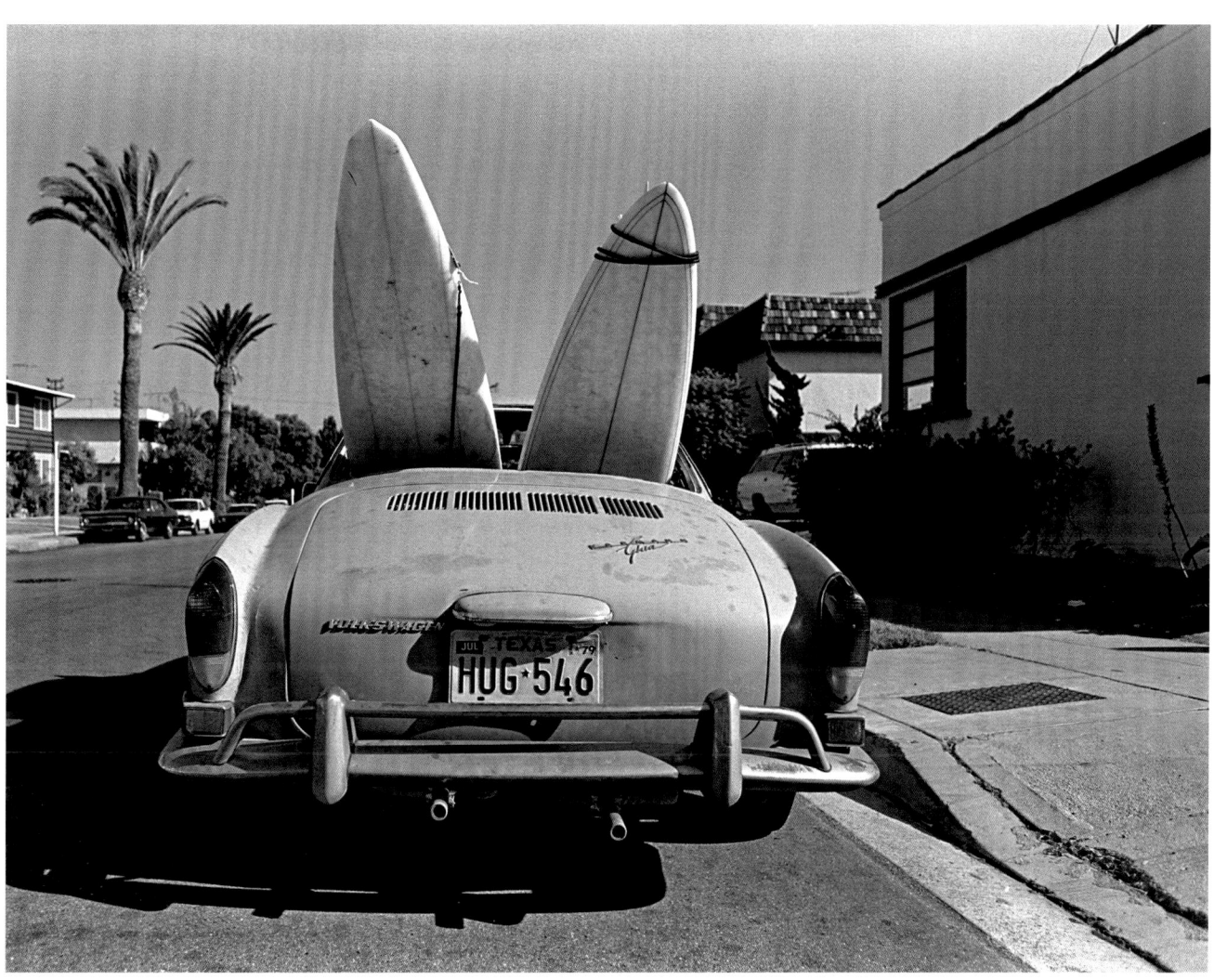

Two Surfboards, Santa Monica, CA 1978

street photos that feature a clever wit, dogs, or both. However, it would be absurd to believe that instead of creating these opportunities for himself, he constantly finds himself surrounded by dogs and people doing amusing things. Isn't it far more likely that he views the world through a "humor filter?" Erwitt, because of his personality and individual perspective on life, sees humorous situations where other might see nothing special at all. The result is that when you look at an Elliott Erwitt photograph you see not just the subject, but how that subject looks to Elliott Erwitt.

For any such sensibility to appear in your photographs, you too have to have a particular point of view or attitude you feel driven to express. The more perceptive you are, the stronger and more persuasive the message of your photographs will be. If you're more internally focused, consider that having something particular you want to express through your street photography gives you a more compelling reason to shoot than if you were only taking random photos of miscellaneous strangers on the street.

The same could be said of landscape photography, portraiture, sports photography — you name it. Regardless of genre, most photographs these days are unexceptional, mainly because they are produced by unexceptional photographers. I assume, however, that you are either an exceptional photographer or aspire to be one, which is why you're reading this book and this chapter.

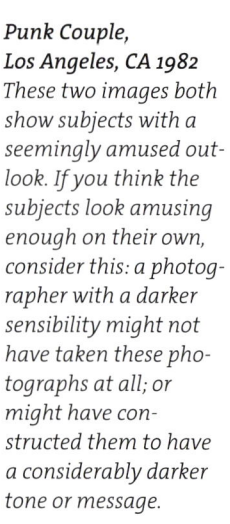

Punk Couple,
Los Angeles, CA 1982
These two images both show subjects with a seemingly amused outlook. If you think the subjects look amusing enough on their own, consider this: a photographer with a darker sensibility might not have taken these photographs at all; or might have constructed them to have a considerably darker tone or message.

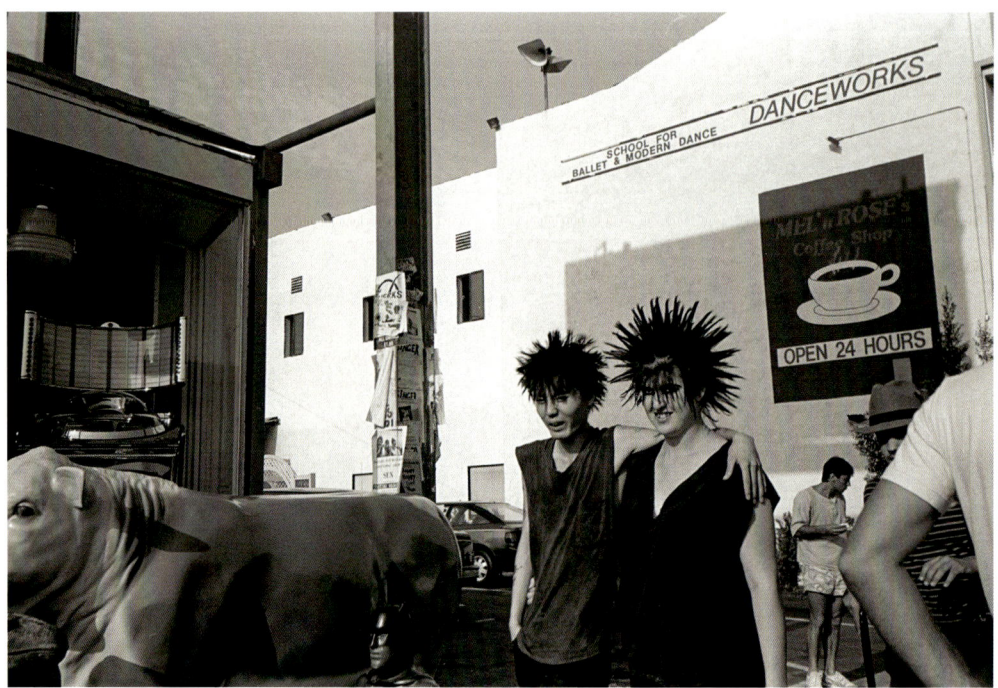

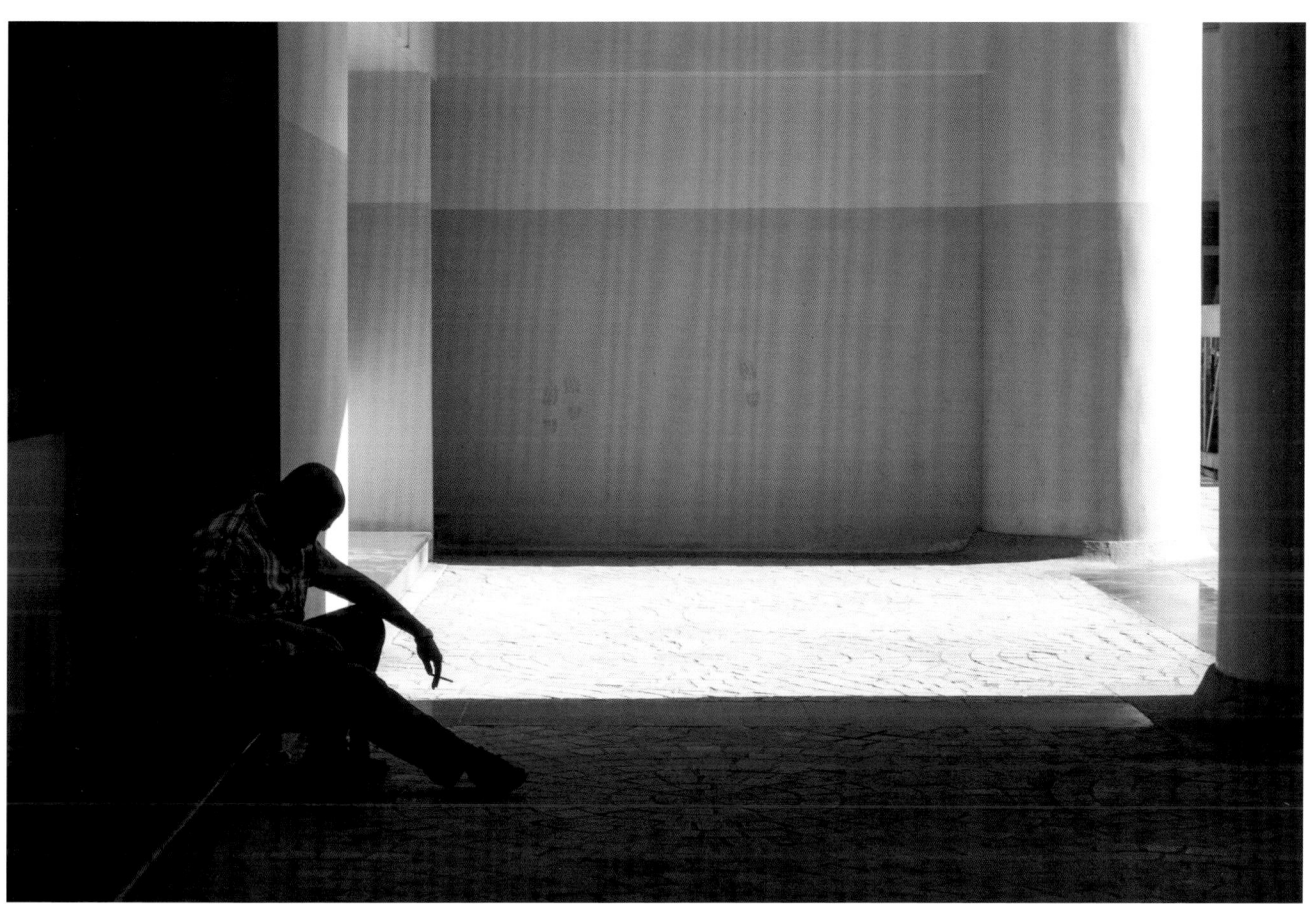

Quiet Smoke, Beijing Railway Station, Beijing 2012

The photographs I've used to illustrate the various style categories have been pulled from over three decades of my work. (I've used examples drawn from other street shooters, as well.) As a result, you will see a variety of styles, from black-and-white to color, from images shot with film cameras to images shot digitally. What they all have in common, at least in my opinion, is a feel for graphic design and composition. Although many of my images may appear as if my camera was mounted on a tripod and I told the subject exactly where to stand and what to do, they are actually spontaneous compositions, shot in only a few seconds. The only control I had was where to stand, what lens and exposure to use, and when to release the shutter. I use color selectively and as key elements in the overall composition to draw the viewer's eye where I want it. I like to think of it as my way of imposing order on a random and disorderly world. In any case, it's self-taught, so if you don't care for it, there's no one to blame but me. It's just the way I like to shoot, or to be more specific, it reflects which types of images I like most.

Your style should be characteristic of who *you* are: *your* personality, *your* experiences and how they've informed *your* outlook on life. Regardless of whether you prefer to shoot in black-and-white or color, with a wide-angle lens or a normal lens, methodically or intuitively, you should do so because it works best for *you,* not because you think it's the way you're supposed to shoot or because you think it's the way everyone else does it. What makes the great photographers great is that they open our eyes to their own individual way of seeing the world.

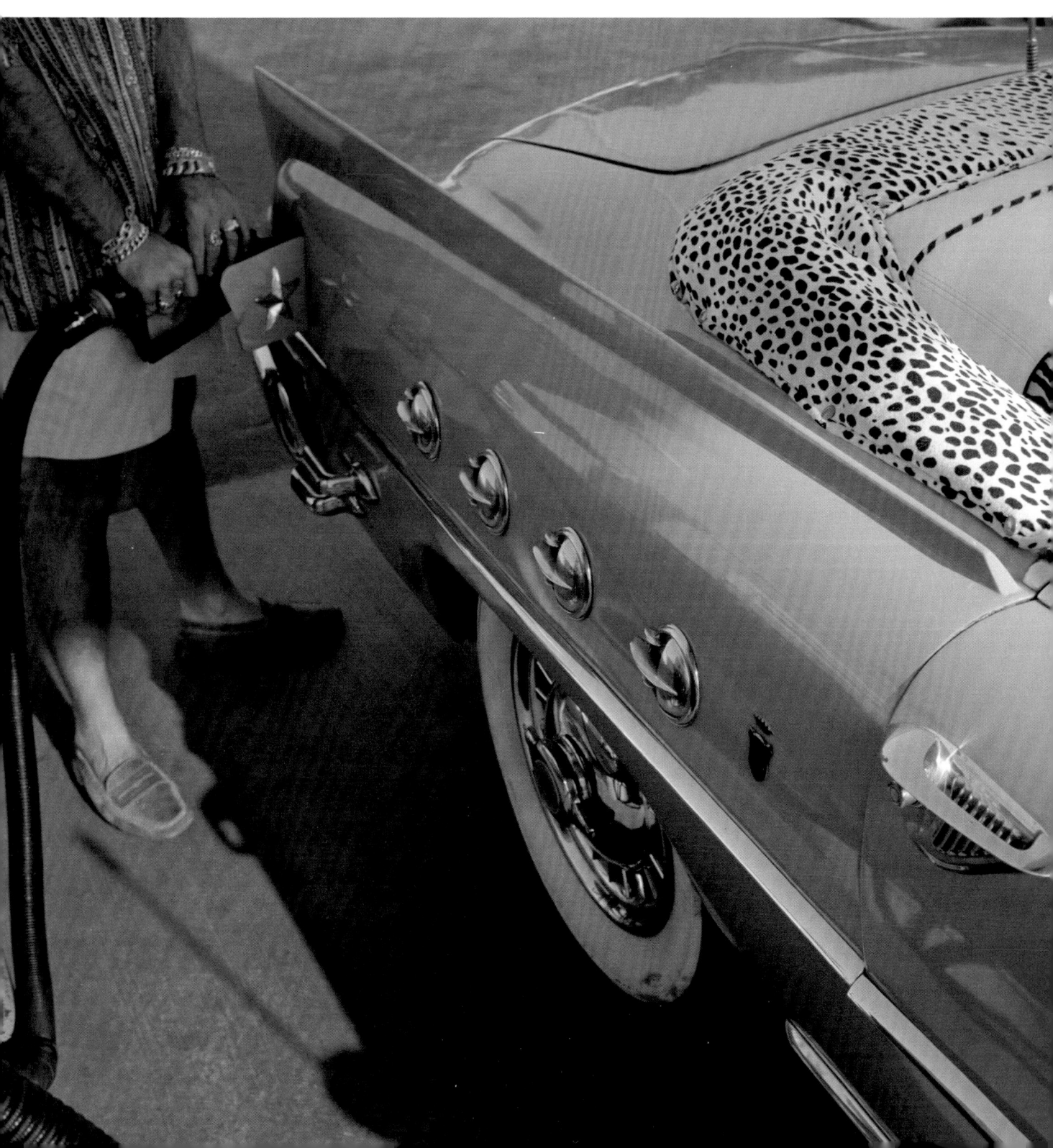

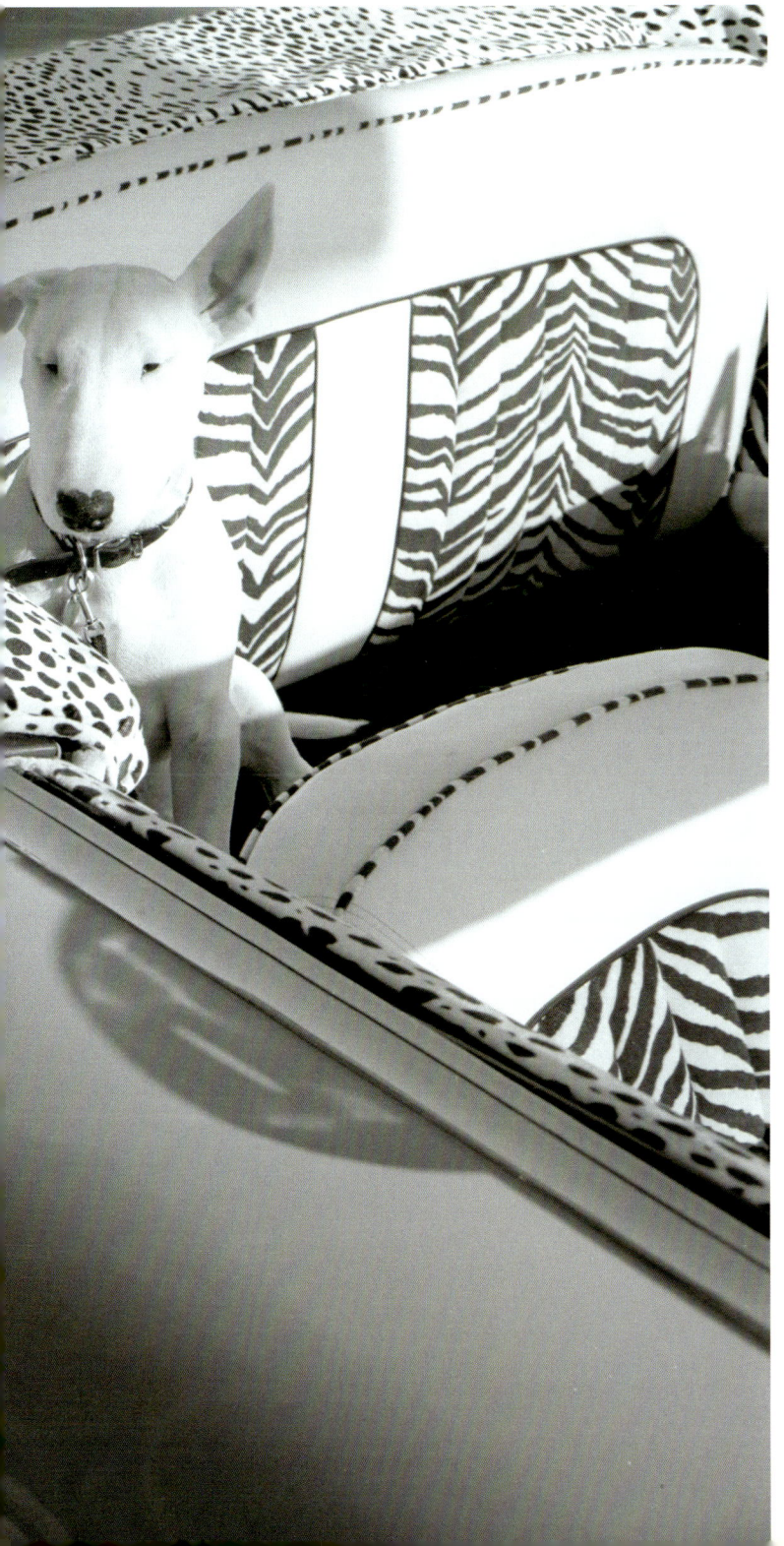

CHAPTER 6

What Makes a Great Street Photo?

Before I begin to expound on the subject of what elements contribute to producing a great street photograph, let me state upfront that what I intend to offer are well-informed *opinions,* not dogma. I don't claim to have any academic training, professional certifications, or divine insights. I do, however, have 40 years of experience as a street and semi-professional photographer. I've won international photo contests, had my work published in several magazines and a few books, and have even sold a few hundred prints to buyers around the world.

This section is written for a broad cross-section of street photographers who may be at different stages of their artistic development. Keep in mind that the qualities I'm about to describe aren't like a feature checklist, where the more of them you have in each photograph, the better. Some great street photos may have several of these qualities, some only one or two. Think of them as ingredients in a recipe: although the individual ingredients are important, what matters most is how they all come together.

Finally, we should all acknowledge that it's one thing to recognize the qualities of a great photograph when you have one in front of you; it's something else entirely to produce one yourself. Knowledge does not necessarily translate into ability. What it *does* provide is a sense of possibility and a standard to strive for. So with all that out of the way, let's get started.

Strong Composition

Composition is the arrangement of visual elements (lines, objects, colors, textures, patterns, light and dark tones, etc.) in a way that suits your artistic purpose and holds a viewer's attention. Your purpose could be to tell a story, convey an emotion, record a special moment in time—there's really no limit. Whatever your purpose might be, the composition is the *means* you use to express an idea, not the idea itself. Great composition alone doesn't make a great photograph any more than correct grammar and punctuation can mask the absence of interesting ideas in an essay.

Content aside, good composition helps direct the viewer's eye, almost as if you were leading it along a specific path in a particular direction. With weak composition, viewers not only don't know where to look, they also don't see much reason to look at all. Good composition has certain elegance: it includes everything you need to suit your purpose and little extraneous information. Excess of visual information becomes a distraction. Too little information leaves the viewer feeling unsatisfied and wanting more.

Apropos of eliminating excess visual information, you have two options. The first is via framing. You can either change lenses, zoom, or change your distance from the subject to include or exclude elements. Your second option is cropping. If the full image frame still includes too much extraneous information, you can crop it out later. Some photographers are devoutly opposed to cropping, often based on the belief that not cropping is somehow more pure. I have no argument with this approach as long as the resulting images don't look as if they could benefit from reframing. You can't expect viewers to give you points

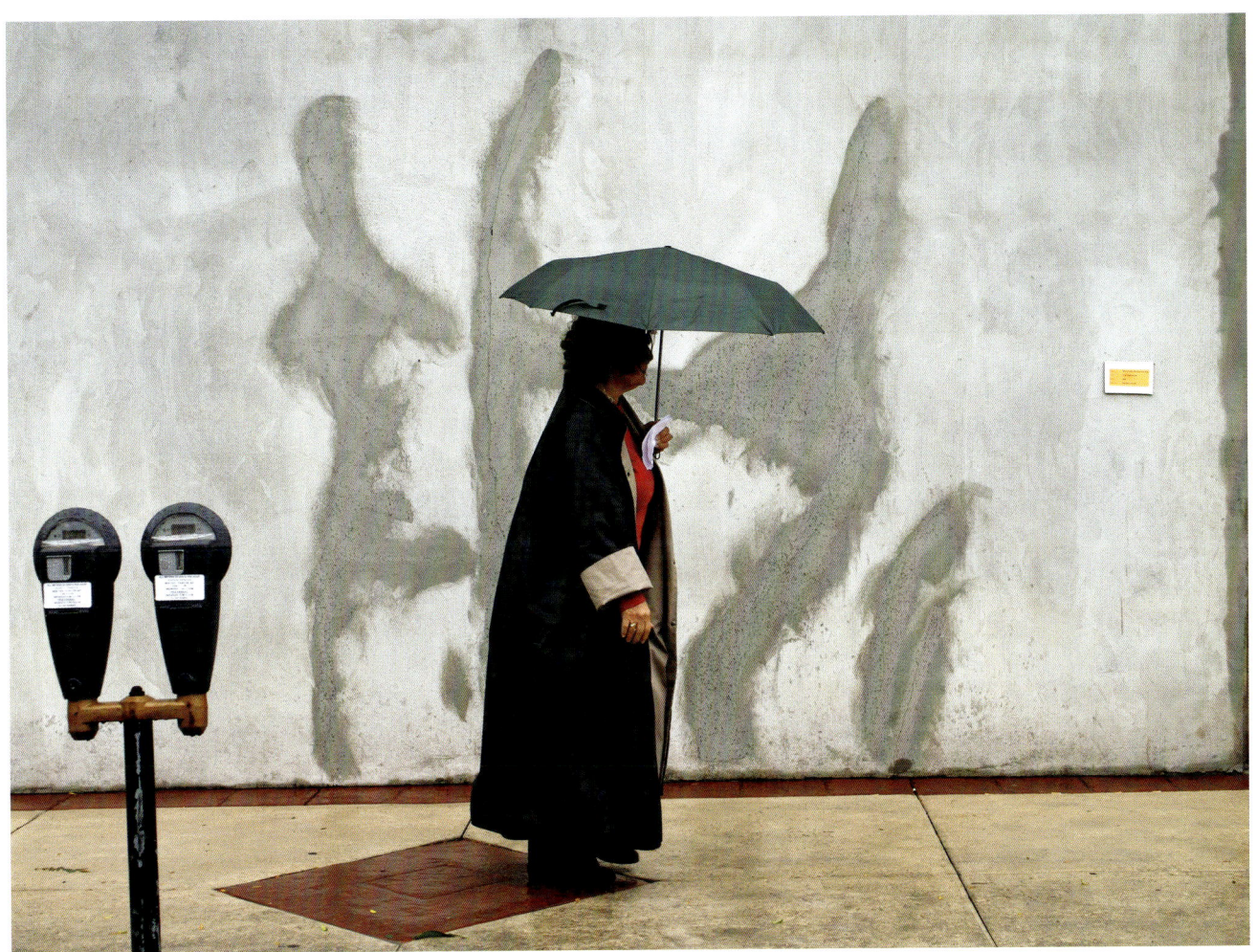

Precipitation, Jenkintown, PA 2009
This photograph is an example of being in the right place at the right time.
This woman turned the corner and stepped onto exactly the spot I wanted:
her raincoat and umbrella against the patching on the wall create a sense of
design and movement.

for purity if the image doesn't have strong composition and content. Personally, if I think I can improve a composition by cropping, then I crop. On the other hand, I also try to get the framing right without cropping, if only because it encourages rigor and discourages laziness.

I imagine you're well aware that you should strive for strong composition in your photographs. This can be a challenge when you're shooting on the street. Unlike, for example, still life photography, you don't have the luxury of lighting and micro-adjusting your subjects to your heart's content, all while your camera is mounted on a tripod. In street photography you're often faced with multiple subjects moving in different directions at once. By the time your brain registers a perfect composition and signals your finger to release the shutter, the moment may have passed. You can, however, learn to recognize and anticipate when a composition is just about to come together, where to position yourself, and when to release the shutter.

A Magic Moment

A mistake novice street photographers often make is to assume that photographing an interesting subject will result in a great photograph. Although it certainly helps to photograph a fascinating person, place, or thing, it's how you photograph the subject that makes the photo interesting, not the subject itself. In fact, in street photography, more often than not it's the *moment* you capture that becomes the true subject of your photograph.

Here's an example: As you're walking down the street, you notice an old man sitting on a bench, feeding pigeons. You could photograph this scene in a straightforward way and all you'd have is a sentimental photo we've all seen many times before. Instead, you position yourself, wait, and observe. A pigeon lands on the man's head. You take a photo. Another pigeon lands on the man's knee. You take another photo. Both shots are better than the first, but still nothing special. Suddenly, a boisterous child causes the pigeons to take flight. Now, instead of a few clichéd images of a man feeding pigeons, you have a photo of a man who appears swarmed by a dense flock of ravenous birds. The physical objects in your photo are the same. What has changed is how they are positioned relative to each other and when you decided to release the shutter. In other words, it's a different *moment*. In a situation such as this, the *moment* is the true subject of your photograph.

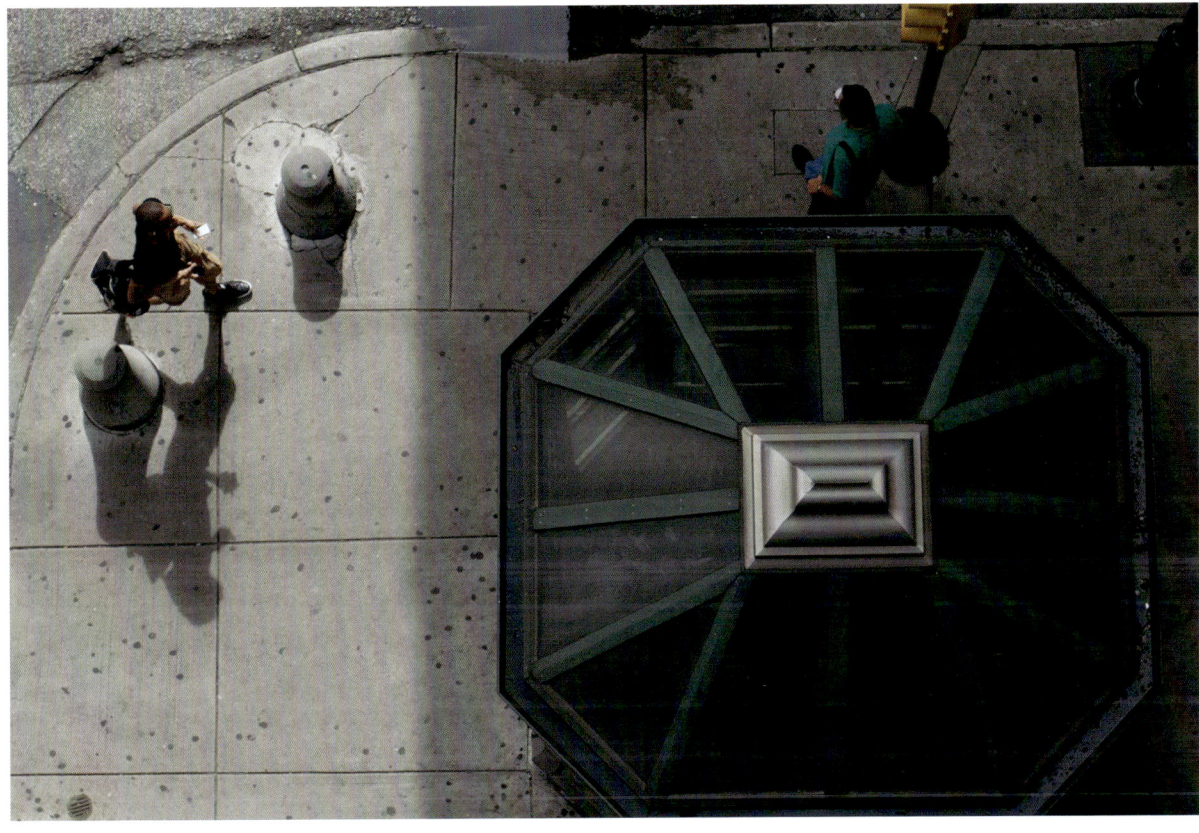

Bird's-Eye View, Philadelphia, PA 2010
I leaned over the railing of a parking structure and saw this kiosk below.
Nothing looked particularly promising about it until this gentleman passed
by with the perfect position, stride, and shadow.

This is just one example. The moment in question could just as easily be a gesture—or many people gesturing. It could be a particular facial expression, or someone caught in the middle of some action. **Henri Cartier-Bresson** defined his famous phrase, "the decisive moment," as "the simultaneous recognition, in a fraction of a second, of the significance of an event as well as the precise organization of forms which gives that event its proper expression." In other words, "the decisive moment" is all about knowing the best moment to release the shutter.

The moment can be one that evokes any number of reactions, from laughter to sadness, from mystery to insight, from empathy to disdain. The reaction you get may not be the one you intended, but if the moment you choose engages a viewer, you've separated that image from the countless images that make our eyes glaze over.

No one can tell you when that moment is. Sometimes it's when the light or composition is just right; other times it's an interesting expression or gesture. Sometimes you'll release the shutter too soon, other times too late; but when you've captured a magic moment, you'll know—and so will the people who view and admire the resulting photograph.

An Exceptional Subject

Sometimes it can actually be the subject itself that makes the photo. **Brandon Stanton's** book and website, *Humans of New York,* is full of street portraits of everyday people—but some of his most fascinating images are of New York's eccentrics. **Diane Arbus** photographed people who mainstream society would label as freaks and outcasts. Her legacy is being carried forward by photographers such as **Zoe Strauss,** who, among other things, photographs people and storefronts in Philadelphia's low-income neighborhoods.

Exceptional subjects don't have to be people. They can be animals, cars, buildings, or signs—practically anything that strikes you as being worth a second look, even when others may give it no more than a glance.

In any case, the key to success with this type of subject is to have a clear concept of how you want the resulting photograph to look. Do you want to use selective focus to make the background or foreground less distracting or are you making an environmental portrait that requires great depth of field? Do you want flat lighting or directional lighting? Do you want a bold color palette or a subtle one? These are questions to which you should give serious thought, especially when you have the time to do so. Even if the subject is more significant than the moment you choose to release the shutter, you can still make a conscious choice about how you want the subject to look. Worried? Proud? Strong? Decrepit? Relaxed? It's up to you.

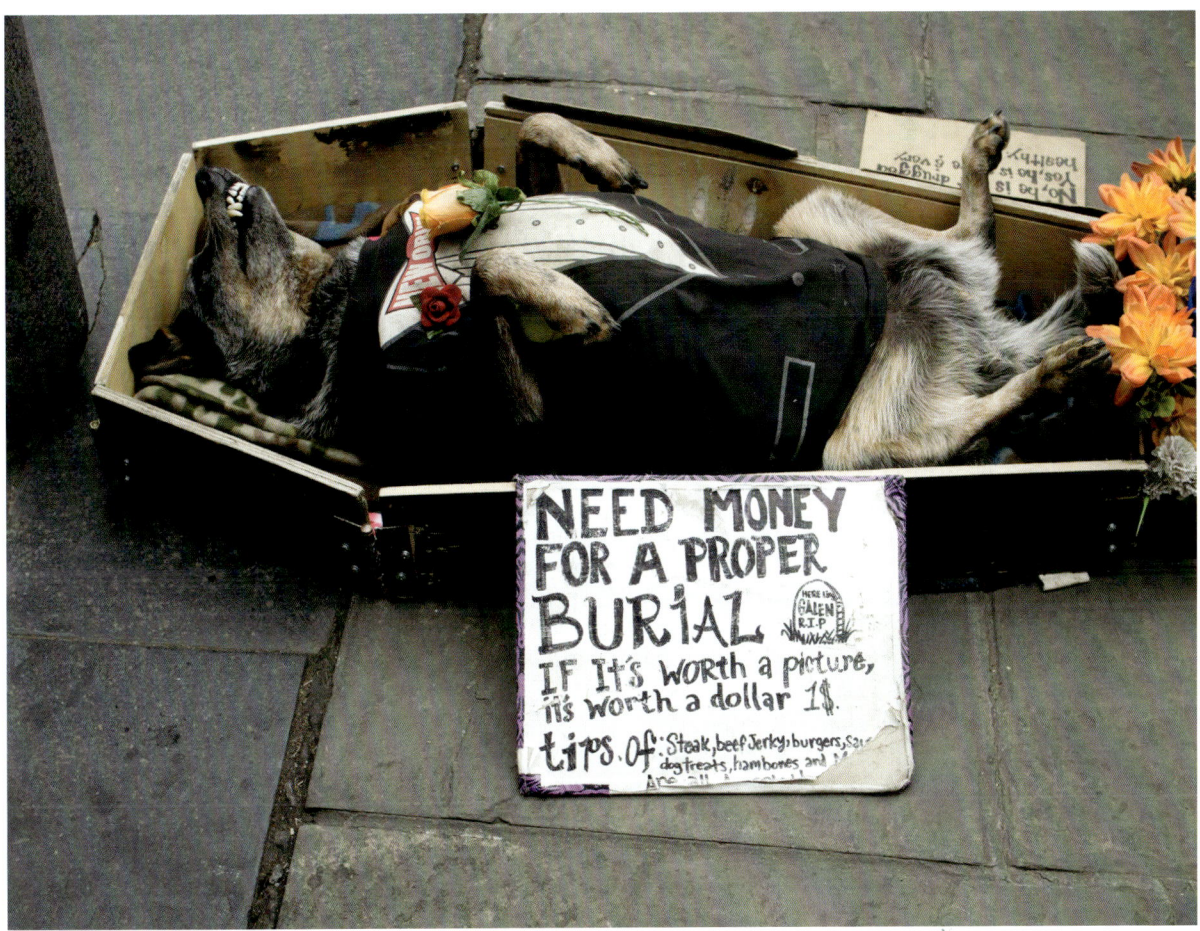

Dead Dog, New Orleans, LA 2014

This dog earned spare change for his owner by playing dead. The "dead dog" is an unusual subject, and the low angle of the camera differentiates this image from a straightforward documentary shot.

OPPOSITE PAGE:
**Market Street,
Philadelphia, PA 2014**

Exceptional Light

Some street photos catch our attention mainly because of the dramatic quality and direction of light. Direct early morning or late afternoon sunlight can cast long, sharp, deep shadows. Backlighting conveys a sense of mystery. Sunlight reflected by mirrored windows or cutting through narrow breaks between buildings can cast intense pools of light onto people and city streets. The same sunlight reflected off of a white wall can create a huge softbox for evenly lit portraits. In some cases, such as **Bruce Gilden's** flash-lit photos of New York pedestrians, you can even carry your exceptional lighting along with you.

Practically speaking, you can't actually photograph light itself; you can only photograph the way it reflects from surfaces. This brings us back to the physical subject, moment, or idea you're photographing. What matters most is how exceptional light helps to create a mood: mystery, tension, wonder, drama—whatever suits your artistic purpose.

Keep in mind that "correct" exposure is a lot more subjective in dramatic or strongly directional lighting situations than if you were photographing in flat, shadowless light. Spot, side, or backlighting can create such strong

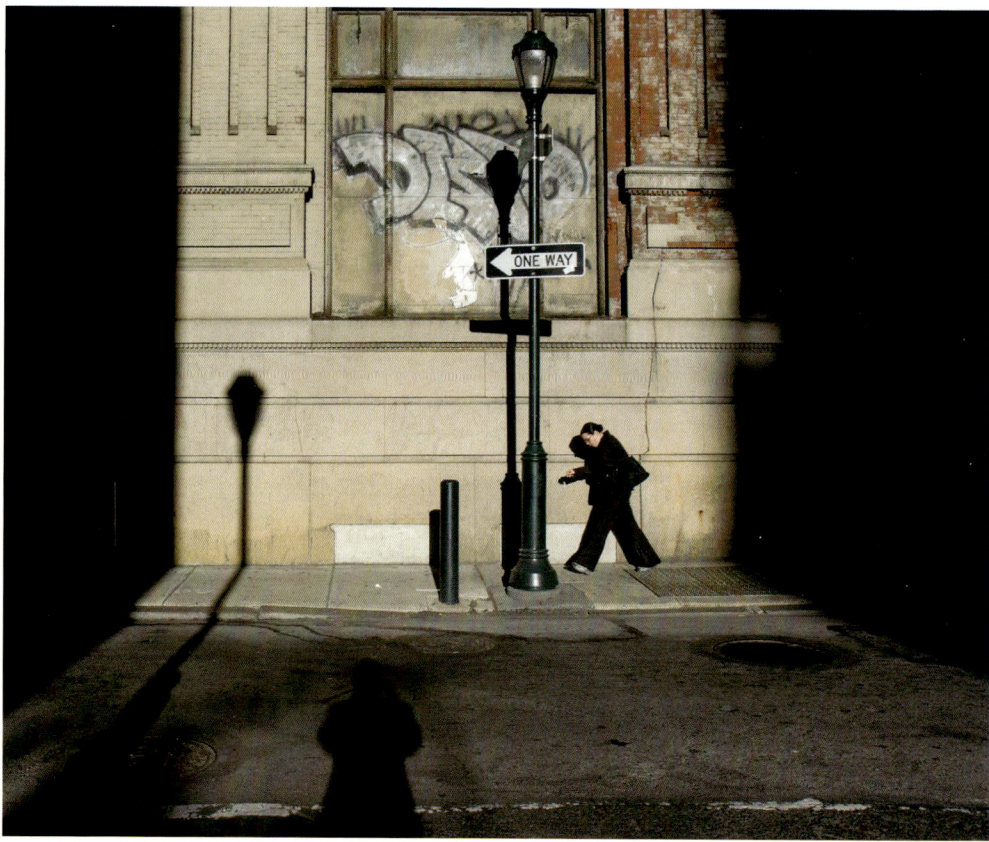

Sidestreet, Philadelphia, PA 2012
The narrow alleys found in older cities can make direct sunlight even more directional and high-contrast. Using this light can add a dramatic boost to compositions that already have strong graphic design or architectural elements.

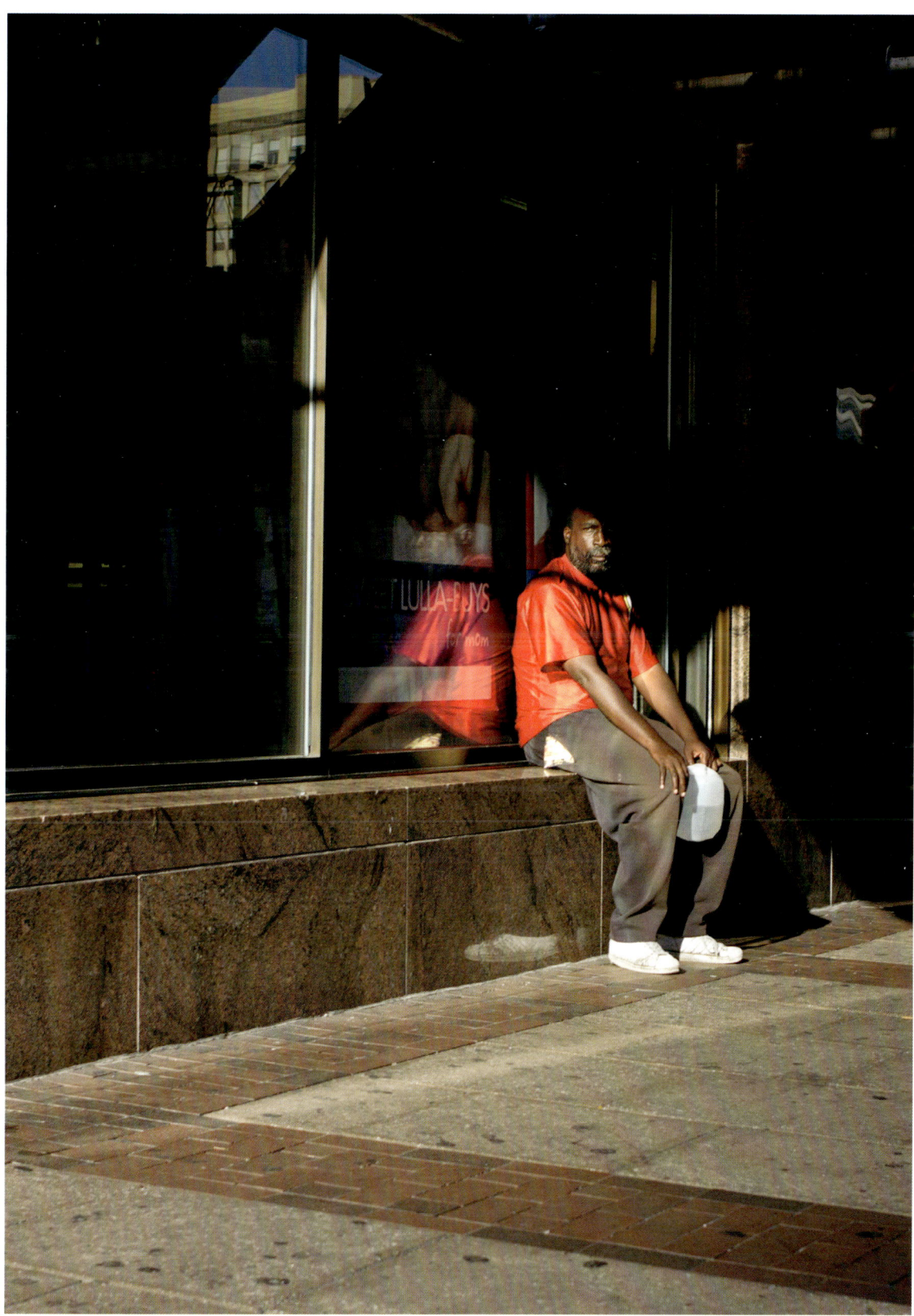

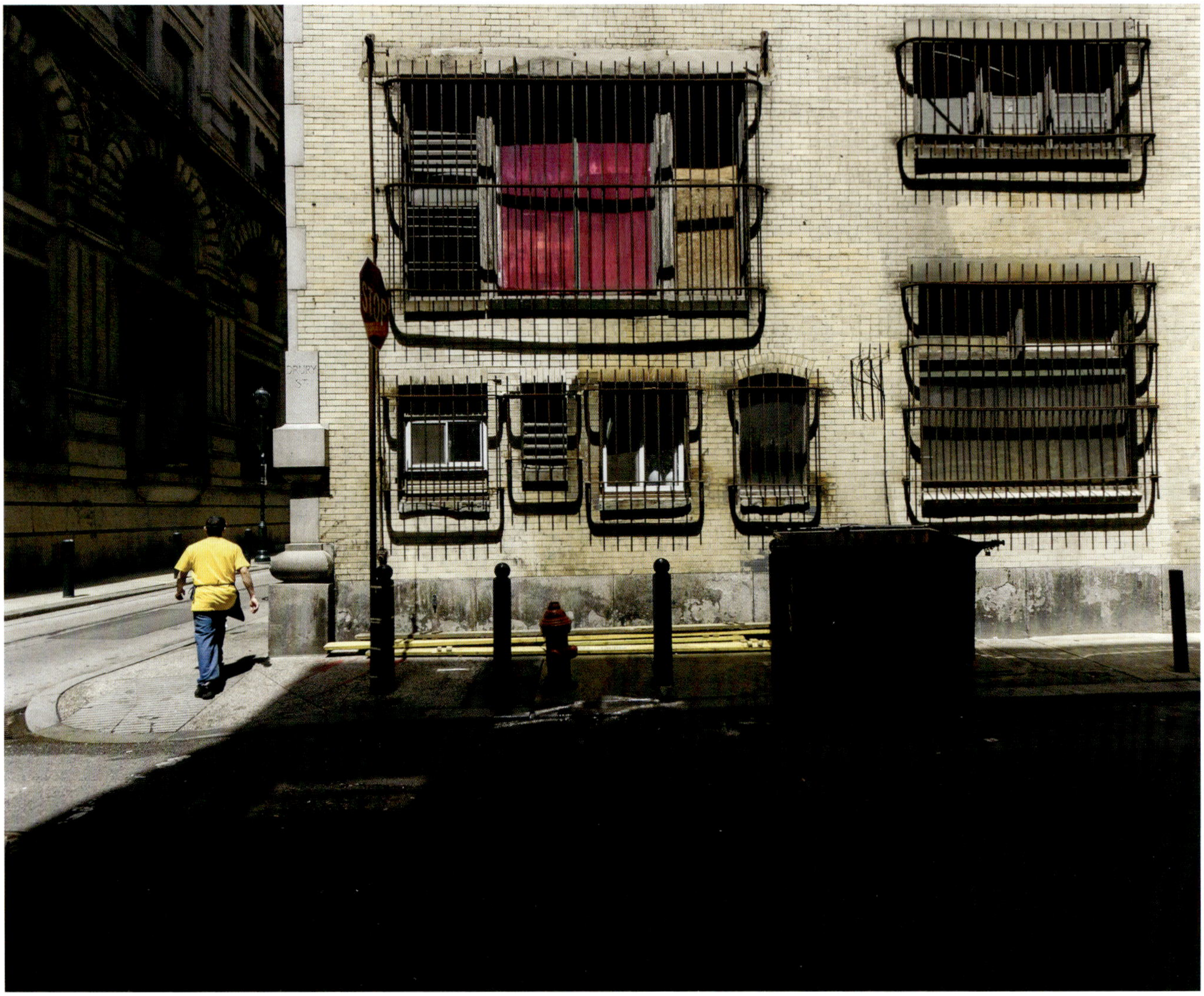

Back Alley, Philadelphia, PA 2009

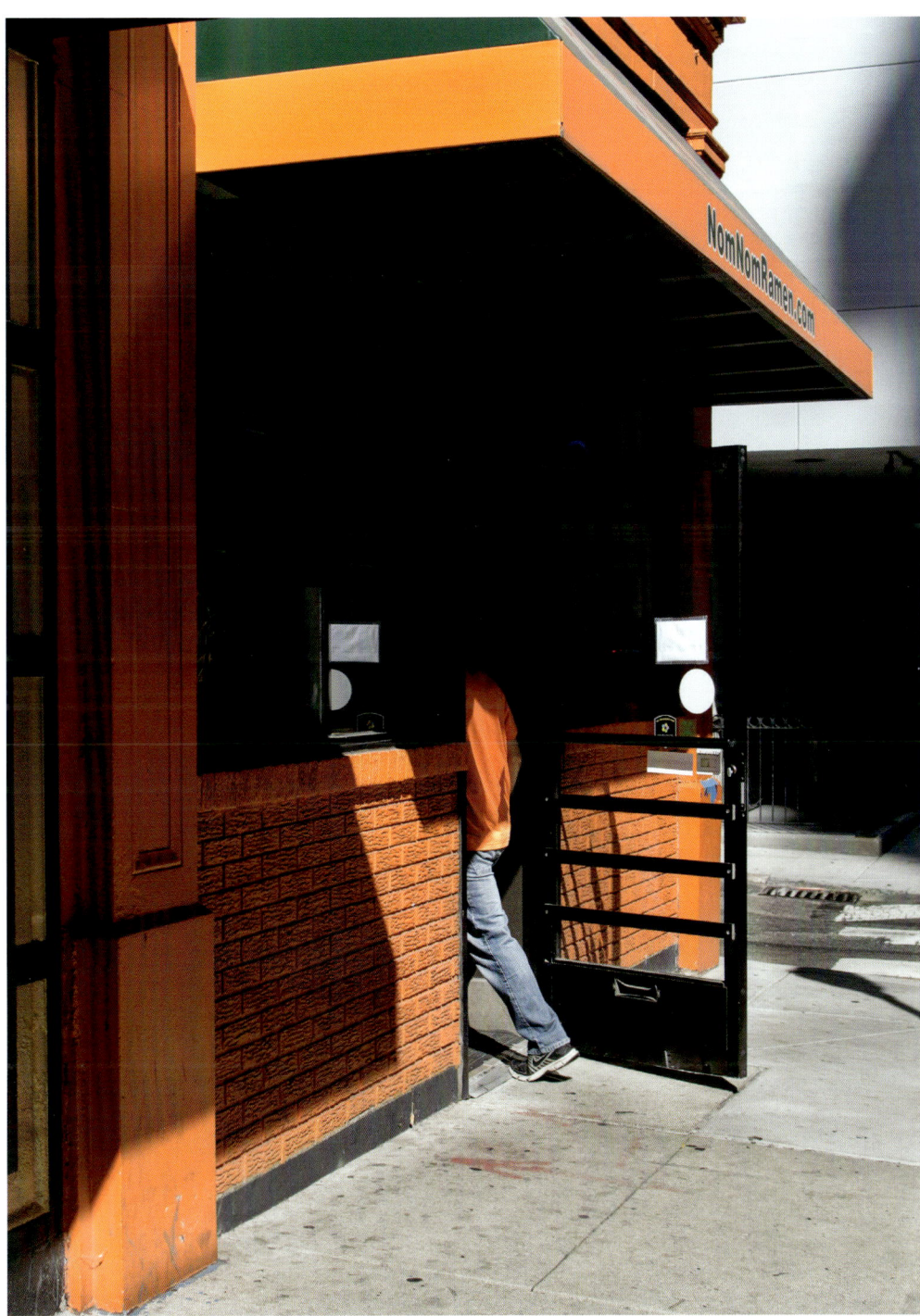

Orange on Orange,
Philadelphia, PA 2014

OPPOSITE PAGE:
Encroached by
Shadows, Philadelphia,
PA 2012

contrast that it exceeds the dynamic range of your film or sensor. You may have to choose whether to expose for the highlights and let the shadows drop to black, expose for the

shadows and let the highlights clip to pure white, split the difference and hope for the best, or bracket exposures to cover your butt. Luck is always a factor in street photography. I can't count the number of times I thought I had screwed up an exposure and missed the moment I was shooting, only to find that my "mistake" was better than what I had originally imagined and intended.

Selective Use of Color

Classic street photography was done in black-and-white for more than just aesthetic reasons. In the early days of the genre, color films weren't available. Color films became generally available in the early 1940s, but because of their expense, slow speed (low sensitivity to light), and high contrast, they were seldom used for street photography. It wasn't until the 1950s that fashion and street photographer **Saul Leiter,** who was also a skilled painter, demonstrated just how powerful and evocative street photographs could be if shot in color. What you'll see if you explore Leiter's work, such as the photographs seen in *Early Color* (Steidl, 2014), is a painter's eye for color and composition. From the barrage of color that might appear in a typical street scene, Leiter manages to select only a few dominant colors and then combine them into a composition where the colors complement or contrast with each other for maximum artistic effect.

This is not at all to imply that you or anyone else should copy Leiter's style, but rather to think of color as a design element that you can control. To put it another way, just because your camera's default rendering is in color and the world you see is in color does

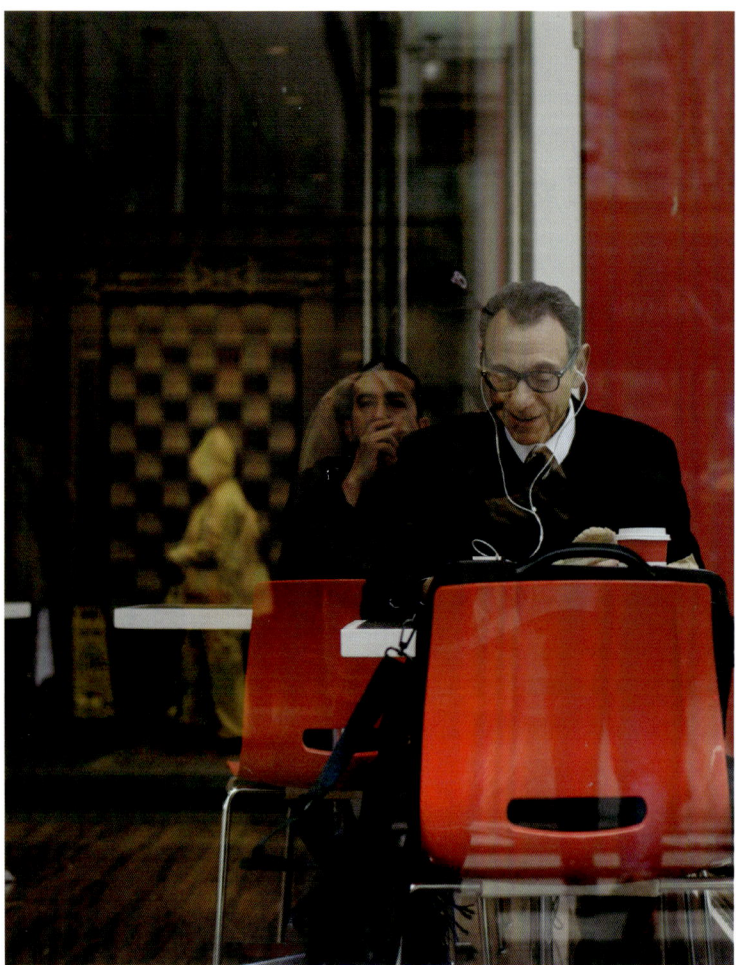

Music Lover, Philadelphia, PA 2013
In each one of these photographs, what initially attracted my eye was not the people or what they were doing, but rather the similarities and contrasts between a limited palette of distinct colors and shapes. This is a technique that painters use often. It's more difficult to do in candid photographs, but it's certainly possible, and it adds another mode of expression to your toolbox.

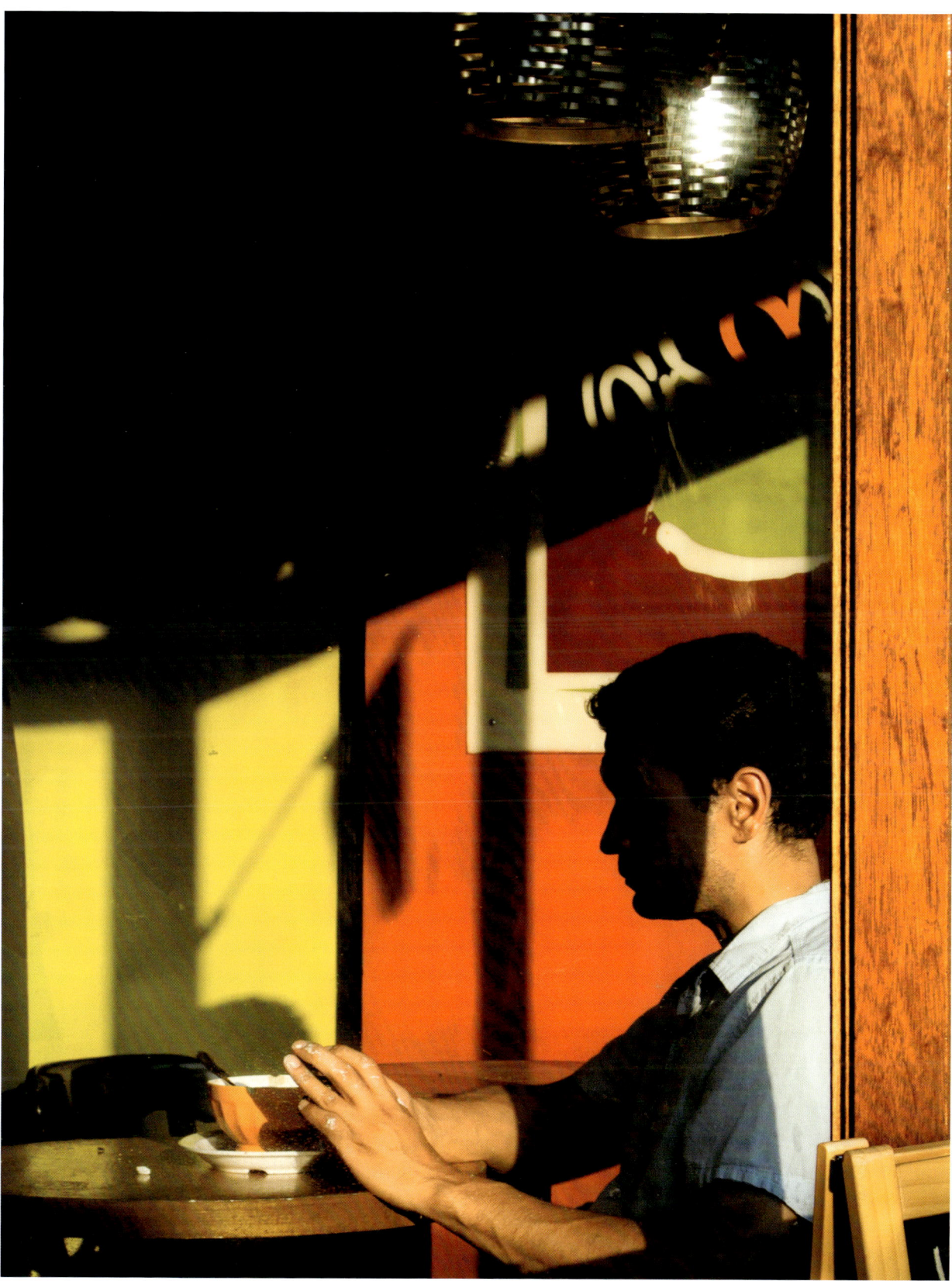

not mean that there's no benefit to being conscious and intentional in how you use color to convey certain emotions or artistic sensibilities.

The selective use of color also includes the choice *not* to use color. Shooting in monochrome eliminates the need to factor color and all of its potential distractions into your compositions. It also provides a type of visual abstraction you can't get with color. On the other hand, it increases the need to be that much more conscious and aware of the other compositional elements, such as contrast, tonality, texture, shape, and line. Let's be clear: it's not monochrome itself that contributes to a great street image—it's the skillful use of monochrome. When it's done right, viewers won't notice the absence of color so much as they'll notice the tonality of the image.

Serendipity

Some of the most memorable street photographs feature those unexpected, unplanned, yet totally amazing moments that happen by sheer luck. Page through any book or exhibition of street photography and you'll be struck by how many images are a product of being in the right place at the right time. Of course, there's not much you can do to prepare for the unexpected. You can, however, improve your odds of success by increasing how often you're roaming the streets and other public places, camera in hand or in your pocket, watching and waiting, ready to respond when you see something out of the ordinary.

The possibility that you might literally have only three seconds to capture a once-in-a-lifetime situation can be sobering. It's the

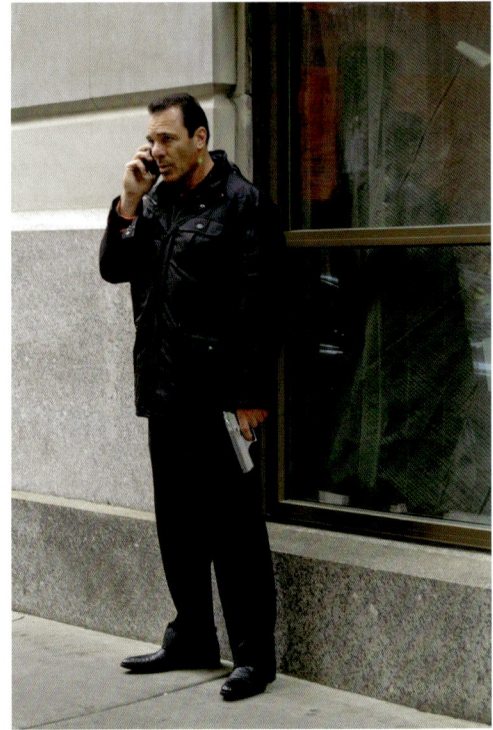

Man With Gun and Cell Phone, Philadelphia, PA 2012
The situation behind this photo was less dangerous than it might look: this man was a movie actor, chatting with a friend or perhaps his agent during a break between takes. I didn't expect to see him when I turned the corner, but I was ready to photograph him as soon as I saw him. Three seconds later he got called back to work.

main reason why dedicated street photographers insist on becoming intimately familiar with how their equipment operates. It's also why they hate cameras and lenses that are slow to operate or don't behave predictably and reliably: you will never be able to predict when serendipity will strike, but it's important to be prepared for when it does.

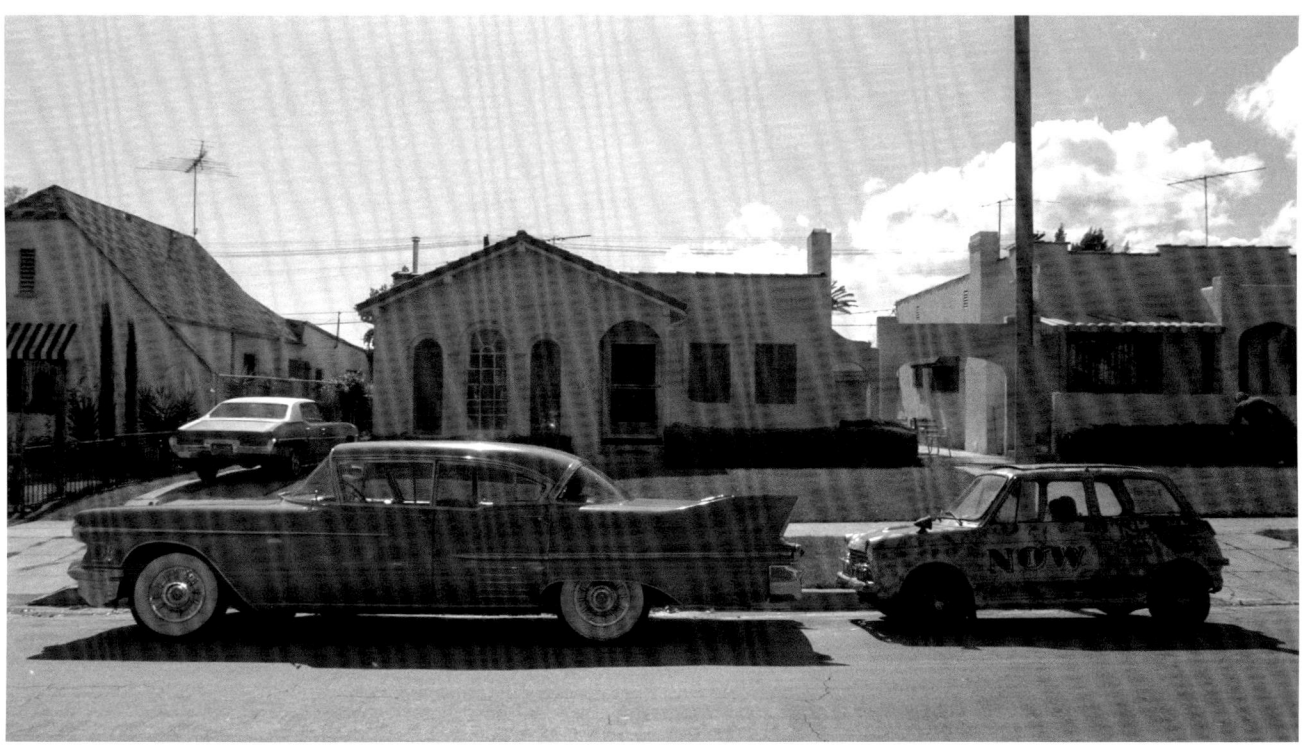

Caddy vs. Honda, Los Angeles, CA 1990
There's no place like the streets of Southern California for finding cars that hint at the personalities of their owners. Just as with the photo of the man holding a gun, my window of opportunity for capturing this shot was small. I photographed this scene, and within minutes of capture the owner of this tiny Honda got in her car and drove away.

Distinctive Style

This book has an entire chapter devoted to style, so it should be obvious how much I think a distinctive style contributes to great street photographs—or at least to differentiating yourself from other street photographers. What I would add here is that style is something that becomes most obvious when you look at someone's work in the aggregate rather than individual images. In other words, although you might see evidence of a distinctive stylistic approach from looking at one image, you wouldn't know whether it was a *consistent* style until you saw several more images with the same approach from the same photographer.

Keep in mind that a style doesn't have to be exaggerated to be distinctive. **Cartier-Bresson,** for example, preferred to shoot in flat lighting conditions. Even when he was forced to shoot in direct sunlight, he preferred prints with extended, luminous gray tones rather than strong blacks and sparkling whites. The same could be said of many other masters of street photography. That being said, today's photographers have options at their disposal that would have been unimaginable even 20 years ago—so many options, in fact, that it can be a challenge to choose among them, especially for photographers who are struggling to decide how they want their work to look. The benefit to finding a style that works for you and your subject matter is that people who like your work will seek it out, buy your books, attend your exhibitions, and purchase your prints.

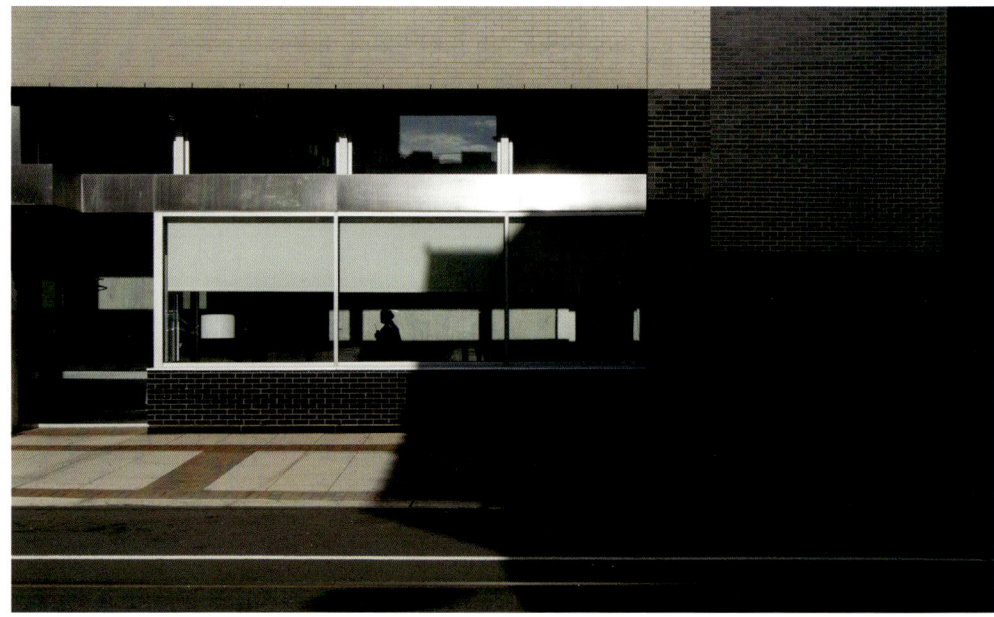

Shadowy Figure, Philadelphia, PA 2013
All of these photographs have strong stylistic elements, but it's only when you look at a collection of photographs by the same photographer that exhibit similar elements that you begin to see evidence of a style. You should have no trouble seeing similar elements in other photographs of mine throughout this book.

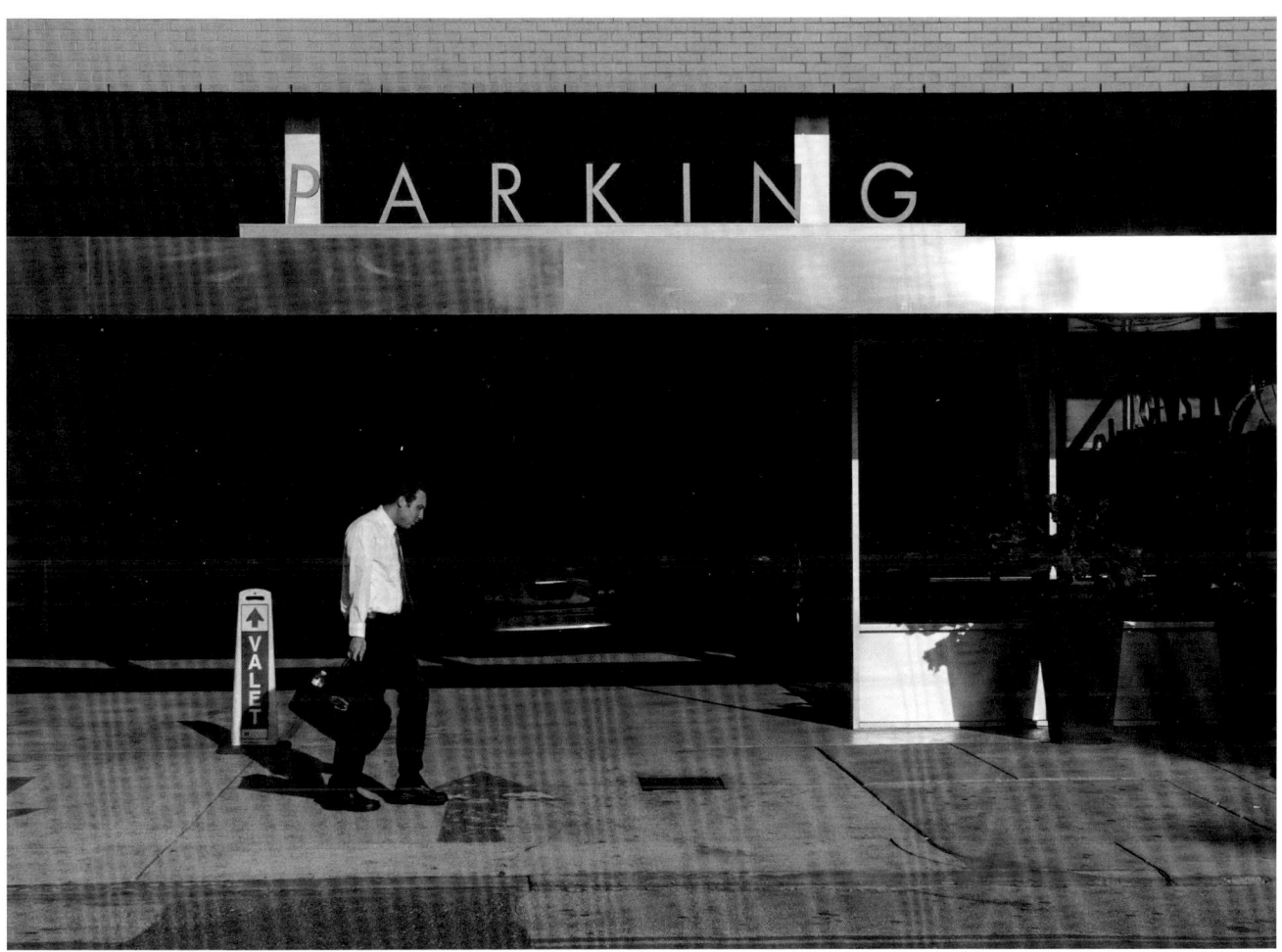

Walking Past Parking, Philadelphia, PA 2013

So in Other Words...

Greatness is the exception, not the norm. Regardless of whether it's because of great composition, the moment, the subject, lighting, color, luck, or style, the quest for great photographs is a quest for images that offer remarkable insights into how we live our lives and the environments we live them in. Life may be a continuous flow of events from start to finish, but it's specific moments in time that we remember most. It's great photographs of these moments that make the most lasting impressions.

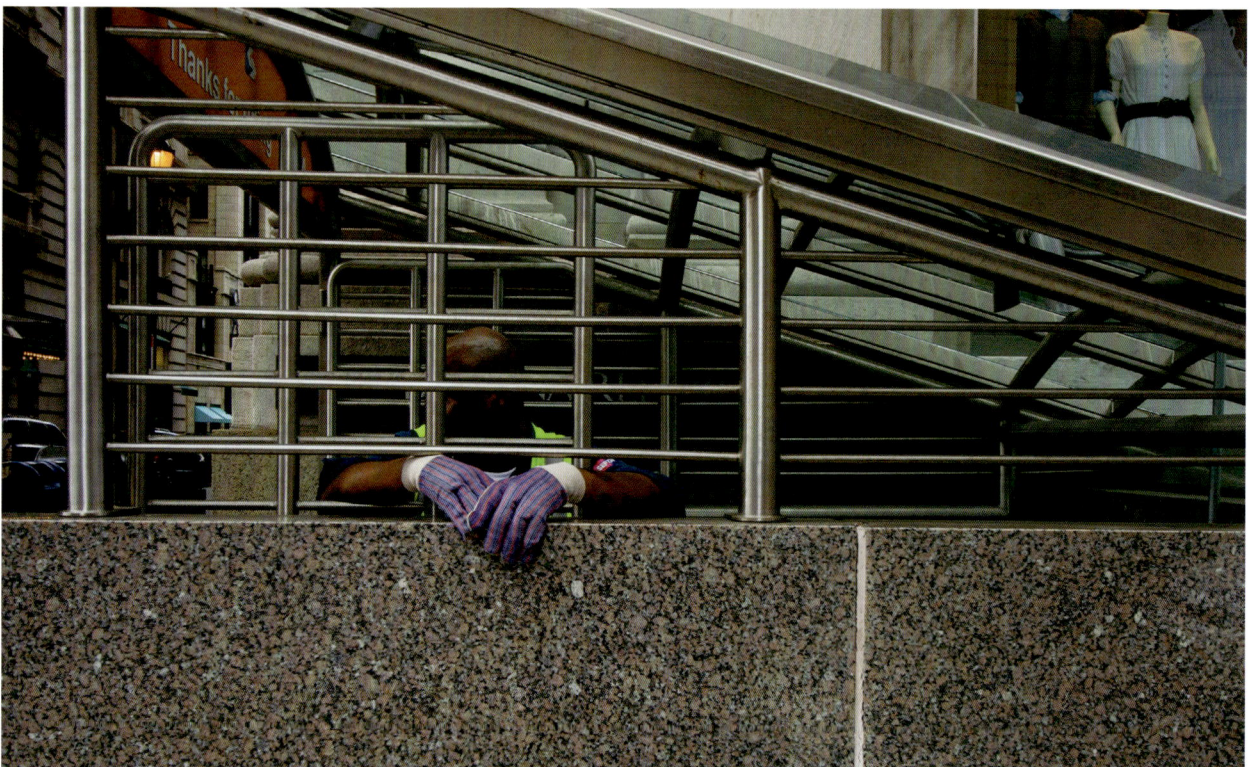

Man Behind Bars, Philadelphia, PA 2009

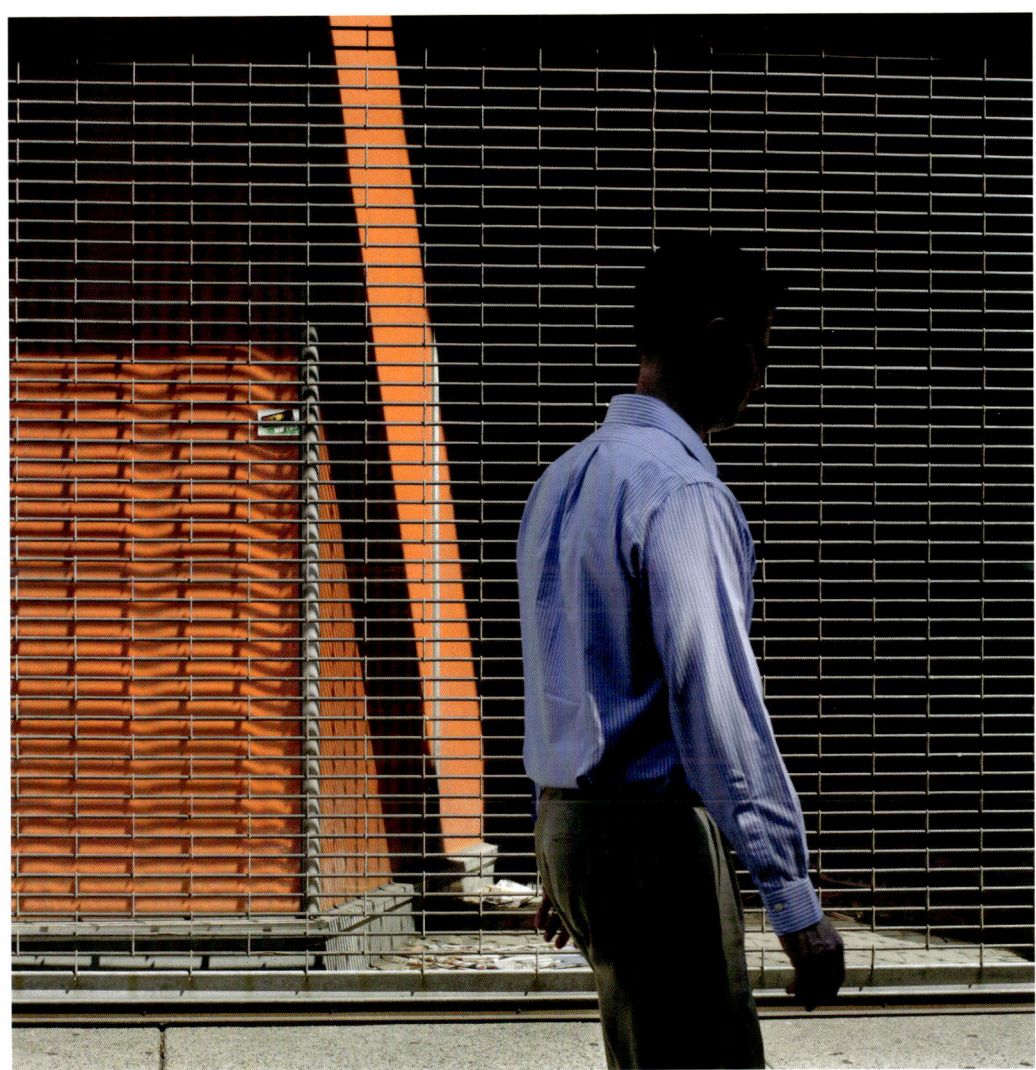

Blue Against Orange, Philadelphia, PA 2011

Get in the Picture!

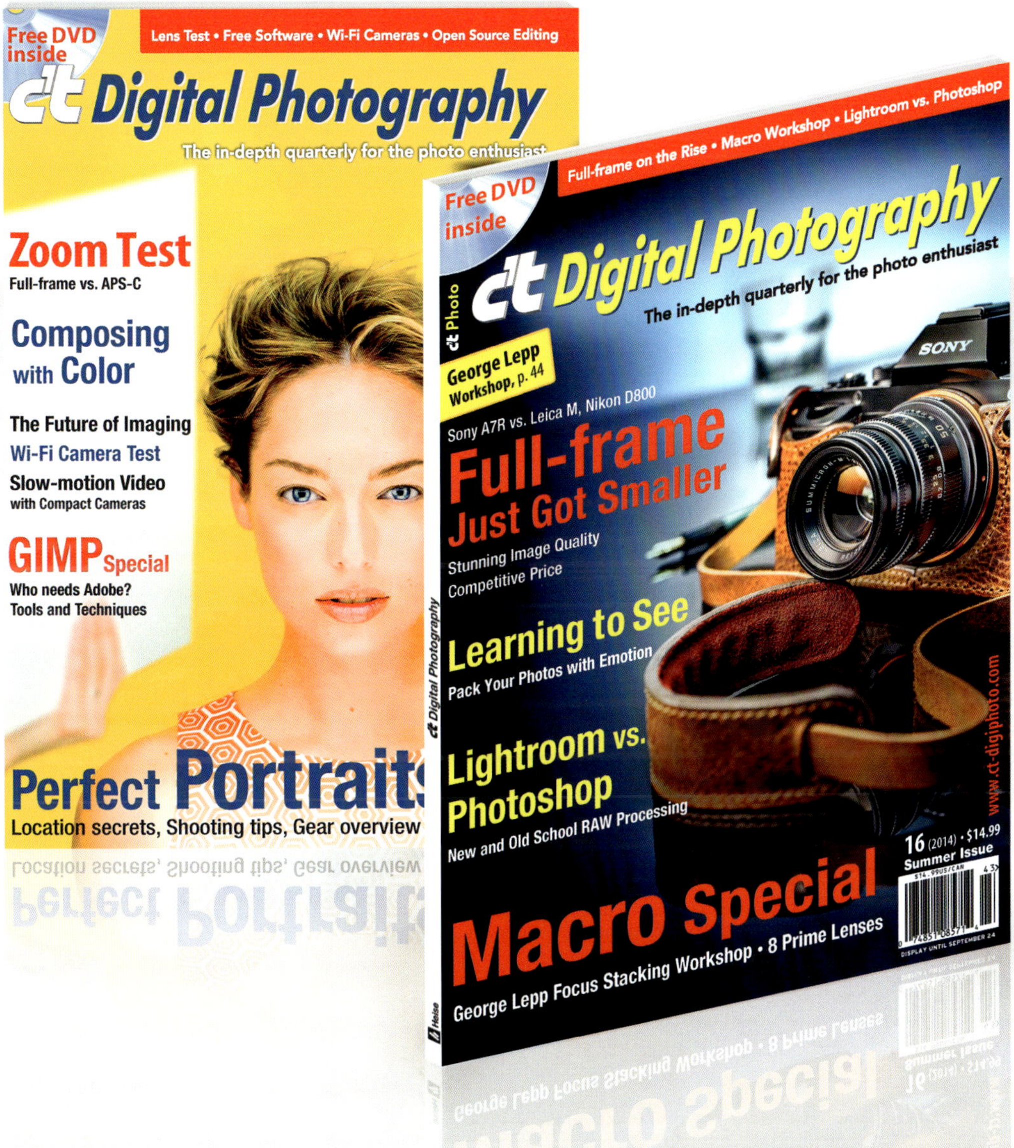

Free DVD inside

Lens Test • Free Software • Wi-Fi Cameras • Open Source Editing

c't Digital Photography

The in-depth quarterly for the photo enthusiast

Zoom Test
Full-frame vs. APS-C

Composing with Color

The Future of Imaging
Wi-Fi Camera Test
Slow-motion Video with Compact Cameras

GIMP Special
Who needs Adobe?
Tools and Techniques

Perfect Portraits
Location secrets, Shooting tips, Gear overview

Full-frame on the Rise • Macro Workshop • Lightroom vs. Photoshop

Free DVD inside

c't Photo **Digital Photography**

The in-depth quarterly for the photo enthusiast

George Lepp Workshop, p. 44

Sony A7R vs. Leica M, Nikon D800

Full-frame Just Got Smaller
Stunning Image Quality
Competitive Price

Learning to See
Pack Your Photos with Emotion

Lightroom vs. Photoshop
New and Old School RAW Processing

16 (2014) • $14.99
Summer Issue

Macro Special
George Lepp Focus Stacking Workshop • 8 Prime Lenses

www.ct-digiphoto.com

---

c't Digital Photography gives you exclusive access to the techniques of the pros and the technology behind great images.

Every issue includes tips and tutorials from experienced pro photographers as well as independent gear and software tests. There are also regular advanced image processing and management workshops to help you create your own perfect portfolio.

Each issue includes a free DVD with full and special version software, practical photo tools, eBooks, and comprehensive video tutorials.

Don't miss out – subscribe today!

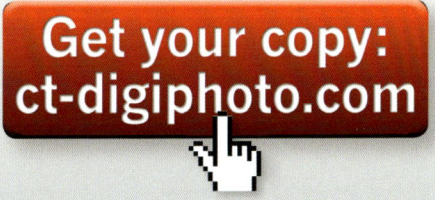

Get your copy:
ct-digiphoto.com

ROCKYNOOK.COM

Don't close
the book on us yet

Interested in learning more on
the art and craft of photography?

Looking for tips and tricks
to share with friends?

Visit

rockynook.com/information/newsletter

for updates on new titles, access to free
downloads, blog posts, our eBook store,
author gallery, and so much more.

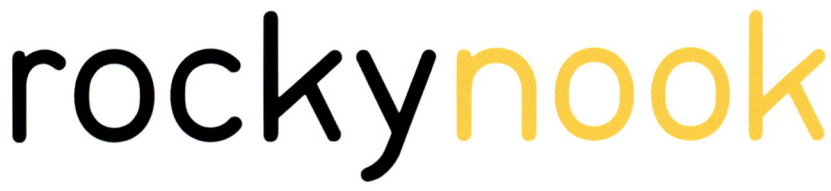

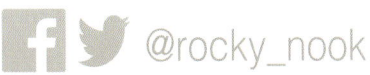 @rocky_nook